Table of Contents

viii	Acknowledgments
1	Introduction
3	Chapter One: Getting Policy Right
39	Chapter Two: Building Professionalism in the Acquisition Workforce
65	Chapter Three: Managing Technical Complexity
93	Chapter Four: Working With Industry
127	Chapter Five: Responding to External Forces and Events
179	Chapter Six: Measuring Progress in Improving Acquisition
203	Conclusion

Articles From *Defense AT&L* Magazine

10	"Better Buying Power Principles—What Are They?," January-February 2016
15	"Original Better Buying Power—David Packard Acquisition Rules 1971," May-June 2013
21	"The Challenges We Face—And How We Will Meet Them," November-December 2012
25	"Innovation in the Defense Acquisition Enterprise," November-December 2015
32	"Real Acquisition Reform (or Improvement) Must Come From Within," May-June 2016
41	"What Does It Mean To Be 'a Defense Acquisition Professional'?," March-April 2014
44	"Ethics and Acquisition Professionalism—It Is All About Trust," September-October 2014
49	"Program Manager Assessments—Professionalism Personified," July-August 2015
53	"Improving Acquisition From Within—Suggestions From Our PEOs," July-August 2016
62	"What Really Matters In Defense Acquisition," January-February 2016
71	"The Optimal Program Structure," July-August 2012
73	"Risk and Risk Mitigation—Don't Be a Spectator," January-February 2015
79	"The Trouble With TRLs (With Thanks to Gene Roddenberry and David Gerrold)," September-October 2013
89	"Manufacturing Innovation and Technological Superiority," September-October 2016
100	"Our Relationship With Industry," November-December 2013
104	"Use of Fixed-Price Incentive Firm (FPIF) Contracts in Development and Production," March-April, 2013
109	"DoD Use of Commercial Acquisition Practices—When They Apply and When They Do Not," September-October 2015

114	"Tying Profit to Performance—A Valuable Tool, But Use With Good Judgment," May-June 2015
121	"Getting 'Best Value' For the Warfighter and the Taxpayer," March-April 2015
142	"Moving Forward," January-February 2013
144	"What Lies Ahead," July-August 2013
149	"Protecting the Future," May-June 2014
153	"Technological Superiority and Better Buying Power 3.0," November-December 2014
156	"Our Theme for 2016—Sustaining Momentum," March-April 2016
174	"When and When Not to Accelerate Acquisitions," November-December 2016
189	"Better Buying Power—A Progress Assessment," July-August 2014
207	"Adventures in Defense Acquisition," January-February 2017

Article from *The ITEA Journal*

82	"Perspectives on Developmental Test and Evaluation," March 2013

Figures and Tables

6	Figure 1. Better Buying Power 1.0
6	Figure 2. Better Buying Power 2.0
7	Figure 3. Better Buying Power 3.0
179	Figure 4. Contract Cost Growth on Highest Risk (Major) Programs
181	Figure 5. Profits of the Six Largest DoD Primes
182	Figure 6. Percent of Major Programs With Cost Reductions
183	Figure 7. Major Programs Crossing Critical Congressional Cost-Growth Thresholds

184	Table 1. Root Causes for Major Programs Crossing Critical Congressional Cost-Growth Thresholds or Other Major Problems
185	Figure 8. Planned Length of Active Development Contracts for Major Programs
186	Figure 9. Planned Major Information System Development Time
186	Figure 10. Contract Schedule Growth on Highest Risk (Major) Program
187	Figure 11. Cost Growth on Highest Risk (Major) Programs Started in Different Budget Climates

E-mails, Correspondence and Statements

4	Under Secretary Frank Kendall's Memorandum for the Acquisition Workforce, Jan. 7, 2015
67	Kendall E-Mail about 2016 Program Executive Officer Assessment
96	Kendall Statement on Consolidation in the Defense Industry, September 30, 2015
97	Joint Statement of the Department of Justice and the Federal Trade Commission on Preserving Competition in the Defense Industry, autumn of 2015
128	Kendall letter to Senator John McCain, June 13, 2014
133	Kendall Memorandum on "Department of Defense Management of Unobligated Funds; Obligated Rate Tenets," September 10, 2012
136	Kendall E-Mail to Acquisition, Technology, and Logistics personnel titled "Guidance During FY13 Sequestration and Furloughs," July 9, 2013
163	Kendall Letter to Service Secretaries and Chiefs on Defense Acquisition
200	Foreword from the *Fourth Annual Report on the Performance of the Defense Acquisition System*, October 24, 2016

Dedicated to all the professionals, in the military, government, and industry, who create and sustain the products our military depends upon to keep us free and secure,

And to Beth, Scott, Eric, and James, for the sacrifices they have made so that I could make my very limited contributions to that effort.

FRANK KENDALL
Under Secretary of Defense for Acquisition, Technology, and Logistics

Frank Kendall was confirmed by the U.S. Senate in May 2012 as the Under Secretary of Defense for Acquisition, Technology, and Logistics. In that position, he has been responsible to the Secretary of Defense for all matters pertaining to acquisition; research and engineering; developmental testing; contract administration; logistics and materiel readiness; installations and environment; operational energy; chemical, biological, and nuclear weapons; the acquisition workforce; and the defense industrial base. He is the leader of the Department of Defense (DoD) efforts to increase the DoD's buying power and improve the performance of the defense acquisition enterprise. Prior to this appointment, he served from March 2010–May 2012 as the Principal Deputy Under Secretary and also as the Acting Under Secretary.

Mr. Kendall has more than 45 years of experience in engineering, management, defense acquisition, and national security affairs in private industry, government, and the military. He has been a consultant to defense industry firms, nonprofit research organizations, and the DoD in the areas of strategic planning, engineering management, and technology assessment. Mr. Kendall formerly was Vice President of Engineering for Raytheon Company, where he was responsible for directing the management of the company's engineering functions and internal research and development. Before joining the administration, Mr. Kendall was a managing partner at Renaissance Strategic Advisors, a Virginia-based aerospace and defense sector consulting firm. In addition, Mr. Kendall is an attorney and has been active in the field of human rights, working primarily on a *pro bono* basis.

Within government, Mr. Kendall held the position of Director of Tactical Warfare Programs in the Office of the Secretary of Defense and the position of Assistant Deputy Under Secretary of Defense for Strategic Defense Systems. Mr. Kendall is a former member of the Army Science Board and the Defense Intelligence Agency's Science and Technology Advisory Board and he has been a consultant to the Defense Science Board and a

Senior Advisor to the Center for Strategic and International Studies. Mr. Kendall also spent 10 years on active duty with the Army serving in Germany, teaching Engineering at West Point and holding research and development positions.

Over the course of his public-service career, Mr. Kendall was awarded the following federal civilian awards: The Defense Distinguished Public Service Award, Defense Distinguished Civilian Service Medal, the Secretary of Defense Meritorious Civilian Service Medal, the Presidential Rank Award of Distinguished Executive (Senior Executive Service), the Presidential Rank Award of Meritorious Executive (Senior Executive Service), and the Army Commander's Award for Civilian Service. He also holds the following military awards from the U.S. Army: the Meritorious Service Medal with oak leaf cluster, Army Commendation Medal, and National Defense Service Medal.

Mr. Kendall is a Distinguished Graduate of the U.S. Military Academy at West Point, as well as an Army War College graduate, and holds a master's degree in Aerospace Engineering from the California Institute of Technology, a master's degree in business administration degree from the C.W. Post Center of Long Island University, and a juris doctorate from the Georgetown University Law Center.

Acknowledgments

I would like to acknowledge the many operational, government acquisition, and industry professionals who contributed to the content of this volume through more than 45 years of experience, collaborative discussion and idea sharing. I am particularly indebted to the support of the Service Acquisition Executives and the entire AT&L staff, particularly my Deputy, the Honorable Alan Estevez, who all played an important role in the creation of the articles included in this volume. Many thanks go out to the Acquisition Policy Analysis Center Team led by Dr. Phil Anton who brought data and analysis to the world of acquisition policy. Thanks also to CAPT Dan Mackin, my Military Assistant, who served as my advisor and editor-in-chief, assisted by President Jim Woolsey and the fine team at the Defense Acquisition University.

Introduction

> "There are two ways of spreading light:
> to be the candle or the mirror that reflects it."
>
> —Edith Wharton

For most of my adult life, a span of over 45 years, I have worked on some aspect of the operation, development, production, and support of American weapon systems. The so-called "defense acquisition system" has produced a long series of diverse advanced technology-based products that are widely recognized as the best in the world. At the same time, however, this acquisition system has come under constant criticism and numerous attempts at "acquisition reform."

Some of the criticism is well founded, and some of the acquisition reform efforts have produced positive results. Others have had the opposite effect. In my role as Under Secretary of Defense for Acquisition, Technology, and Logistics (USD[AT&L]) for several years, I have worked hard to pass on to the rest of the acquisition workforce of the Defense Department (DoD), and to all the stakeholders in defense acquisition, some of the hard-won lessons of my decades of experience in the development of new defense products. This volume assembles some of the results of that effort, organized by logical topics and preceded by a summary of the specific items discussed.

During my tenure as Under Secretary, I have written and published a short article dealing with some aspect of defense acquisition management roughly every 2 months. These articles were published in the DoD's *Defense AT&L* magazine and also sent to the acquisition workforce by e-mail. Roughly 5 years in, it occurred to me that this body of work could be integrated into a short volume in a way that might be useful to both acquisition professionals and also to anyone looking for a deeper understanding of the subject. In looking back over the last several years, it also occurred to me that there were a handful of other items that were produced during the course of my tenure that should be included to provide a more complete picture.

This volume begins with acquisition policy and then discusses the most important ingredient for successful programs: people—more specifically, the acquisition professionals who work in government and industry.

Following these sections, some specific aspects of managing technical complexity in large programs are addressed. Because almost all of our weapons systems are designed and produced by private industry under government contracts, the next section deals with the relationship between government and industry, and how that should be managed for mutual benefit—while supporting our warfighters and protecting the American taxpayers' investments in defense systems. Next, the subject of outside influences on defense acquisition is covered, including the impact of budget pressures, legislative initiatives, and customer desires. The "customer" for Defense Acquisition is the military operator, and this relationship is addressed in detail. The penultimate chapter deals with measuring progress. It addresses the questions of how we know if things are getting better or worse. Acquisition policy has been changed many times, often out of frustration when results were not what was desired. But have those changes had any impact? Finally, I try to draw some general conclusions from the preceding chapters. Readers are encouraged to enter or leave this volume at any point based on their interests—the whole volume, each chapter, and each article in a chapter, can be read in its entirety or individually.

Chapter One
Getting Acquisition Policy Right

> "Experience is never limited and it is never complete;
> it is an immense sensibility, a kind of huge spider-web of the finest
> silken threads, suspended in the chamber of consciousness and catching
> every air-borne particle in its tissue."
>
> —Henry James

Here is all the acquisition policy we ought to need:
- Set reasonable requirements.
- Put professionals in charge.
- Give them the resources they need.
- Provide strong incentives for success.

Unfortunately, there is a whole universe of complexity in each of those four items. Because of that complexity, because of our imperfect results in delivering new capabilities, and because of the interests of a wide array of stakeholders, formal acquisition policy in the United States is expansive and embedded in multiple publications. The basic acquisition policy document for the Department is a DoD Instruction, DoDI 5000.02, titled "The Defense Acquisition System." It has been rewritten numerous times during my career, but the underlying substance has never really changed much. New product development is new product development. The major decisions are generic—starting risk reduction, starting design for production, and starting production itself. When I came back into government in 2010 as the Principal Deputy to then Under Secretary Ashton Carter, I was resolved to not rewrite 5000.02 again ... but then I did. I personally wrote the basic document and heavily edited the dozen or so enclosures that comprise half of the content.

I was motivated partly by the fact that a number of legislative changes had to be implemented in 5000.02 but most of all I wanted to use the document to communicate some overarching principles. The most important of these principles was the necessity to thoughtfully tailor program plans to address the unique circumstances and nature of the product being created. Form follows function, not the reverse. Another motivator was the implementation of the Better Buying Power acquisition improvement initiatives my predecessor and I had put in place in 2010 and that I modified significantly in 2012 as Better Buying Power 2.0 (and again in 2014 as 3.0) As I discuss in more detail below, I was also concerned about the morass of statutorily required regulations our managers were tasked to comply with. My intent was reflected in the cover letter that I put out with the new DoDI 5000.02—which is reproduced here:

THE UNDER SECRETARY OF DEFENSE
3010 DEFENSE PENTAGON
WASHINGTON, DC 20301-3010

ACQUISITION,
TECHNOLOGY,
AND LOGISTICS

JAN 0 7 2015

MEMORANDUM FOR THE ACQUISITION WORKFORCE

SUBJECT: Department of Defense Instruction 5000.02

This memorandum issues the new Department of Defense Instruction (DoDI) 5000.02 and cancels the interim version that was implemented on November 25, 2013. This version implements many of the policies and practices included in the sequence of three sets of Better Buying Power initiatives.

Successful defense acquisition depends on careful thinking and sound professional judgments about the best acquisition strategy to use for a given product. Even more than previous versions, this DoDI 5000.02 emphasizes tailoring of program structures, content, and decision points to the product being acquired. DoDI 5000.02 contains several program structure models instead of a single model. These models, however, are not alternatives from which a Program Manager must choose; they serve as examples and starting points that can and should be tailored to the actual product being acquired. Program Managers and Program Executive Officers should use these models as references to assist their thought processes and analysis of the best structure to use on a given program. Milestone Decision Authorities have been given broad authority to tailor program acquisition strategies.

Better Buying Power is based on the concept of continuous process improvement. We will never stop learning from our experience, and we will never completely exhaust the potential for improvement in how we acquire weapons and other systems for the Department. Therefore, I do not consider this or any version of DoDI 5000.02 to be the final word on acquisition policy. In fact, I hope that some positive changes to this DoDI 5000.02 can be implemented soon. One of them, which we are working closely with the Congress on, is to simplify and rationalize the complex set of statutory requirements that have been levied on our managers over the past few decades. These burdensome and overlapping requirements are reflected in the dense tables in Enclosure 1. I am hopeful that a much shorter set of the tables in Enclosure 1 can be published as a result of our ongoing legislative initiative in acquisition reform that we are working in collaboration with Congress. I have also already initiated work on a new enclosure that will deal with the increasingly serious problem of designing for and managing cyber-security in our programs. We must do a better job of protecting our systems and everything associated with them from cyber threats.

DoDI 5000.02 provides policy guidance, but it is also a tool that should be used by acquisition professionals, and the operational, programming, and intelligence professionals we work with, to deliver products that meet our warfighters' needs and deliver value to the American taxpayer.

Frank Kendall

CHAPTER ONE: GETTING ACQUISITION POLICY RIGHT

In addition to DoDI 5000.02, there are many regulatory provisions that govern federal and defense contracting. These are embedded in the thousands of pages of the Defense Federal Acquisition Regulation (DFAR) governing defense contracting. These rules have to be administered by our contracting professionals and managers. As new legislation is passed or new Executive Orders are issued, the DFAR is constantly updated to reflect that new guidance. The trend is almost entirely in the direction of adding volume to the regulation, not reducing it. In response to legislative direction, I recently chartered a 2-year effort to review the DFAR with the hope that it can be dramatically streamlined. This is a very worthwhile endeavor, but I hold only limited hope for its success—every provision in the DFAR is rooted in some stakeholders' belief that it will accomplish a desired result, often a result only indirectly associated with defense acquisition itself.

During the last several years, the DoD has used an evolving set of acquisition policy initiatives that then Under Secretary Carter and I started in 2010. As noted above, they were called the "Better Buying Power" initiatives and were mentioned in the DoDI 5000.02 cover letter. Over the last few years, I have used a management philosophy of continuous improvement to modify these initiatives; some have been dropped, and some have been added. As we have learned from our experience and made progress, we have kept the most significant initiatives but shifted our efforts to emphasize other areas needing improvement. As of 2016, there had been three versions or releases of Better Buying Power initiatives. The latest version, Better Buying Power 3.0, continues the highest payoff initiatives from earlier versions, addressing cost consciousness, incentives, and building professionalism in particular, and adds an emphasis on increasing technical excellence and innovation. All three iterations are summarized in Figures 1, 2, and 3 so that you can track both the continuity and the change in policy.

Figure 1. Better Buying Power 1.0

Figure 2. Better Buying Power 2.0

Figure 3. Better Buying Power 3.0

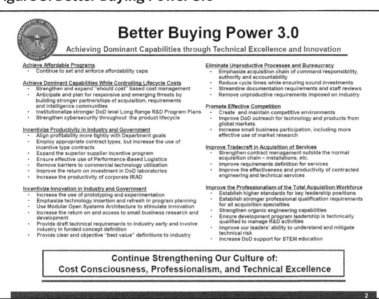

The underlying premise, and one I continue to strongly advocate, has always been that acquisition improvement would be incremental, that there was no "acquisition magic" that could be applied to all situations and that could dramatically improve results. The Better Buying Power initiatives sweat the details; that's where progress has to be achieved. As a result, there is a large number of initiatives, and more detailed implementation actions behind each initiative. All of the Better Buying Power releases, however, have been based on some underlying principles that I decided were worth articulating. The first piece in this chapter describes those acquisition management and policy principles. The list of principles is presented in this article in its original sequence. I was correctly chastised after I published the article for not putting people and professionalism first on this list, and I subsequently made this important modification to the sequence.

The process of creating cutting-edge weapon systems isn't new. The pace of change in technology advances accelerated dramatically in the 19th and, particularly, the 20th centuries. This trend continues today in the 21st century. However, the American reliance on technological superiority for military advantage really didn't take shape until World War II and afterward. With this reliance came the problems associated with accepting technological risk in new products, problems that we still confront—cost increases, schedule slips, and sometimes failure to deliver an acceptable or affordable product. In 1971, the year I graduated from West Point, David Packard was Deputy Secretary of Defense. This is the David Packard who helped found Hewlett-Packard, and who led the "Packard Commission," which influenced the acquisition reform legislation that accompanied the Goldwater-Nichols reforms of 1986. Deputy Secretary Packard published a set of "Acquisition Rules." I had this list put on posters and hung in the Pentagon meeting room where the Defense Acquisition Board (the committee that advises the Under Secretary on major acquisition decisions) meets. I consider this list to be the original Better Buying Power. It is discussed in the second piece in this chapter.

The next article in this chapter is a more detailed discussion of some of what I have referred to as "core" elements of all the Better Buying Power initiatives. Written shortly after the second version—Better Buying Power 2.0—this article goes into more detail about these core concepts. They include affordability constraints on requirements and designs, the use of "should cost" to actively target costs for reduction, and the importance of defining "best value" so that industry is motivated to offer optimized product designs in line with warfighter priorities. These concepts should be core elements of acquisition policy and embedded deeply in the Department's culture. Instilling these values and concepts in the workforce and into the DoD culture was a priority throughout my tenure as USD(AT&L) and a major reason that I stayed much longer then my predecessors.

The overarching goal of defense acquisition is to give our warfighters a significant military advantage over any opponent they might face. One key to meeting that goal is the ability to create innovative, even game-changing products that enable innovative operational concepts. The need for continuing technological superiority was the motivator for the third version of Better Buying Power. Starting with Secretary Hagel's Defense Innovation Initiative, later endorsed by Secretary Ashton Carter, for the last few years we have been emphasizing the importance of innovation across the Department. Secretary Carter's innovation initiatives included the Defense Innovation Unit Experimental or DIU-X, the Strategic Capabilities Office, and the Force of the Future personnel initiatives. Deputy Secretary Robert Work introduced the concept of a Third Offset Strategy. All three of us have been working toward the common goal of encouraging, seeking, and integrating more innovation into our processes. In the next article in this chapter, I took up the subject of innovation and discussed the ingredients needed in an organization for innovation to occur. They include technical expertise, freedom, risk tolerance, persistence, and teamwork or collaboration. I closed with a discussion of the need for capital (funding). While the development of good ideas is essential to innovation, so too is the need for money to convert those ideas into reality. In my view, all the focus on innovation by the Department over the last few years may have obscured the fact that our fundamental problem has not been lack of ideas, but the lack of resources to make them into products.

The final piece in this chapter is the most recent. It was written in part in reaction to the latest round of acquisition reform coming from the Congress. This article discusses the basic structure in which acquisition policy must operate, points out some of the inherent limitations in legislative attempts to improve acquisition, and charges our acquisition professionals with the goal that ultimately only they can achieve—lasting and significant improvement in our acquisition performance. The next section will take up the topic of those acquisition professionals who are central to executing any improvement effort.

Better Buying Power Principles— What Are They?

Reprinted from Defense AT&L: *January-February 2016*

Inevitably, whenever any senior leader embarks on a set of initiatives intended to improve an organization's performance and labels that set of initiatives, he or she can expect one reaction for certain. That reaction is what I would describe as genuflecting in the direction of the title of the initiative by various stakeholders who are trying to show the leader that they are aligned with his or her intent.

Sometimes—usually, I hope—this is sincere and backed up by real actions that reflect the intention of the initiative. Sometimes it is just, for lack of a better word, gratuitous. Better Buying Power (BBP) is no exception. One form this takes is assertions, which I see often enough to be writing this piece, that the recommended course of action is consistent with "BBP principles." (Presumably, the idea is that this will lead to instant support, but that is not a reliable assumption.)

I find this amusing, because so far as I know we've never articulated any BBP principles. When I do see this in a briefing, I ask the presenter what those principles are. So far, no one has been able to articulate them very well.

Under the circumstances, it seems like a good idea for me to provide some help answering this question. So here are some BBP principles. I also want to thank the 24 acquisition experts in the Defense Acquisition University's fall 2015 Executive Program Manager's Course who provided a number of suggestions for this list and article.

The Principles Suggested by Acquisition Experts:

- Principle 1: Continuous improvement will be more effective than radical change.
- Principle 2: Data should drive policy.
- Principle 3: Critical thinking is necessary for success; fixed rules are too constraining.
- Principle 4: Controlling life-cycle cost is one of our jobs; staying on budget isn't enough.
- Principle 5: People matter most; we can never be too professional or too competent.
- Principle 6: Incentives work—we get what we reward.

- Principle 7: Competition and the threat of competition are the most effective incentives.
- Principle 8: Defense acquisition is a team sport.
- Principle 9: Our technological superiority is at risk and we must respond.
- Principle 10: We should have the courage to challenge bad policy.

Principle 1

Continuous improvement will be more effective than radical change. All of BBP is based on this concept. It's the reason there have been three editions of BBP. We make incremental change focused on the biggest problems we see. Then we monitor the results and evaluate progress. We drop or modify ideas that aren't working, and we attack the next set of problems in order of importance, priority or expected impact. Those ideas and policies that work are not abandoned for the next shiny object we see. I have seen any number of acquisition reform fads that had little discernible impact on the acquisition performance of the Department of Defense (DoD). Some had adverse impacts. During my career, we have had the following: Blanket Firm Fixed Price Development Contracting, Total Quality Management, Reinventing Government, and Total System Performance—to name just a few.

I generally am not a fan of broad management theories and slogan-based programs. Sometimes they contain sound ideas and policies—but they seldom outlast the leaders who sponsor them, and the hype associated with them usually exceeds their value. The complexity of acquiring defense products and services makes simple solutions untenable; we have to work hard on many fronts to consistently improve our results.

Principle 2

Data should drive policy. Outside my door a sign is posted that reads, "In God We Trust; All Others Must Bring Data." The quote is attributed to W. Edwards Deming, the American management genius who built Japan's manufacturing industry after World War II. The three annual reports on *The Performance of the Defense Acquisition System* that we have published are based on this premise. It is difficult to manage something you cannot measure. Despite the noise in the data, it is possible to pull out the correlations that matter most and to discover those that have no discernible impact. As we have progressed through the various editions of BBP guided by the results of this analysis, we have adjusted policy, such as preferred contract type and incentive structure.

Principle 3

Critical thinking is necessary for success; fixed rules are too constraining. This principle was the core concept behind BBP 2.0, which was subtitled "a guide to help you think." Our world is complex. One-size-fits-all cookbook solutions simply don't work in many cases. The one question I most often ask program managers (PMs) and other leaders is "Why?" When we formulate acquisition strategies, plan logistics support programs, schedule a series of tests, decide which technology project to fund or do any other of the myriad tasks that acquisition, technology and logistics professionals are asked to do every day, we have to apply our skills experience and understanding of cost, benefits, and relative priorities to arrive at the best answer. There is no shortage of policy or history to assist us, but at the end of the day we have to figure out the best course of action in a specific circumstance, balancing all the complex factors that apply to a given situation.

Principle 4

Controlling life-cycle cost is one of our jobs; staying on budget isn't enough. This idea, that managing cost is a core responsibility, is at odds with a long history of focusing on execution (spending) in order to maintain budgets. The idea introduced in BBP 1.0 of "should cost" was intended to compel our managers (all of our managers) to pay attention to their cost structure, identify opportunities for savings, set targets for themselves and do their utmost to achieve those targets. I am hopeful that this idea is becoming institutionalized and, what is more important, is becoming part of a culture that values proactive efforts to control cost. Once in a while, I still see token savings targets. But, for the most part, our managers are implementing this concept and doing so effectively. One cautionary note is that this does not imply we should make poor decisions that result in short-term savings at the expense of high long-term costs.

Over the last 5 years, we have billions of dollars in savings that we can point to. In all cases, those dollars have gone to higher-priority Service, portfolio or program/activity needs. The result is more capability for the warfighter at less cost to the taxpayer.

Principle 5

People matter most; we can never be too professional or too competent. We introduced an entire section on building professionalism in BBP 2.0. It was a major oversight that former Under Secretary of Defense for Acquisition, Technology, and Logistics Ashton Carter and I left this out of BBP 1.0. Improving over time the expertise, values and competencies of our professionals is the best way to improve defense acquisition, technology and logistics outcomes. This was never intended to imply that the workforce is not already professional—of course it is. But more is better, and every one of us can be better at what we do—including me. The best statutes, processes and policies in the world will not by themselves make us or anyone in industry better managers, engineers, business people or logisticians. We should all constantly increase the DoD's professionalism, for ourselves and the people who work for us.

Principle 6

Incentives work and we get what we reward. Policies related to incentives are found everywhere in the various editions of BBP, most obviously those associated with contract types and incentive structures. Others include the use of open systems, how we manage intellectual property, the monetization of performance in source selection, and the use of prototypes to encourage innovation. In BBP 1.0 and BBP 2.0, we focused on getting the business incentives right. In BBP 3.0, we focused on incentives to innovation and technical excellence.

Principle 7

Competition and the threat of competition provide the most effective incentive. All businesses exist in large part for the purpose of making a profit for their investors. The opportunity to gain business through competition and the threat that an existing market position will be lost as a result of competition are powerful motivators. One thing I enjoyed about my time working in the defense industry was the simplicity of the metric and the fact that everyone in the firms I worked with understood that metric: If something increased profit, it was good; if it didn't do so, it wasn't good. When we rolled out the first set of BBP initiatives, industry was concerned that we were waging a "war on profit." That was never our intention. What we wanted and still want to do is align profit with the desired performance for the warfighter and the taxpayer. Many BPP initiatives are designed to foster competition or the threat of competition.

Principle 8

Defense acquisition is a team sport. Over the three editions of BBP, we have pointed to the importance of close cooperation and coordination between participants and stakeholders. The importance of the requirements and intelligence communities were highlighted in BBP 2.0 and 3.0, respectively. The nonacquisition leaders who are responsible for much of the DoD's service contracts are another important community. Defense acquisition can only be successful and efficient if all participants recognize and respect other participants' roles and responsibilities.

Principle 9

Our technological superiority is at risk, and we must respond. This fact is the reason for BBP 3.0. The combination of cutting-edge, strategic and increasing investments made by potential adversaries, coupled with our own budgetary stress and global commitments, are causes for alarm. We need to do everything we can to maximize the return on all our investments in new capability, wherever those investments are made. BBP 3.0 focuses on all the ways in which we expend research and development (R&D) funding (DoD laboratories, industry independent R&D, contracted R&D, etc.) and on the opportunities to spend those funds more productively. The Long-Range Research and Development Planning Program recommendations are intended to provide guidance on how to achieve this. BBP 3.0 also includes the increased use of experimental prototypes and other measures designed to spur innovation—such as early concept definition by industry and monetary incentives to industry to develop and offer higher-than-threshold performance levels. We need to reduce cycle time, eliminate unproductive bureaucracy, and increase our agility by accepting more risk when it is warranted. All of these measures are BBP initiatives.

Principle 10

We should have the courage to challenge bad policy. One of Deming's principles was that successful organizations "drive out fear." He meant that a healthy organizational culture encourages members to speak out and contribute ideas and inform management about things that are not as they should be. We should not be afraid to speak up when we see bad policy, or policy applied too rigidly where that clearly isn't the best course of action. We should not be afraid to offer creative ideas or to challenge conventional wisdom, and we should encourage others to do so as well. None of the BBP initiatives, or their more detailed implementation guidance, are intended to apply in every possible situation. All of us should be willing to "speak truth to power" about situations in which policies simply are not working or will not achieve the intended result. The annual PM Program Assessments that I started last year and included in BBP 3.0 proved to me that the chain of command has a lot to learn from the very professional people on the front lines of defense acquisition. This applies to all the professionals who support or work for those PMs also. Continuous improvement comes from the willingness to challenge the status quo.

CHAPTER ONE: GETTING ACQUISITION POLICY RIGHT

The Original Better Buying Power— David Packard Acquisition Rules 1971

Reprinted from Defense AT&L: *May-June 2013*

In this article, I thought I would give us all a break from our budget woes, sequestration, and continuing resolutions—issues I hope will be resolved before this goes to print.

In 1971, I graduated from West Point. This was also the same year that David Packard, the Packard in Hewlett Packard, who was then the Deputy Secretary of Defense (there was no Under Secretary for Acquisition), published his rules for Defense Acquisition. I wouldn't say there has been nothing new under the sun since then, but some things do endure.

Recall that by 1971 we had already been to the moon, and the digital age, enabled by solid state electronics, had just begun. By the fall of 1971, I was at Caltech where I designed logic circuits using solid state integrated components that included a few specific logic functions—several orders of magnitude from current technology, and I was reducing experimental data using the first engineering math function digital calculator. My slide rule had become obsolete. Deputy Secretary Packard's rules, however, still resonate. I recently had them put on a poster and hung it in the Pentagon in the room we use for Defense Acquisition Board (DAB) meetings. Here they are with a little commentary from both David Packard and me. You should recognize a number of areas of overlap with Better Buying Power.

1. Help the Services Do a Better Job. Improvement in the development and acquisition of new weapons systems will be achieved to the extent the Services are willing and able to improve their management practices. The Services have the primary responsibility to get the job done. OSD offices should see that appropriate policies are established and evaluate the performance of the Services in implementing these policies.

I continue to struggle with achieving the appropriate degree of staff "oversight," but I certainly agree with this sentiment. Services manage programs. As Defense Acquisition Executive (DAE), I set policy and I make specific decisions about major investment commitments for large programs, usually at Milestone Reviews. The staff supports me in those decisions, and I expect solid independent "due diligence" assessments for those decisions from the staff of the Office of the Secretary of Defense (OSD). All other staff activities should be about helping the Services be more effective, ensuring that our policies are well defined, and getting feedback on what works and what needs to be improved in our acquisition practices.

2. Have Good Program Managers with Authority and Responsibility. If the Services are to do a better job, they must assign better program managers to these projects. These managers must be given an appropriate staff and the responsibility and the authority to do the job, and they must be kept in the job long enough to get something done.

I don't know anything more basic and important to our success than this imperative. Having seen more than 4 decades of defense acquisition policy changes, I am absolutely convinced that nothing matters as much as competent, professional leadership. Once you have that, the rest is details. It was my concern for the professionalism of the acquisition workforce that led to the inclusion of an additional category of initiatives focused on our workforce in BBP 2.0. We have a lot of good, even great, extremely dedicated, professionals working in Defense Acquisition. But we need a deeper bench, and every one of us can improve on our own abilities. In the tough budget climate of today, managers at all levels, including Military Department and Agency leadership, should pay a great deal of attention to retaining and managing our talent pool. At the tactical level, I'm looking for some opportunities to take a "skunk works"-like approach to a pilot program in each Service. The key to implementing this approach, however, and what I want to be sure of before I authorize it, will be a highly qualified and appropriately staffed government team that will be with the project until the product is delivered.

3. Control Cost by Trade-offs. The most effective way to control the cost of a development program is to make practical trade-offs between operating requirements and engineering design.

The affordability as a requirement element of Better Buying Power is intended to provide a forcing function for just this purpose. I've seen several variations of this; during my first tour of duty in OSD, we used "Cost as an Independent Variable" to try to capture this idea. The approach we are using now relies on the affordability caps (which are based on future budget expectations—not on cost estimates) that we are establishing early in the design process or product life cycle (Milestones A and B). The requirement to deliver products that meet the affordability caps is intended to force requirements prioritization and trade-offs among competing needs. I plan to insert a Requirements Decision Point prior to Milestone (MS) B to help facilitate this. I will continue to put these affordability caps in place and will be enforcing them over the next several years. For non-ACAT I programs, the Services and Agencies should be doing the same.

4. Make the First Decision Right. The initial decision to go ahead with full-scale development of a particular program is the most important decision of the program. If this decision is wrong, the program is doomed to failure. To make this decision correctly generally will require that the program be kept in advanced development long enough to resolve the key technical uncertainties, and to see that they are matched with key operating requirements before the decision to go ahead is made.

I have long regarded the decision to enter Engineering and Manufacturing Development (EMD) as the single most important decision in a program's life cycle. The name has changed several times over my career, and Deputy Secretary Packard refers to it as full-scale development—but we are talking about the commitment to go on contract for design of a producible product that meets stated requirements, engineering development test articles, and for the tests that will be necessary to confirm performance prior to starting production.

At this point, we are committing to on average about 10 percent to 20 percent of the product's life-cycle cost to years of development work, and to getting a product that we will field ready for production. Among the most disturbing sources of waste in our system are the programs we put into EMD, spend billions on, and then cancel—sometimes before EMD is complete and sometimes after some initial production. Part of getting this decision right (in addition to affordability) is having the risk associated with the product and its requirements under control and sufficiently understood and reduced so EMD can be executed efficiently and successfully. In recent years, we have focused on the Technology Readiness Level (TRL) as a metric for maturity. I find this metric to be useful, but not adequate to the task of assuring readiness to enter EMD, and not a substitute for a thorough understanding of the actual risk in the program—necessary but not sufficient, in other words. In addition to technology risk, we have to manage engineering and integration risks. More importantly, we have to deeply understand the actual risk, what it implies, and what the tools are to mitigate it before and during EMD. I commissioned a review of programs transitioning from Technology Development into EMD over a year ago and discovered we are not paying adequate attention to the actual risk associated with the actual product we intend to acquire. In many cases, industry was not being incentivized to reduce the actual risk in a product it would produce; it was being incentivized to claim a TRL and to do a demonstration. This isn't necessarily the same thing as reducing the risk in an actual product. The label of a TRL isn't enough to ensure that the risks of a product development are under control; we have to look deeper. This decision is too important to get wrong.

5. Fly Before You Buy. Engineering development must be completed before substantial commitment to production is made.

If you have read any article about the F-35 Joint Strike Fighter in the last year, you probably saw a quote of my comment about "acquisition malpractice." I was talking specifically about the decision to enter production well before the first flight of a production representative EMD prototype. The earlier Milestones in our Materiel Development Decisions (MDD) system for weapons acquisition—MS A and MS B—generally are based on planning documents and analysis. MS B also is based on risk-reduction activities, but if these have been completed, the balance of the review is about intended business approaches, engineering, test planning, and funding adequacy. The decision to enter production at MS C is different. Here the emphasis is on whether the design meets requirements and is stable. I would regard this decision as a close second to the EMD decision in importance. Once we start production, we are effectively committed, and it will be very difficult to stop. I seriously considered stopping F-35 production a year ago, but I believe I made the right decision to continue. We shouldn't put ourselves in the position of having to make that sort of a choice.

Before the commitment to production, the ability to meet requirements and the stability of the design should be demonstrated by developmental testing of EMD prototypes that are close to the production design. Some degree of concurrency usually is acceptable; all testing doesn't usually have to be complete before the start of low-rate production. The degree of concurrency will vary with the urgency of the need for the product and the specific risks remaining. But as a general practice, we should "fly before we buy."

6. Put More Emphasis on Hardware, Less on Paper Studies. Logistics support, training, and maintenance problems must be considered early in the development, but premature implementation of these matters tends to be wasteful.

Most of the costs of our products are neither development nor production costs. It is support costs that predominate. These costs do need to be considered up front, early in the requirements and design processes and as the acquisition strategy is being formulated. They drive considerations of the data and property rights we will acquire and the implementation of open systems and modular designs (all features of Better Buying Power). While we should avoid setting up support functions too much in advance of need, we also should ensure that the ability to meet support requirements is designed in and tested at the appropriate places in the development program, and we must ensure that an adequate budget will be available to sustain the product. Better Buying Power's affordability caps on sustainment costs are designed to ensure that these upfront analyses are conducted early in development, preferably while there is still competition for the development work, and before the design concept has matured to the point that trade-offs to improve supportability no longer are possible.

7. Eliminate Total Package Procurement. It is not possible to determine the production cost of a complex new weapon before it is developed. The total package procurement procedure is unworkable. It should not be used.

Total Package Procurement is one of those acquisition ideas that come along occasionally and are embraced for a time until it becomes apparent they are not panaceas. I'm speculating, but I would guess the Deputy Secretary had seen some disasters come out of this approach. The idea is to get prices (as options, presumably) for the production run at the time we start development. I'm not quite as pessimistic as Deputy Secretary Packard was about the ability to predict production costs, but I'm pretty close. We are tempted occasionally to ask for production prices as options at the time we are doing a competitive down-select for EMD. This is tempting because we can take advantage of competitive pressure that we will lose after we enter EMD. While I wouldn't close out this idea entirely as Deputy Secretary Packard did in this rule, I think we have to consider this approach carefully before adopting it. There are other ways to provide incentives to control production costs, and we need to consider the full range of options and the pros and cons and the risks associated with them before we decide on an acquisition strategy or a contract structure for a specific product. BBP 2.0 takes this approach.

8. Use the Type of Contract Appropriate for the Job. Development contracts for new major weapons systems should be cost-incentive type contracts. (a) Cost control of a development program can be achieved by better management. (b) A prime objective of every development program must be to minimize the life-cycle cost as well as the production cost of the article or system being developed. (c) Price competition is virtually meaningless in selecting a contractor for a cost-incentive program. Other factors must control the selection.

We seem to work in 20-year cycles. In 1971, David Packard supported the use of cost-plus contracts for development. About 20 years later in the late 1980s, we tried a policy or requiring firm fixed-price contracts for development. I lived that dream from the perspective of having, in the early 1990s, to extricate the Department from the disasters that ensued—not least among them the Navy's A-12 program cancellation, which still is in litigation more than 20 years later. Fast forward another 20 years, and we are seeing suggestions of using this approach again. Recently, I wrote at length about the times when a fixed-price development approach might be appropriate, and I won't repeat that material here. There are times when fixed price is the right approach to development contracts, but it is the exception rather than the rule. I completely agree with David Packard that costs can be controlled on a cost-plus contract by better management. It requires hands-on management and a willingness to confront industry about excessive and unnecessary costs or activities. It also requires strong incentives to reward the performance we should expect, coupled with the will and expertise to use those incentives effectively. The importance of controlling life-cycle costs has been discussed earlier. I don't entirely agree that price competition is meaningless in selecting a contractor for a development contract, but I do agree that other factors should usually be of greater significance to the government. Most of all, I fully concur with Deputy Secretary Packard's overarching point: Use the contract type appropriate for the job. If you get a chance to attend a DAB or DAES meeting, or just to come into the Pentagon, you can see David Packard's rules on the wall in Room 3B912. They still resonate. We have tough jobs, and the professionalism needed to do them effectively is a constant. There are no rules that can be a substitute for that.

CHAPTER ONE: GETTING ACQUISITION POLICY RIGHT

The Challenges We Face—
And How We Will Meet Them

Reprinted from Defense AT&L: *November-December 2012*

"Supporting the warfighter, protecting the taxpayer"—these words were suggested by my military assistant for a small sign outside the door to my office in the Pentagon. They succinctly express the challenges those of us who work in defense acquisition, technology, and logistics face in the austere times we have entered. We will have to provide the services and products our warfighters need and protect the taxpayers' interest by obtaining as much value as we possibly can for every dollar entrusted to us.

This is nothing new; we have always tried to do this. Going forward, however, we will have to accomplish this goal without reliance on large overseas contingency funding and in the face of continued pressure on defense budgets brought about not by a change in the national security environment, which is increasingly challenging particularly with the emergence of more technologically and operationally sophisticated potential opponents, but by the policy imperative to reduce the annual budget deficit.

Hopefully, the specter of more than $50 billion in sequestration cuts next year will be avoided, but, even if it is, we can expect the pressure on defense budgets to increase. Last winter, the department published new strategic guidance as well as a budget designed to implement that strategy. Like all budgets, this one did not make any allowance for overruns, schedule slips, or increases in costs for services beyond the standard indices assumed by the Office of Management and Budget, indices that often are exceeded. We have our work cut out for us today and for as far into the future as we can see.

The overriding imperative of obtaining the greatest value possible for the dollars entrusted to us is not just an acquisition problem; it encompasses all facets of defense planning, as well as execution of acquisition programs and contracted services. We have to begin by understanding and controlling everything that drives cost or leads to waste. The budgeting/programming and requirements communities are as important to success as our planning and management and industry's execution of acquisition contracts. The quest for value includes an understanding of: (1) the constraints we must live within; (2) a willingness to prioritize our needs and accept less than we might prefer; (3) an understanding of the relative value of the capabilities we could acquire; and (4) an activist approach to controlling costs while we deliver the needed capability. Only the last of these is solely an acquisition responsibility.

For the last 2 years, and as part of the original Better Buying Power initiative, we required that affordability caps be placed on programs entering the acquisition process. These caps are not the result of anticipated costs; they are the result of an analysis of anticipated budgets. Here is a simple example of what I mean: If we have to maintain a fleet of 100,000 trucks that we expect to last 20 years, then we will have to buy an average of 5,000 trucks per year. If we can only expect to have $1 billion a year to spend on trucks, we must buy trucks that cost no more than $200,000 each. That $200,000 is our affordability cap. Affordability is not derived from cost; it dictates cost constraints that we have to live within. The source of the type of analysis illustrated here is generally not the acquisition community; it comes primarily from force planners and programmers, working in collaboration with acquisition people. We have affordability caps on a number of programs now, both for production costs and sustainment costs. Our greatest challenge going forward will be to enforce those caps.

To achieve affordability caps, we will need a willingness to identify and trade off less important sources of cost. In other words, we will have to prioritize requirements, identify the costs associated with meeting those requirements, and drop or defer the capabilities that do not make the affordability cut. This is a simple formula, but one the department has been reluctant to act on in the past. Too often, our history has been one of starting programs with desirable but ambitious requirements, spending years and billions of dollars in development, and perhaps in low rate production, and then finally realizing that our reach had exceeded our grasp. The most recent example of this is the Expeditionary Fighting Vehicle, which was canceled after many years in development because it was unaffordable. There are many others.

The acquisition community and the requirements communities must work together to understand priorities and make these choices as early as possible. Delay in confronting difficult trade-offs will only lead to waste. If a 1 percent or 2 percent change in a performance goal will result in a 10 percent or 20 percent cost reduction, that trade should be considered as early as possible. Configuration Steering Boards are one mechanism to address requirements trade-offs, but they must meet often, be empowered, and have the data they need to make informed decisions. When the affordability of the full requirements for a new product that hasn't been developed yet is uncertain, industry must be given prioritized requirements so that its offerings can be optimized to meet the highest-priority user needs within the cost cap. Again, this takes close cooperation between communities and the willingness on the part of

Chapter One: Getting Acquisition Policy Right

the requirements community to articulate priorities and to take into consideration the costs of meeting less essential requirements.

One situation I have seen on occasion in the last few years, and one I expect we will see more in the future, is the case in which "best value" has to be clearly defined. Often in these cases there is a competition between companies offering dissimilar capability levels based on existing products that may be modified to meet a need. The Air Force tanker program is an example of this: Both offerings were based on commercial aircraft and both could meet the basic requirements, but they also had differing capabilities with disparate military utility as well. In situations like this, the onus is on us, primarily on the user, to determine the value to the government of the different levels of capability and to apply that understanding objectively in the source selection process. Defining the value of a capability to the customer (what the customer is willing to pay for something) has nothing to do with the cost of the capability. Read that last sentence again—it is very important. In the KC-46 tanker situation, the Air Force determined that it was only willing to pay up to 1 percent more for the extra features that might be offered. Again, this had nothing to do with what those features cost. The bottom line is that, in the austere times we can expect going forward, we will need to understand how much we are willing to pay in total (the affordability cap) and how much of a premium we are willing to pay for additional capability beyond the threshold requirement. We will also have to communicate these parameters clearly to industry.

If we have constrained our appetites to what we can afford and to what we consider best value, now we have to execute more effectively than we have in the past. Historically, we have overrun development programs in the high 20 percent range, and we have overrun early production lots by almost 10 percent. This has to stop. It will not stop because of any one thing we do or any one set of policies. If controlling acquisition costs were easy, we would have done it decades ago.

Soon I will be publishing the next round of Better Buying Power initiatives (BBP 2.0), perhaps by the time this article goes to press. However, the central idea of Better Buying Power is not the list of specific management practices or policies we are currently emphasizing. The central idea is that we must all continuously look for ways to improve how we do business and the outcomes we achieve. We have to understand our costs; we have to look for opportunities to reduce them; and we have to attack unnecessary costs as the enemy of the department that they are. The whole idea of "should cost" management approaches and goals reflects this concept. So too do the various policy, management, and contracting initiatives we are pursuing under the Better Buying Power rubric and throughout everything we do.

We should not be content with staying within our budgets. It is not our job to spend the budget. It is our job to provide our warfighters with the greatest value we can for every penny of the money the taxpayers provide to us. If we keep this always firmly in mind, we will successfully meet the challenges we face.

CHAPTER ONE: GETTING ACQUISITION POLICY RIGHT

Innovation in the Defense Acquisition Enterprise

Reprinted from Defense AT&L: *November-December 2015*

Innovation has become a very popular word lately. Former Secretary of Defense Chuck Hagel announced the Defense Innovation Initiative about a year ago. At about the same time, the draft Better Buying Power 3.0 set of initiatives, focusing on technical excellence and innovation, were published for comment. Deputy Defense Secretary Robert O. Work has led the effort to develop an innovative "Third Offset Strategy." Most recently, Secretary of Defense Ashton Carter announced the opening of the Defense Innovation Unit—Experimental, or DIU-X, in California's Silicon Valley. President Obama has led the administration's successful opening of several Manufacturing Innovation Institutes, most of which are sponsored by the Department of Defense (DoD). And more institutes are on the way.

Today it is possible to obtain advanced degrees at major universities in the fields of innovation and entrepreneurship. Many books and articles have been written on innovation, perhaps none more well-known than Clayton Christianson's "The Innovators Dilemma." I would like to add a few thoughts to that body of work by making some very unscientific (meaning unsupported by data) comments on the ingredients needed to foster and encourage innovation—and on the extent to which the DoD acquisition enterprise has or does not have those ingredients today.

The first and absolutely necessary ingredient is knowledge. Technical innovation is itself, almost by definition, a new idea. But new ideas are rooted in the knowledge that makes the new idea conceivable and practical. Part of Better Buying Power 3.0 involves increased support for education in STEM (science, technology, engineering, and mathematics). Our educational system provides the foundation of our knowledge, but that is just the beginning. Experience, exposure to a wide and diverse range of technical fields, and continuing in-depth study are all important. For the more exciting areas of technical innovation today, this knowledge is increasingly highly specialized and deep. I recently visited the Massachusetts Institute of Technology and spoke to researchers in the fields of biological process-based materials production, novel computational architectures, and autonomy. These are areas in which it is not possible to enable innovation unless one has a deep knowledge of the science and associated technology. I believe that we are in the early stages of some explosive growth in the products that these and other technologies will make possible, but some very specialized advanced technology work will have to be accomplished to achieve that potential. Once that occurs, innovative applications of these technologies will be created at an exponential rate. In many cases today, the DoD is not the primary financial supporter of the relevant work. Nevertheless, the DoD's basic research program still represents an important contributor, and it provides a basis by which the DoD can shape and capitalize on new technical knowledge as it is created. By reaching out to nontraditional sources, such as through the DIU-X, the DoD intends to increase its knowledge of the possibilities that commercial cutting edge technology can offer to DoD.

My second ingredient is freedom. By this, I mean the freedom to have a new idea and to take action in pursuit of that idea. I mean the freedom to fail and start again. I also mean freedom from bureaucratic constraints. Our free enterprise system provides this ingredient on a national scale, and it is the most powerful economic engine ever created. The United States stands out as a place where it is amazingly easy to start a new business. I've done it a couple of times.

Within the DoD, one of our most effective and successful institutions—the Defense Advanced Research Projects Agency (DARPA)—is a living testament to the value of freedom. I zealously guard DARPA's freedom from the many parts of the DoD that see DARPA's budget as an opportunity to fund something they need. The whole concept of DARPA is that the organization has the freedom to choose its own high-risk but high-payoff investments.

In DoD more broadly, we set strategic goals for technology investment, require a certain fraction of the Services Science and Technology work to be in these areas and leave those organizations the freedom to choose their own priorities for the balance of their work. Within DoD, we also allow our contractors to pursue Independent Research and Development (IR&D) as an allowable overhead cost with very little constraint.

I made industry a little nervous recently by proposing in Better Buying Power 3.0 to increase the DoD's oversight of this work. The fundamental concern of industry partners has been the possible loss of freedom to make their own IR&D investment decisions. That was never my intent. I once ran a major defense contractor's IR&D program, and I appreciate industry's perspective. I appreciate the value, to industry and the DoD, of allowing industry to place its own bets on technology that might increase a firm's competitiveness.

After carefully considering several alternatives, the policy I propose would merely require industry to brief an appropriate DoD officer or official prior to and after concluding an IR&D project, and to document that the meeting occurred as part of the accounting for the project. This policy would not require sponsorship or approval of an IR&D project by a DoD official, but it would require industry to communicate directly with appropriate DoD personnel and to obtain feedback on the proposed work and to communicate the results when the work is complete. This should not constrain industry's freedom in any way that current regulations and statutes don't already require, and it will provide the benefit of ensuring more frequent and effective communication between industry and government.

Human Intangibles

My next two ingredients enter the area of what I will call subjective human intangibles. These intangibles also are manifested in what we call organizational cultures. One could generate a pretty long list of the human qualities needed for successful innovation. The list might include innate intelligence, creativity or the ability to think "out of the box" and curiosity, to name just a few such qualities. These address the capacity to have a new idea. A great deal of work has gone into structuring organizational environments to encourage and foster creativity. This can include physical arrangements, workplace layouts, and a range of approaches intended to foster cultural norms that support creativity.

Some companies use problem-solving tests to identify candidates with high creativity. I believe all this work has merit, but I also think its goal is to select creative people and to draw out the inherent creativity that people either do or do not possess. I'm only going to mention two human qualities that I think have great importance, and that DoD managers at all levels should be especially conscious of: risk tolerance and persistence.

Accepting Risk

I was asked by a reporter during an interview 2 or 3 years ago if the DoD was taking too much risk in its programs. My response was that we are not taking enough risks. With respect to our major programs, I find myself pushed in two directions simultaneously by the political winds in Washington. At the same time that I am told the expectation for all our programs is to have no schedule slips or cost overruns, I also am told that we should go much faster in our programs and not have so much oversight. I'm sorry, but you can't have it both ways.

To me, both perspectives miss the point. Development of new products, particularly a new generation of cutting-edge and militarily dominant systems, cannot be made risk free. If we want risk-free defense acquisition, we should just buy fully developed products from other countries. If, on the other hand, we want the best military in the world, and one in which our warfighters always have innovative and dominant equipment, then we are going to have risk in our programs.

One of our program managers' most important responsibilities is to understand and proactively manage the risk inherent in any development program. (I wrote about that responsibility in an article in the July-August 2015 issue of *Defense AT&L* magazine.) To borrow a line from the movies, the secret of life is balance. We have to balance risk against urgency and resource constraints. If we are too cautious, our programs will take forever and be too modest in their ambitions. If we gamble wildly, we will waste precious resources and not meet our objectives.

At the enterprise level in DoD today, there is strong support for accepting the risk of embarking on a number of what I will call advanced technology demonstration programs. The recently completed Long Range Research and Development Planning Program has recommended several advanced technology demonstration programs for consideration in the Fiscal Year (FY) 2017 budget. Similarly, the Strategic Capabilities Office is proposing demonstration programs based on novel applications of currently fielded systems or those in development. In the FY 2016 budget, I was able to secure funding for the Aerospace Innovation Initiative that will culminate in X-plane-type and propulsion technology demonstrators that will create options for the systems subsequent to our current Joint Strike Fighter program. This fall, all of these demonstration proposals will collide with budget reality at the President's Budget request level. Needless to say, if sequestration occurs, that collision will be even more violent. In some cases, we could reasonably accept more risk and move directly into Engineering and Manufacturing Development (EMD) programs instead of pursuing concept demonstration programs, but we simply don't have the resources to conduct those EMD programs.

Persistence

The other intangible characteristic successful innovators demonstrate is persistence. When innovators encounter obstacles, they find ways through or around them. Two obvious historical examples are Thomas Edison and his quest for a practical light bulb, and the Wright brothers and their pursuit of controlled, powered flight. (David McCullough has written a new book chronicling the Wright brothers' tenacious pursuit of powered and controlled flight.)

The DoD has sometimes been criticized for sticking with programs that encounter problems. The F-35 fighter is a current example. Earlier ones in my experience include the C-17, the Advanced Medium-Range Air-to-Air Missile, and the F-18E/F fighter. In all those cases, we persevered and achieved good results. In other cases, we have stopped programs that, in retrospect, we probably should have continued. In still other cases, we kept going for far too long on programs that should have been canceled earlier.

In general, my sense is that, for most programs, we can get to a product that meets our requirements if we have the patience and persistence to continue. There are exceptions, however.

There is an important difference between the persistence applied to commercial innovation and that applied to innovative products in DoD. For commercial products, both in start-ups and large corporations, the decision to continue product development when problems are encountered is driven by the judgment of the management (influenced by persistence and risk tolerance) and by the resources available to the firm. In DoD's case, these decisions have a high political content—both internally and externally. My observation is that the politicization of these decisions does not generally lead to better results. We also have frequent leadership changes—which makes persistence in the face of difficulties more problematic. I have no solution to offer for all this other than to continue the work of the last several years to ensure we don't start unaffordable programs, and to manage risk professionally and proactively in our development programs. The DoD spends taxpayer-provided money; we will always be under close public scrutiny, and we will always have internal competition for resources.

Collaboration

Innovation, in the commercial and the DoD context, tends to be based on collaboration. Multiple technical disciplines often have to come together, and the synergy between multiple disciplines may be the central feature of the innovative idea. In the DoD, technical ideas only reach the market when the using military Service decides to embrace the new concept or new product. This is not quite the same as the commercial market where "early adopters" from a large customer base may help a technology establish a foothold and gain credence. Commercial entrepreneurs build the better mouse trap first and expect customers to come. In DoD the customers, the military Departments, ask for fairly specific products and then budget the resources to pay for the development of those products.

The DoD also uses a formalized requirements process that is based on the perception of "gaps" in capability. Requirements are generated to fill these perceived gaps. This approach tends to be self-limiting and to discourage new concepts and innovative approaches that deviate from existing paradigms. Henry Ford's famous quip that if he had asked his customers what they wanted it would have been a better horse has some relevance here. The fact is, however, that despite our formal process, requirements are often based on the priorities of senior Service leadership. For this reason, I welcome the initiative from the U.S. Senate to increase Service leadership involvement in acquisition.

A strong collaboration between Service leadership and the technical acquisition community, starting as early in the product life cycle as possible, is essential to effective innovation in the DoD, and it is a component of Better Buying Power. I would also add that close collaboration with the intelligence community is critical as well: Potential adversaries are moving very quickly to develop products clearly designed to defeat U.S. capabilities. The DoD must be both innovative and quick to market in responding to these emerging threats. Achieving these objectives requires strong and continuous collaboration between operators, the intelligence community and the technical acquisition community.

Funding Is Fundamental

There is one more necessary ingredient that I have not discussed yet. That ingredient is capital. Small start-ups and large businesses alike depend on capital to survive and to bring new products to market. So it is for the DoD, and this is my greatest concern today. Our capital comes from the budgets we receive from Congress. As long as we remain trapped in the grip of sequestration and as long we continue to prepare budgets that are far out of alignment with the funds we may receive, we will not be able to innovate effectively.

Innovation isn't just about thinking outside the box, or about demonstrating new technologies and operational concepts. It is about developing, producing, fielding and training with those new capabilities. Today I believe our pipeline of new products in development is inadequate to deal with emerging threats. We are facing a major recapitalization bill for the strategic deterrent that is about to come due. There is nothing that I or the DoD can do to improve our productivity and efficiency that will fully compensate for inadequate capital. All the efficiencies I can even imagine will not make up this shortfall. By conducting well-chosen demonstrations, we can reduce the lead time to acquiring real operational capability, we can keep an essential fraction of our industrial base gainfully employed, and we can position ourselves for changes in threat perceptions and the availability of additional funds. But, without relief from the specter of sequestration, we cannot increase the relative combat power of the United States against our most capable potential adversaries.

I can point to numerous places in DoD where we are taking steps to improve our access to and use of each of these ingredients: knowledge, freedom, risk tolerance, persistence, collaboration and capital. For the last few years, we have worked hard to emphasize and increase the professionalism of the government acquisition workforce. Secretary Carter's "Force of the Future" initiative is specifically intended to bring high knowledge people into our workforce. With help from the Congress through the Defense

CHAPTER ONE: GETTING ACQUISITION POLICY RIGHT

Acquisition Workforce Development Fund and a number of internal actions, we have continued to build on our strong foundation in this area despite budget constraints.

We are protecting and emphasizing the freedom of our managers to find creative solutions to technical and managerial problems. Last year, I tasked each of our program managers to communicate directly with me about problems, issues and recommended solutions. The result was a huge testament to the creativity, dedication and professionalism of our workforce.

The demonstrations that I mentioned, if they can be funded, show our willingness to take risk on new and nontraditional approaches to operational problems. Deputy Secretary Work's "Third Offset" strategy, by its very nature, will require the DoD to accept the risk associated with new operational concepts and the technologies that enable them. Our ability to persist in bringing all of these initiatives to fruition remains to be seen, but the closely aligned leadership in the DoD—including the Secretary and Deputy Secretary of Defense, myself, and the new Joint and Service uniformed chiefs—makes me optimistic that we can collaborate to do so.

From their inception, the Better Buying Power initiatives, in every edition, have been about getting the most value possible from our available capital. With that possible exception—which is in the hands of the Congress—we possess or can obtain all the ingredients we need to bring innovative solutions to our warfighters.

Real Acquisition Reform (or Improvement) Must Come From Within

Reprinted from Defense AT&L: *May-June 2016*

Since I returned to government 6 years ago, I have been working with the acquisition workforce and defense industry to improve defense acquisition performance. There is a lot of evidence that we are moving in the right direction. We have also effectively partnered with Congress on some initiatives, and we are in the midst of a new cycle of congressionally led efforts to improve defense acquisition—as in other cases with the label of "acquisition reform."

I would like to share some thoughts with you about the limitations of legislative tools, and also explain why I believe that lasting improvements must come from within the Department of Defense (DoD)—from our own efforts. Legislation can make our job easier or harder, but it can't do this job for us. I recently was asked by Chairman Mac Thornberry to attend a roundtable on acquisition reform with the House Armed Services Committee. This article is based in part on the thoughts I communicated to the committee.

First of all, what it takes to be successful at defense acquisition isn't all that complicated—to first order at least. It consists of just these four items: (1) set reasonable requirements, (2) put professionals in charge, (3) give them the resources they need, and (4) provide strong incentives for success. Unfortunately, there is a world of nuance and complexity in each of these phrases and words. They also apply to both government and industry organizations, but not always in the same way. The fact is that none of this is easy.

Reasonable requirements are not all that simple to create, professionals don't exist by chance, resources are subject to budget vagaries and other constraints—including a predisposition toward optimism—and incentives are complicated and often have unintended consequences. The work of making each of these four imperatives real for a given program is not easily accomplished, even with strong hands-on leadership. It is even harder to influence through legislation. I have some sympathy—and even empathy—for the difficulty that the Congress and our oversight committees face when they try to "reform" defense acquisition. Congress has two major challenges as it tries to improve acquisition results. The first is the structure of the

Chapter One: Getting Acquisition Policy Right

defense acquisition enterprise itself. The second is the inherent limitation on the set of tools they have to work with to effect change.

One way to imagine the defense acquisition enterprise is as a layered construct. At the base of this tiered structure are the organizations and people that do the actual work of delivering products and services. These people and organization are almost all defense contractors. (I'm oversimplifying a little here—some services and products are provided within government, but this is an exception.) The next layer consists of the government people who actually supervise the defense contractors. This second layer is also the layer at which requirements—a critical input to the acquisition structure I'm describing—directly impact the work. There is a huge variety of contracted services and product acquisitions, and the government people who plan, issue and administer contracts cover a broad spectrum of roles and professional expertise. These two layers are where the action occurs in terms of delivering products and services. Everything else in the acquisition structure is about making these two layers function as effectively as possible.

Above these layers there are chains of command and direct stakeholders of many types, most but not all of whom are located in the organization (military department or component) acquiring the service or product. Next there is a layer of what we like to call "oversight" within the DoD, some of it in the Office of the Secretary of Defense but also a great deal of it distributed in the military departments and agencies. My own position as Under Secretary is a mix of acquisition chain of command responsibilities and policy or oversight.

Finally, at the top of the whole structure, and furthest from where the work is done, there is the Congress, which has statutory authority over the DoD and the entire Executive Branch and conducts its constitutional oversight role.

In order to achieve its objective of improving acquisition, Congress has to penetrate through all the other layers to get to those where the work is done. This isn't an easy task. The DoD's relationship with our contractors is defined primarily by contracts, so one route available to the Congress to improve acquisition is to write laws governing defense contracts. These laws then are turned into regulations in our Defense Federal Acquisition Regulation Supplement (DFARS) by people in the oversight and policy layer and implemented by the management layers that are in more direct contact with defense contractors.

As a practical matter, Congress tends to react to events as they occur by passing additional statutory provisions. Congress also tends to make changes or additions whenever committee leadership, members and staff change. Of course, lobbyists for industry and other interests play a role in this process. The result over time is a frequently changing, but usually increasingly complex compendium of almost 2,000 pages of DFARS regulations governing how the DoD contracts for work. A serious effort at acquisition reform would include a complete review of everything in both the Federal Acquisition Regulations (FAR) and DFARS with the first-order goal of simplification and rationalization and the second-order goal of eliminating as much content as possible.

This task would take a good-sized, knowledgeable team up to a year to complete and it would take at least a year more for review and modification to the resulting product. The DFARS is based on the FAR, of course, so this would need to be a federal government, not just a defense, endeavor. I believe this task is worth undertaking, but no one should expect it to achieve miracles; almost everything in the FAR and DFARS is there for a reason—usually as an expression of policy goals that are considered worthwhile. The tough questions have to do with whether the costs of all these provisions in terms of inefficiency, higher barriers to entry for industry, and taxpayer expense are outweighed by the benefits achieved. We may only be able to eliminate a subset of existing provisions, but what we could do for certain is have a more consistent, coherent and easily applicable body of regulations. Over time, I have no doubt that Congress would continue to add legislation that would take us down the same path of increasing complexity; a "reset" every decade or so would be necessary, but I still believe the effort would be of value.

In addition to influencing how the DoD contracts with industry, Congress also attempts to improve acquisition by legislating rules that affect the government oversight layers and the people in them. This indirect approach is based on the premise that oversight and supervisory bodies can have a positive or negative impact on acquisition performance and that laws can in turn improve the performance of those layers. The Weapons Systems Acquisition Reform Act (WSARA) was of this nature. It addressed the systems engineering and developmental test and evaluation offices and it created the Performance Assessment and Root Cause Analysis organization (all within the Office of Acquisition, Technology, and Logistics), for example. Congress also has taken some steps to improve professionalism of the government management team by mandating tenure for program managers and selection rates for acquisition corps officers. Many of the steps Congress has taken, like these, have in fact been helpful.

The more indirect approach to improving acquisition by redesigning oversight structures and processes also suffers from the problem that it only impacts what happens in the top layers of the structure—not the layers where the work is done. Many outside observers seem to confuse the efficiency of the defense acquisition system, (i.e., the process by which program plans are approved and program oversight is executed), with the fact of cost and schedule overruns on particular programs. I sometimes make the point that the DoD only has two kinds of acquisition problems—planning and execution. The burden on the military department or component of preparing a plan and getting it approved is an overhead cost we should seek to reduce, but that burden shouldn't be confused with the failure to deliver a product or service on time and within cost. Where the DoD's oversight structure falls short is when it approves an unrealistic plan and thereby fails to prevent overruns and schedule slips. The oversight mechanisms succeed when they produce a more affordable and executable plan. I think we are fairly successful in this regard. Execution itself is where we most often have problems—and that is squarely the responsibility of contractors we hire and the government people who supervise them—in the bottom two layers I described. Changing the oversight layer's structure and processes can improve our planning, but it doesn't lead to better execution.

In my experience, some of Congress' efforts to improve acquisition have been problematic in three ways. In order of significance they are: (1) imposing too much rigidity, (2) adding unnecessary complexity and bureaucracy, (3) failing to learn from experience.

A lot of the work we have done over the past several years has been to identify and promulgate best practices, but a point I have made repeatedly is that the DoD conducts such a huge array of contracted work that it is counterproductive to impose a one-size-fits-all solution or way of doing business on everything that we do. Imposing rigid rules and universal practices is counterproductive. Overly proscribing behaviors also has the unintended impact of relieving our professionals of the core responsibility to think critically and creatively about the best solution to the specific problems they face.

One thing the DoD is very good at is creating bureaucracy. New procurement laws lead to the creation of more bureaucracy. Last year we provided Congress with a number of recommendations to remove reporting requirements and bureaucracy in the acquisition milestone decision making process that our program managers go through. Many of these recommendations were included in the Fiscal Year (FY) 2016 National Defense Authorization Act (NDAA). Unfortunately, while some requirements were removed more were added. As indicated above, the overhead we impose on our managers does not directly impact the cost or schedule to complete a program or deliver a service, but it does have the secondary impact of distracting our managers from their job of getting the most out of our resources, and it does increase overhead costs. Frankly, I think we have enough rules; we need fewer rules—not more.

I've also been in this business long enough to have seen multiple cycles of acquisition reform. I tell a story sometimes about the first congressional hearing I ever attended. It was in 1980. I vividly remember someone on the committee holding up a program schedule and ranting about the presence or absence of concurrency between development and production. He was very passionate, but I don't recall if he was for or against having more concurrency. We've been both for and against high degrees of concurrency several times over the years. Concurrency is one of the many judgments best left to professionals who understand the risks in a particular new product design and the urgency of the need. I also spent several years cleaning up the messes left behind in the late 1980s by an early round of self-imposed fixed price development contracting, which at one time was a presumed panacea to overruns in development. It was a disastrous policy that we swore we would never try again.

The sign outside my door, "In God we trust, all others bring data," isn't there as a joke. We need to learn from our experience, and the data tell us very clearly that fixed price development is usually, but like everything in acquisition, not always, a bad idea. We should not be making arbitrary acquisition policy changes under the guise of reform just because we are not fully happy with the results we've seen recently. Doing something different ought to reflect a factual basis for thinking that change will make things better. At the very least, novel ideas should be tried on a small scale in pilot programs before they are mandated more broadly. We need to learn from our experience, and, in general, passing laws that force us to repeat unsuccessful experiments is not wise.

Let me come back to where I started, with a description of what it takes to succeed in acquisition. Requirements drive what we acquire and they are set by our customers—the warfighters and the organizations that use the services or products we procure. Setting reasonable requirements that meet user needs operationally but are still achievable within a specified timeframe, consistent with the need at an affordable cost is a matter of good professional judgment. These judgments can't be legislated. They occur when operators, intelligence experts, acquisition professionals and technologists work together.

Creating complex new defense products that provide technological superiority is a job for true professionals, in industry and government. It is very hard to write a law that makes someone a better engineer or program manager. We have to develop these professionals over their careers in industry or government. Adequate resources are a concern of Congress, but they are authorized and appropriated in the context of the budgets the DoD submits. Historically, our greatest failing in building those budgets has been to be too optimistic about the resources we needed to deliver a product or service successfully, or about what we expected we could afford in the future.

Sound cost estimating, rational affordability constraints and leadership that insists on the use of realistic costs also are hard to legislate. Incentives for acquisition success in government come from the dedication of our workforce members and how they are encouraged and rewarded by the chain of command and their institutions. Again, this is about leadership, not legislative rules. For industry, it is a matter of aligning financial incentives with the government's objectives in a way that successfully improves contractor behaviors. And this requires professional judgment that must be tailored to the individual situation—not something that can be directed in legislation with broad applicability.

The bottom line of all this is that there won't be meaningful acquisition improvement except by our efforts. Congress can make things easier or harder, but this is still our job. We should be encouraged by the fact that we have made a great deal of progress over the last several years. The data support both that we are making progress and that there is still room to improve. As an example, we recently calculated the net Major Defense Acquisition Program overrun penalty for the Services that the FY 2016 NDAA directed. As of today, because of the savings we have achieved, we have built up a "credit" of more than $25 billion in underruns across the DoD. We also have some programs that have come in above their predicted costs, but the number of programs in which we are beating our original projections for Program Acquisition Unit Cost outnumbers the programs where we are seeing overruns by about 2 to 1. We need to stay on course; keep up the good work.

Chapter Two
Building Professionalism in the Acquisition Workforce

> "I happen to think we've set our ideal on the wrong objects;
> I happen to think that the greatest ideal man can set
> before himself is self-perfection."
>
> —W. Somerset Maugham, "The Razor's Edge"

In the second version of Better Buying Power, I added a category of initiatives associated with building professionalism. I was not implying that our workforce lacked professionalism—quite the contrary. What I wanted to communicate was the importance of constantly improving our capability; all of us can always improve our capabilities as professionals. Doing so is one of our jobs. Even more important, we need to help the people who work for us to grow in their own professional capacities. I firmly believe that the most important legacy any government acquisition professional can leave behind is a more professional workforce then he or she inherited. I also wanted to communicate to outside pundits, critics, and stakeholders, and even other defense communities, that all aspects of acquisition, including program management, engineering, contracting, testing, manufacturing, and logistics require qualified professionals to achieve success.

The first piece in this chapter addresses professionalism itself. What makes the people who work in each of the dozen or so fields associated with the acquisition workforce professional? My answer includes specialized knowledge, standards of performance, the ability to deal with complexity, a distinct culture of continuous improvement, and high ethical standards. In the following article in this chapter, I discuss in more detail some of the ethical standards that apply particularly to acquisition professionals.

The next article provides some real life examples of acquisition professionals at work. Each year I ask each of the Program Managers for our larger programs to write a short assessment of their programs. The total number of assessments is around 150. I read each one and reply to each Program Manager. Many are sources of ideas that can be applied more broadly.

Sometimes they illuminate problems that can be solved with more senior intervention. In nearly every case, they reflect the range of problems, the complexity of those problems, and the dedicated and effective way these acquisition professionals are performing their duties. This article summarizes specific Program Manager experiences in the areas of high-risk development, incremental acquisition of specialized software, the unique problems associated with a space system, and the sustainment, 20 years after it was acquired, of a commerical-off-the-shelf product adapted for military training purposes.

From the Program Managers' assessments, we move up the chain of command to Program Executive Officers (PEOs) who are responsible for a portfolio of programs, usually with similar characteristics. All of our roughly 50 PEOs were asked to provide assessments of their portfolios and recommendations for improvement. If the reader is interested in real acquisition reform (improvement), this is the one section that I would consider mandatory reading. The PEOs have more experience as professionals and a broader portfolio, so they are more inclined to see and focus on problems with wider impact than a single program. Arranged alphabetically by topic and largely as reported by the PEO, this section covers a broad range of areas where the PEOs see opportunity for improvement. This is the work of a very professional group of people. Their suggestions were acted upon.

I close this chapter with a tribute to some exemplary acquisition professionals who have left government service. The individuals whose careers and contributions I describe include two civil servants and two officers. All had exceptional careers. They are representative of the fine professionals in the nation's acquisition workforce. It is a privilege to work with people like this. The United States is fortunate to have such a remarkable cadre of government acquisition professionals and many equally dedicated industry partners.

CHAPTER TWO: BUILDING PROFESSIONALISM
IN THE ACQUISITION WORKFORCE

What Does It Mean To Be "a Defense Acquisition Professional"?

Reprinted from Defense AT&L: *March-April 2014*

One of the seven goals of Better Buying Power 2.0 is to improve the professionalism of the total acquisition workforce. I thought it might be useful to provide some specificity about what I have in mind when I talk about professionalism. The following is based on various experiences over my career, including some formal education on the nature of professionalism in the military, including at venues like West Point and the Army War College, in my on-the-job training in program management and systems engineering by various Air Force colonels in the Ballistic Missile Office, and by mentors in the Army's Ballistic Missile Defense Systems Command. I don't intend this to be an academic discussion, however, but a hands-on practical application of the term "professional" in the context of defense acquisition.

Defense acquisition professionals have a special body of knowledge and experience that is not easily acquired. Other professions such as attorneys, physicians, and military officers also have this characteristic. The situation for defense acquisition professionals is analogous. This characteristic applies equally to professionals in program management, engineering, contracting, test and evaluation, and product support, to name our most obvious examples. One should no more expect a lay person to make good judgments about something in these acquisition fields—be it a program structure, a risk mitigation approach, or the incentive structure of a contract—than one would expect an amateur to tell a lawyer how to argue a case, or a brain surgeon how to do an operation, or a brigade commander how to organize an attack. No one should expect an amateur without acquisition experience to be able to exercise professional judgments in acquisition without the years of training and experience it takes to learn the field. Like these other highly skilled professions, our expertise sets us apart.

Defense acquisition professionals set the standards for members of the profession. One of the reasons we are establishing "qualification boards" for our various key senior leader fields is to infuse a greater element of this characteristic into our workforce. Our senior professionals should know better than anyone else what it takes to be successful as a key acquisition leader. A professional career-field board will make the determination, in a "peer review" context, whether an individual has the experience, education, training, and demonstrated talent to accept responsibility for the success of all, or a major aspect of, a multibillion dollar program. This is not a minor responsibility.

These new boards are an experiment at this stage, but I am hopeful that they will take on a large share of the responsibility for enhancing and sustaining the expected level of preparation and performance of our key leaders. The boards will be joint, so that our professional standards are high and uniform across the defense Services and agencies. Setting standards for other members of the profession also encompasses the development and mentoring responsibilities that leaders at all levels, including AEs, PEOs, and other acquisition leaders, take on to strengthen and maintain the profession. They know that their most important legacy is a stronger—and more professional—workforce than the one they inherited.

Defense acquisition professionals know how to deal with complexity. The problems we have to solve are not simple—we are developing and fielding some of the most complicated and technically advanced systems and technologies in military history. It is therefore an illusion to believe that defense acquisition success is just a matter of applying the right, easily learned "cookbook" or "checklist" approach to doing our jobs. There are no fixed rules that apply to all situations, and as professionals we know that a deeper level of comprehension is needed to understand how to make good decisions about such issues as technical risk mitigation, what incentives will best improve industry's performance, what it will take to ensure that a product is mature enough to enter production, or how much testing is needed to verify compliance with a requirement. It is not enough to know acquisition best practices; acquisition professionals must understand the "why" behind the best practices—that is, the underlying principles at play. Many of our products consist of thousands of parts and millions of lines of code. They must satisfy hundreds of requirements, and it takes several years to bring them into production. Understanding and managing complexity is central to our work.

Defense acquisition professionals embrace a culture of continuous improvement. The concept of continuous improvement should apply to our own capabilities as individuals, to the teams we lead, to the processes we create and manage, and to the acquisition outcomes we seek. Better Buying Power is built on the idea of continuous improvement, of measuring performance, of setting targets for improving that performance, and striving to reach them ("should cost" for example). We are willing to examine our own results and think critically about where we can achieve more, and we have the courage and character to learn from our mistakes and to implement constantly ideas for better performance. As leaders we encourage these behaviors in the people who work for us and who collaborate with us.

Defense acquisition professionals practice and require ethical standards of behavior and conduct. Our ethical values guide how we interact with one another, with our supervisors, with industry, and with stakeholders including the public, media, and Congress. An Under Secretary whom I worked for decades ago told me once that when you lose your credibility you have nothing left—and you won't get it back. We must speak truth to power about problems within our programs and about ill-advised guidance that will lead to poor results. Successful acquisition requires a culture of "telling bad news fast," and that values accountability without a "shoot the messenger" mentality. Finally, it is particularly important that we treat industry fairly and with complete transparency.

I hope that this doesn't all come across as either preachy or aspirational. I believe that these are realistic expectations for defense acquisition professionals. I believe that they go a long way to defining what being a professional really means. My West Point class (1971) motto is "Professionally Done." I have always thought that this is a pretty good motto, and a pretty good way to look back on a successful career or a completed project, including in defense acquisition.

Ethics and Acquisition Professionalism— It Is All About Trust

Reprinted from Defense AT&L: *September-October 2014*

One of my predecessors as Under Secretary for Acquisition, Technology, and Logistics, and my former boss, John Betti, once commented to me, "The most valuable thing any one of us has is our credibility; once credibility is gone, it can never be recovered."

Credibility, or our capacity to have other people trust what we say, is essential to any successful acquisition professional. Trust in our credibility matters when we interact with our supervisors, subordinates, customers (military operators), the media, Congress and industry—in other words with everyone we encounter. Once we lose credibility with any one of these groups, we aren't far from losing it—and our effectiveness—with all of them.

There are a lot of ethics-related topics I could write about. I've chosen this one partly because of its importance, but also because of the frequency with which I've seen problems in this area and finally because it takes us into an area where there are a lot of shades of gray. I won't say much about the basic rules we are required to follow as a matter of integrity and public confidence, but I will mention them briefly. If you are a dishonest person who would violate fundamental ethical requirements, say by accepting a bribe in some form, then there probably isn't anything I can write that would change that fact. If you are likely to yield to that sort of temptation, we will do all that we can to catch you and put you in jail. If that doesn't deter you, I don't think an article will have much effect.

Sustaining trust in our integrity as public servants also demands that we be very careful about avoiding any appearance of unethical conduct. We are reminded of these requirements frequently and all of us should follow them. The ethical problems I'd like to address instead involve times when one of us might be tempted to do something wrong in our professional lives because of a goal we believe has real merit; in other words, to rationalize that good ends justify unethical means. In my experience, those unethical means often involve misleading a decision maker, authority or stakeholder in some manner. People generally don't go to jail for this type of behavior and we aren't talking about appearances only. The people who commit

Chapter Two: Building Professionalism in the Acquisition Workforce

these ethical lapses do, however, sacrifice their credibility—and sometimes their careers.

I'm sometimes asked about why the government or, more specifically, the Office of the Secretary of Defense, doesn't trust one party or another more—or even why I personally do not do so. When I'm asked this, it is usually in the context of someone asking for a decision such as a business commitment, or reducing the oversight used, or a milestone delegation, or agreement to limit risk mitigation activities and expenses. The party asking can be someone from industry or a military department program manager or another senior leader. The answer, I'm afraid, is simple enough: experience.

My life in the military, government and industry taught me that it isn't wise to give trust away for free; it should be earned. We are all involved in situations where we are trying to persuade someone to accept our point of view. It can be for approval of a milestone or authorization of funding or continuation of a program. There can be strong temptations in these cases to be something less than fully honest. This is the gray area I want to discuss.

I'll start with what I consider unethical attempts to influence decision makers or stakeholders. The extreme form of this is simply lying. I have very rarely, as far as I know, been directly lied to by a government acquisition professional. I did have one well-reported occasion when direct lying was practiced. It originated in a program executive office associated with the infamous Navy A-12 program. That individual was relieved and forced to retire when it was revealed that he had directed his subordinates to report lies about the program.

It shouldn't be necessary for me to exhort anyone in defense acquisition not to cover up problems in a program by actively lying about them. If you are doing that, my advice to you is to get out of our profession. The rest of us do not want to work with you. The form of ethical lapse I have seen too often consists of more subtle attempts to mislead decision makers in order to obtain a desired result. There are two forms of conduct that in my experience are much more common. The first is simply omitting information that would support a conclusion that is different from the desired one. The second one I'll refer to as "marketing," which falls short of direct lying but not by a wide margin.

I think I'm a realist, and I know that when a Military Department asks me for a decision when it has already decided what that decision should be. As the Defense Acquisition Executive (DAE), I'm not being asked by the Service to figure out the right decision; I'm being asked to ratify the one the Service believes it has already effectively made.

Going back to John Betti for a moment, John came into the Department of Defense (DoD) from a nondefense company where he was a senior executive. Originally, John approached his job as DAE as being similar to a corporate chief executive officer being asked to make a decision about an investment for a company. I explained to John that DoD worked a little differently. I told him he should think of it more as if he were a banker being asked to approve a loan.

The applicant (Service) already knows it should get the loan; its only interest is in getting the loan approved. There is no incentive for a loan applicant to explain in detail all the reasons his credit rating is overstated or to emphasize risks that the business plan might not be successful. Despite this disincentive, we do have an ethical obligation to provide senior decision makers with all the relevant information they should have before they can make an informed decision, whether or not it supports the decision we would prefer. In this regard, the best way to ensure credibility is to tell the whole story. It's fine to make recommendations, and even to advocate for a decision you support, but it is not fine to omit important facts of which the decision maker should be aware before he or she makes the decision.

Another of my bosses was Dr. John Deutch, also a former Under Secretary for Acquisition. John is one of the smartest people I've ever met. When I worked for him, John had a habit, however, of leaping ahead on a subject and reaching a conclusion before I could give him all the information he needed. On more than one occasion, I had to physically grab him and insist that he have the patience to wait for some more information from me before making a decision. Even if I thought he was right and making the decision I supported, I still wanted him to have all the relevant information. This was partly out of self-interest as well as a sense of the duty I owed to my boss. If I didn't give him the full story and his decision was later proven wrong by events, I didn't want to be in the position of not having given him all the relevant data—my future credibility with him was at stake.

The second type of behavior I see fairly often can be described as "marketing." A friend of mine in business was once appalled at the lies her associate was telling a prospective client. When challenged, the sales person responded, "That wasn't lying; it was marketing." In this case, what I'm referring to is a little more of a gray area; it consists of claims about judgments, such as risk levels, or future implications of decisions that stretch the truth instead of breaking it.

More extreme versions of "marketing," as opposed to objective presentation, are easy to spot. It doesn't take too many questions to find out whether there is real substance behind an assertion or, to use a phrase from the legal world, to discover that the claim being made is "mere puffery." I've found it to be an

Chapter Two: Building Professionalism in the Acquisition Workforce

important practice to try to find out if a program manager (PM) is trying to "sell" me, or if he or she is really on top of the program and has a real basis for the assertions made. (As a style comment, a "just the facts ma'am" delivery works a lot better with me than that of a used car salesman.)

Most PMs are very professional about this; some are not. Once a PM told me his optimistic schedule projection was made because he planned to do things "differently." Unfortunately, when I probed a little more deeply, he had no specifics whatsoever about what he was going to do "differently." In short, we shouldn't make claims we can't back up just to get someone's approval.

In another instance, a PM told me the new design turbine engine for his UAV [unmanned aerial vehicle] program was low-risk because it had over 100 hours of testing on a prototype. I asked him based on past experience how many hours of testing a new engine should have before it is ready to enter serial production. He had no idea. (Hint: It's a lot more than 100.)

It doesn't take too many questions to find out if a PM, or anyone else, knows his business and has done his or her homework. If you haven't done your homework and get caught trying to fake it, you can forget about trust or credibility as an asset.

I'll also mention similar behaviors that don't occur as often, but which I have seen, including relatively recently. One that particularly galls me is the "let's hope he doesn't read it" approach to getting something approved. Occasionally people will insert an action that they know I'm likely to disagree with into a document in the apparent hope I will miss it and grant approval. Even if I discover what I've done later, I would be in the unfortunate position of having to reverse myself. This doesn't happen often, but when it does the major impact is that I will read all the documents from the same organization very carefully in the future.

A variation on this approach is to insert elements into a program option the Service or the PM doesn't support largely to make that option look less attractive from a cost or schedule perspective. I've seen this done to try to prevent congressional action that was opposed by the Service, and I've seen it done to try to dissuade me from a course of action I as the DAE thought was worth considering. When I see such actions, the organization does not earn my trust, nor do the responsible individuals.

One other behavior I see on occasion is what lawyers call "the parade of horribles." (Although I'm about 80 percent engineer, legal training provides some useful insights.) The phrase "parade of horribles" refers to the use in legal argument of a long list of all the really bad things that will happen if the judge makes a ruling the party opposes. These lists tend to be very speculative and inflated but not entirely fanciful. I do find it amusing when I'm told that any decision to change a requested program, in any direction other than precisely the requested one, will have equally negative consequences for cost or risk. In short, adding a lot of weak or speculative arguments to a recommendation can have the opposite of the desired effect.

While I've focused on some gray areas within my own interactions in the Department, the points I'm trying to make about earning and sustaining credibility apply equally well when we deal with outside stakeholders, especially Congress, industry and the media. For supervisors especially, please note that when we do any of the things I have described we are effectively training our workforce that these practices are "OK." One reaps what one sows.

The bottom line is that we should not let advocacy for a position, no matter how sure we are that it is correct, push us outside of ethical constraints. We don't just need to tell the people we are responsible to the truth, we need to tell them the whole truth. We need to be clear about what we know and what we don't know. We need to clearly distinguish between things we know and things we have informed opinions about. We must be able to back up our assertions with facts and sound logic or we shouldn't make them. We certainly should not try to sneak anything by the people or institutions that make decisions we are bound by. Building our credibility as defense acquisition professionals is a career-long effort. Destroying it only takes a moment. John Betti was right; our credibility is our most valuable possession.

Program Manager Assessments—Professionalism Personified

Reprinted from Defense AT&L: *July-August 2015*

A few months ago, I decided to ask all of our Acquisition Category I and Major Automated Information System (MAIS) program managers (PMs) to provide me with a one- to three-page assessment of the state of their programs. At the time, this was an experiment. From the feedback I received, most PMs were delighted to have this opportunity. I have incorporated these assessments into Better Buying Power (BBP) 3.0 as an activity that will continue on an annual basis. The assessments are intended to strengthen the role of the acquisition chain of command. The assessments are simultaneously sent to me, the Service or Component acquisition executive, and the program executive officer. It was, however, an experiment that seemed to make a lot of people nervous.

Some of the nervousness stemmed from concerns that I was putting the PMs in an awkward position, where they might fear that being too honest with me could jeopardize their program or get them into trouble with a senior stakeholder in the Service or on the Office of the Secretary of Defense (OSD) staff. I could understand this concern, and I hesitated briefly. However, one of the management principles I've picked up over the years (like the sign outside my door reading "In God We Trust, All Others Must Bring Data," this comes from W. Edwards Deming) is that one must drive fear out of an organization to achieve success. No fear is more crippling or dysfunctional to an organization than fear of negative consequences of telling the truth. Close behind that is fear that a new idea will be dismissed or ridiculed. I decided that any institutional fear of the consequences of an honest assessment should not be appeased; it should be confronted.

There was also a concern, which I took more seriously, that the PM would have to obtain approval and go through multiple drafts and reviews before being allowed to send me an assessment. To overcome this concern, I required each PM to certify to me that no one had reviewed the PM's assessment in draft or final form. That seems to have been successful, although I expect I have caused some people to worry.

The results, from my perspective at least, have been terrific. I'm still working my way through roughly 150 assessments, but I've already learned a great deal about Department of Defense (DoD) programs and the people who are managing them. It was no surprise to me that the assessments have reflected the high degree of professionalism and dedication in our key leaders. I expected that. What I hadn't expected, but probably should have, was the window these documents provide into the many complex challenges our PMs face, and the creative and innovative ways they are dealing with those challenges. In this article, I would like to summarize some of the inputs I received. They say a great deal about the work we are doing—and how well we are doing it. I hope, with the permission of the writers, to publish a subset of these assessments soon, but here is a sampling without the names of the programs or PMs.

The cutting-edge weapon system; high-risk development: This assessment was probably the most impressive of the ones I have read to date. It was the smallest font the PM thought he could get away with—narrow margins, filled all three pages, and was packed with detail about the design, the technical issues and risks and what the PM was doing about them. It left me with no doubt that this PM was doing what Air Force Assistant Secretary Acquisition Bill LaPlante calls "owning the technical baseline." After a short overview of the program, the PM dug into the precise risks he is managing and mitigating. It wasn't quite a textbook or professional journal article on electrical engineering and systems engineering, but it was pretty close. One feature of this PM's approach that is noteworthy, and a program management or systems engineering best practice, was the use of knowledge points associated with each technical risk area. The use of actual test results at sub-scale, component testing, modeling, simulation, and field testing were all described in fair detail. Key near-term tests were highlighted. This is not a low-risk program, and there are numerous ways for this design to encounter problems before it matures, but the PM left me with the strong impression that he is on top of the risks and well positioned to deliver this critical product.

The legacy Command and Control (C2) system; incremental acquisition: This program is a large, complex C2 system that was built up over time from literally dozens of legacy systems. A few years ago, the idea of modernizing this collection in a "big bang" approach was rejected in favor of a lower-risk and lower-cost incremental approach (Model 2 of the new DoD Instruction 5000.02). The PM has the challenge of coordinating and managing numerous interfaces with systems that cannot go offline, while rebuilding part of this conglomeration of applications and supporting infrastructure with the government in the role of lead system integrator. A Service-Oriented Architecture is being implemented in sections as infrastructure and legacy programs are replaced. This PM is dealing with several builds of software in various stages of maturity, testing, and fielding. He also is dealing with the transition of DoD traditional information assurance approaches to the

CHAPTER TWO: BUILDING PROFESSIONALISM
IN THE ACQUISITION WORKFORCE

recently implemented Risk Management Framework. What this means on the ground is that the compliance measures have grown from about 100 to more than 400. At the same time, the PM is reacting to the "cyber shift left" and other recently published Operational Test and Evaluation cyber procedures. In attempting to implement Agile software development practices this PM has run into constraints from MAIS and DoD acquisition processes that have stymied modern software development best practices. This PM is trying to do the right thing, but we're getting in his way. He needs some help, and, because of his assessment, I plan to see that he gets it.

The space; achieving stability: Our space systems generally have struggled to get through development and make the transition to production. This is often a challenging step in a product's life cycle, but space programs have a particularly troubled history. Over the last few years, several DoD satellite systems have made this transition with great difficulty and are now at relatively stable phases of their life cycles. This PM's program is no exception. Software and hardware issues caused major delays and overruns. These problems have been largely overcome and the program is in serial production for the space segment, but the PM has no shortage of challenges. The ground segment, an incremental software-intensive program, has lagged significantly and only now seems to be stabilizing. An aggressive team effort by government and industry has been required to deliver capability. The PM's assessment reflects the successful use of Earned Value and Software productivity metrics to identify problem areas early and focus effort on corrective actions. While the PM generously (as I see fairly often) gives earlier versions of BBP some credit for his corrective actions, I would prefer less drama in our programs and less need for corrective action in the first place.

Like many of our PMs, this one is managing several programs at once. In this case, they are various separable components of an integrated system. Each has its own prime contractor, its own business arrangements, its own technical challenges and its own place in the product life cycle.

The Commercial Off-the-Shelf (COTS) product; sustainment 20 years on: Most of the attention in the acquisition system falls on programs in development, where delays and overruns are most likely, but where the contributions to life-cycle cost are lowest. This PM is dealing with a platform that has been in the inventory for almost 20 years. It is nearing the end of production and was based on a COTS product. The program has myriad supply chain, aging, and obsolescence issues. Originally a Contractor Logistic Support for life of the program (acquisition reform circa late 1990s), the program has bounced back and forth between Federal Acquisition Regulation (FAR) Part 12 and FAR Part 15—ending up in Part 15. The program has moved to introduce competition for sustainment, but the

PM continues to deal with high costs of spare parts and issues associated with the commercial design that has not stood up well to military use. Bad assumptions (commercial product, life-cycle support by the producer) that may have reduced cost up front are being paid for now. The PM is dealing with a supply chain that sources nearly 500,000 parts and sees more than 10,000 issues per month across the fielded systems. Moving to competition and standing up a new support contractor has been painful: Protests, claims, uncooperative suppliers, and intellectual property issues have all been problems. The PM has worked hard to understand the lessons learned from this experience and is preparing for the next round of competition. The bottom line: Sustainment is every bit as challenging as development. It demands attention to detail, strong leadership, tenacity, solid business acumen and innovation in dealing with support contractors.

What I find fascinating about all of these assessments is the complexity and scale of the problems described and the candor and depth of understanding demonstrated by the writers. They personify the professionalism we all have to continue building throughout our workforce. BBP 3.0 focuses on innovation, technical excellence and the importance of U.S. technological superiority, while continuing to build on our earlier efforts to control cost and to extract as much value as possible from the dollars the taxpayers provide us. None of these initiatives in any edition of BBP is more important than continuing to build the human capital that is responsible for the successful delivery of every product or service the DoD acquires.

I asked a number of senior people to provide articles for this edition of *Defense AT&L* magazine, but for my submission I wanted to highlight the contributions that our very talented and dedicated PMs, together with their staffs and supporting organizations, are providing to the department and the nation. Well done.

Improving Acquisition From Within—Suggestions From Our PEOs

Reprinted from Defense AT&L: *July-August 2016*

This year I asked all of our Program Executive Officers (PEOs) to provide short assessments and recommendations to me directly. The result, as it was for the Program Manager Assessments I've received for the last 2 years, has been a treasure trove of observations and recommendations covering a wide range of topics. I thought it would be useful and insightful for the entire workforce to see some of these professional, and very frank, comments. I've removed most inputs that were about specific programs and edited lightly to make some of the inputs less Service specific. Arranged alphabetically by topic, and presented without comment, here is a sampling of the topics on our senior line managers' minds as they confront the many challenges we face.

Acquisition Education: Cybersecurity requirements continue to grow impacting virtually everything we do in acquisition from daily workplace activities, to Enterprise Resource Planning (ERP) system development, to weapon system development. Additionally, the Department of Defense (DoD) is required to certify audit readiness in Fiscal Year (FY) 2017. Audit readiness affects every career field in acquisition, not just financial management professionals. Ensure that the Defense Acquisition University curriculum is updated to reflect audit readiness and cybersecurity considerations and requirements for all of the career fields.

Also, an executive level Acquisition seminar for our senior General/Flag Officers, especially those assigned in the Pentagon, would advance acquisition reform. We consistently find ourselves answering questions to our Service Chiefs and members of Congress that are far outside of acquisition responsibilities. This is a team sport, and DoD would be better served if all of our most senior leaders had a basic understanding of the Defense Acquisition process and their respective roles in it.

Business Cases and AoAs (Analysis of Alternatives): Why would we do both? There is too much complexity and lack of clarity between the Deputy Chief Management Officer and the role of the Office of Acquisition, Technology, and Logistics.

Clinger-Cohen Act (CCA) Compliance: CCA mandates the completion and approval of numerous other programmatic documents as supporting documentation before a program's CCA can be certified. The Army Chief Information Officer (CIO)/G6 estimates the staffing and approval for a program CCA compliance determination to take up to 120 days to complete. Two supporting documents required for submission for a CCA compliance determination are (1) Test and Evaluation Master Plan (TEMP) and (2) Acquisition Program Baseline (APB). Because of the potential lead time required to support a CCA determination (120 days), we recommend that draft versions of the TEMP and APB be authorized for submission for CCA compliance purposes. We also recommend that significant programmatic changes identified during documentation staffing that would alter the CCA compliance determination be presented during an abbreviated and accelerated update to allow programs to simultaneously staff critical documents without delaying program schedules.

Configuration Steering Boards (CSBs) and Testing: CSBs have been especially helpful in adjusting requirements (both to provide a forum for the deliberate addition of some requirements as well as removing some requirements where they don't make sense). This process should be extended to include using the CSB process to adjust test plans and requirements as well rather than allowing independent members of the test community virtually unlimited authority to commit programs to cost and schedule of tests that the operational leaders of the Service do not believe are warranted. Similarly, it would provide a forum for those same uniformed leaders to insist on testing that might otherwise be overlooked.

COTS and NDI Acquisition: Financial Management Regulation must be clarified to provide consistent guidance on the use of procurement funds in lieu of research, development, test and evaluation (RDT&E) funds to test Commercial Off the Shelf (COTS) and NonDevelopmental Items (NDI). This has tremendous impacts across my portfolio, which is heavily reliant on COTS/NDI and could mitigate additional funding stability risks if properly clarified where both the budget analysts and the lawyers agree on the flexibility to use either procurement or RDT&E to test COTS/NDI.

Cyber Security Testing: Cyber testing and the ability to achieve a "Survivable" rating in an official operational test environment continues to be nearly impossible for a Program of Record (POR) to achieve. Test criteria are not well defined and, even if requirements are met, the standards and scope is "independently" determined by the OTA or DOT&E for success. The threat portrayal often exceeds the capabilities of a Blue Force Team (i.e., nation-state threat going against a brigade-level formation), focuses more on "insider" threat of unreasonable proportions, and minimizes the importance of "defense in depth" approach. Recommend better definition for standard cyber rules of engagement at operational test, the allowance

CHAPTER TWO: BUILDING PROFESSIONALISM
IN THE ACQUISITION WORKFORCE

for external cyber protection teams, and that test reports focus on the program under test (not the overall "network").

Fiscal Law Constraints: It is likely pie in the sky, but to operate with a single color of money would greatly improve our efficiency and effectiveness. We spend far too much time trying to discern the gray areas that exist between the appropriations. Functioning with Operation and Maintenance dollars during periods of continuing resolutions and severe cash distribution challenges, makes continuity of support a challenge and results in all sorts of bizarre contract actions. If we operated primarily in an Other Procurement world with narrow definition on true RDT&E (introduction of truly new functional envelopes), we would be much more efficient and effective stewards.

Funding Concerns (10 USC Section 2282): I continue to bring this up to anyone who will listen to me. This pseudo-Foreign Military Sales (FMS) funding is an excellent tool in that it allows us to deliver capability and build Combat Command (COCOM) military partnerships, particularly in countries that can't afford to invest in our weapon systems. That said, the funding is restrictive in that we need to figure out what we're going to buy, put together an acquisition strategy, and get it on contract in the year appropriated (which drives some bad acquisition behaviors). The biggest challenge is that we can only use Section 2282 funding to sustain the system for 2 years. After that, the receiving country must create/fund an FMS case or the COCOM must provide funding. Bottom line is that there is a high risk that these great capabilities will be left to rot and quickly become useless.

Funding Stability and Flexibility: For the last several years, we have started each fiscal year under Continuing Resolution Authority (CRA) for 3 to 4 months before the budget is enacted and funding begins to flow. The CRA creates instability in the year of execution because we can't have any new start programs and the amount of funding available under CRA typically is some percentage of our prior year funding. This instability is exacerbated by the fact that our funding execution is measured against the Office of the Secretary of Defense (OSD) obligation and expenditure goals that do not take into consideration the delay in receipt of funding caused by operating under a CRA. As a result of missing OSD execution goals, funding often is rephased in the outyears, which perpetuates the situation as the cycle has consistently repeated itself and is likely to do so in the future. It would be helpful if the OSD Comptroller could adjust the OSD obligation and expenditure goals to "start the 12-month clock" when the Defense budget is actually passed and not on Oct. 1, as they do now.

Hiring Authority: The agility of a PEO to support its portfolio with appropriate personnel is not adequate with the formal billeting and staffing process and needs to move to a management to budget construct that allows the hiring of additional government personnel.

Human Capital: As the military service begins to reduce force structure, similar reductions are taking place across the civilian workforce. Additionally, there is pressure from Congress to reduce the number of support contractors across DoD. My workforce is comprised of military members (4 percent), core DoD civilians (15 percent), matrixed DoD civilians—combining the traditional and product organization structure—(46 percent) and support contractors (35 percent). With all of these components being driven to reduce numbers and no relief from the mission requirements and expectations, my PEO organization will be challenged severely, even after realizing process efficiencies, to effectively perform the mission unless some portion of the workforce can be stabilized.

Innovation: In intelligence, surveillance and reconnaissance and in working with Special Operations Forces, we are working hard at giving people the tools to bring out their innovative side and give them the confidence to be creative. It is probably the most enjoyable part of my job. I have numerous examples of recent initiatives, but will mention just two of them. First, the Rapid Development and Integration Facility (RDIF) continues to grow as a place where government program managers (PMs) and engineers (sometimes in partnership with small business) are rapidly modifying everything from gunships to B2s to helicopters. They are taking back the technical base line, learning how to innovate and growing confidence in our government teams. Second, is the Revolutionary Acquisition Techniques Procedures and Collaboration (RATPAC) forum run jointly between the Air Force and Special Operations Command. Twice a year we select about 50 junior acquisition professionals to attend an intense week of engagement with our most innovative acquisition, warfighter and congressional thinkers. They leave RATPAC fired up to be acquisition combat enablers, and it is really special to see.

Obsolescence: We face an ever-growing challenge dealing with obsolete parts when we build on a COTS-based infrastructure. Components over the life cycle of our programs become obsolete when supply chain providers move on to next efforts or divest in the business area. We have seen cases where we are replacing obsolete components on a system prior to fielding the initial capability. Many vendors are updating their products at an increasing rate and do not maintain or support older versions of their equipment. This is true for both software and hardware. Programs need to ensure they adequately budget for these activities and have the correct personnel to address these issues throughout the life cycle of programs. We also need to engage with vendors early to ensure we have long term sustainment strategies that may include extended lifetime buys for key components early in a program to ensure long-term supportability as well, and address the ability to upgrade at the component level to meet any potential obsolescence issues. Help is needed in supporting continuous low-level modification lines to deal with obsolescence issues.

Protests: I recommend that there be a penalty for protesting to discourage weak protests. Example: paying the DoD's legal costs, or paying some penalty for the program disruption.

Quality and Clarity of High Level Taskers: I would like to address the quality of taskers or assignments received at my level. Often a broad-based tasker is issued and, as it flows down the chain of command, it is interpreted in various ways by a number of different people to the point where nobody really understands what information is required. These taskers should be clear and concise from the beginning and follow established staffing chains to ensure that we are not wasting precious resources (time, money and people) providing data and information that does not properly respond to the issue.

Quick Reaction Capabilities: This year alone, I had 42 Quick Reaction Capabilities (QRCs) that I managed and reviewed as separate programs and resolved that 5 be closed, had 10 pending closure once 100 percent accountability of assets is resolved, 7 transitions to existing Programs of Records (PORs), and 20 that will continue to be managed as stand alone QRCs. Note that no QRC comes with organic personnel resources and must be managed with allocated POR resources and the heavy use of matrix and contractor support. This is not a sustainable model. The military Service is working the requirements process that supports these transitions. However, the alignment with the Program Objectives Memorandum (POM) process inherently results in a 2-year gap that we have only been able to solve because of the availability of supplemental appropriations. If supplemental dollars did not exist, we would have been unable to transition and/or retain QRC capabilities to the degree we have successfully done to date. The delay in obtaining updated requirements documents hinders the ability to compete in the POM process and exacerbates the gap. A second issue with QRC transitions is balancing the adequacy of testing to support POR transition and milestone decisions. In many cases, these capabilities have been operated effectively for thousands of hours in combat—meeting requirements as specified for military utility, which ought to be the goal of an Operational Test event. Testing a QRC now for integration into a POR, should only verify any changes caused by modifying/integrating on platforms or needed changes to address usability/human factors of the system when we transition from contractor to green suit sustainment/operations. In many cases, we are spending extensive resources (time, money, test ranges, personnel expertise) to retest basic sensor performance on capabilities which have been operating in combat for more than 10 years as a QRC. The Service Test and Evaluation Organization, the OSD Offices of Developmental Test and Evaluation and of Operational Test and Evaluation need to adjust to a more continuous evaluation process and away from the big bang, all-inclusive testing. Finally, overall, the DoD Instruction (DoDI) 5000 series guidance does not address the process of the transition of QRCs to PORs. For example, personnel Concept Plans to support program office manning take forever, material release tailoring is all but nonexistent to deal with COTS, and timely requirements documentation and integration of funding into the appropriate Program Evaluation Groups/base are challenging tasks. The aforementioned conditions cause PMs to focus on near-term resourcing and not effective/efficient program management. Help is needed from an institutional perspective to take lessons learned and update policies and provide tailoring procedures for improved transitions.

Reprogramming Authority: Another way to provide additional flexibility would be to allow greater reprogramming thresholds (this requires approval from Congress). Higher Below Threshold Reprogramming limits go hand in hand with giving PEOs/PMs greater authority to move cost savings realized from successful Better Buying Power (BBP) initiatives within our funding lines. This would also act as a strong incentive for the Defense Acquisition Workforce to inculcate BBP principles into our programs.

Requirements Process: I suggest that both the operational and acquisition communities focus serious attention at the most senior levels on implementing a simplified requirements process which better facilitates the rapid technology/threat cycles within the cyber domain.

Risk Management Framework (RMF): The construct has added time to the process with, in my opinion, no added benefit to date. This process needs quick efficiency reviews and updating. Help is needed in making the RMF more efficient and shorter.

The new RMF process (which replaced the DoD Information Assurance Certification and Accreditation Process), providing for certification and accreditation of weapon systems, has been too unwieldy for the speed and agility needed in approving cybersystem solutions. Specifically, we have identified the following issues with the RMF process as applied to cyber weapon systems:

- RMF levies heavy requirements for monitoring, software updates and policy controls that are less bound by operational concerns than previous systems.

CHAPTER TWO: BUILDING PROFESSIONALISM
IN THE ACQUISITION WORKFORCE

- RMF causes a large resource burden of time and manpower. With the volume of work entailed in RMF, it is difficult to make consistent progress or to develop reliable schedules to inform our operational user. Additionally, the unplanned burden on program offices to apply RMF is taking resources from fixing user issues and addressing modernization needs.

- There was little structure put into phasing the RMF requirement into weapon systems. The full requirement was mandated with less than 2 years to prepare, with limited waiver opportunities provided.

- While new systems in development can accommodate RMF during the design process, legacy systems were not designed with RMF security controls in place, so there are significant programmatic and operational impacts to meeting the RMF controls. Thus, applying RMF to currently fielded operational systems puts undue burden on the operational user.

- Control of and accountability for system cybersecurity is spread over numerous organizations and is poorly integrated, resulting in diminished accountability and unity of command and control for cybersecurity. These overlapping roles create ambiguity regarding whether the commander or the authorizing official can make the final decisions regarding risk to a mission.

- The coordination process for RMF approval packages continues to evolve. Changes in expectation, standards and formats are not communicated well, and this often creates much rework, further delaying approval and impacting program cost and schedule.

- The vast majority of our systems currently are accredited under the old structure and the RMF process does not allow previous accreditations to be easily absorbed into the new structure.

- There has been a shift in focus from simply managing risk to now ensuring all facets of system vulnerabilities are addressed. While this will improve cybersecurity, there is simply not enough manpower to adequately perform all of the required processes, specifically within the Approving Official and the Security Compliance Assessor communities.

- Approving Officials have not been issuing Plans of Actions and Milestones during this transition process, which has led to an expiration of Authority To Operate during the lengthy process.

In considering improvement opportunities since RMF has been in use and lessons learned have become available, I suggest that the application of RMF to currently fielded cyber weapon systems be reexamined and tailored to reduce heavy RMF resource demands and impact to the operational user. In addition, as stated earlier, it is imperative that the acquisition and lifecycle management tools and processes for both new and fielded cyber weapons systems be streamlined to maximize speed and agility within reasonable levels cybersecurity risk.

Sustainment in DoDI 5000.02: I see a difference between a system in the sustainment phase and a sustainment program. Because DoDI 5000.2 is silent on sustainment programs, we sometimes treat sustainment programs the same as efforts to modernize a program in the sustainment phase, in terms of systems engineering, milestones and documentation. Modernizing a program in the sustainment phase usually fits pretty clearly into one of the "Defense Acquisition Program Models." But a sustainment program such as a Service Life Extension Program, Diminishing Manufacturing Sources Program or a Contractor Logistics Sustainment Program doesn't fit well within those models. Yet there are some nuances, best practices and common tailoring that could apply to these types of programs. I thought the "model" concept was a great addition to the DoDI 5000 series, so I think adding a model for sustainment type programs would be helpful. I have also recommended this at the military Service level to address in our documents. I see a lot of teams struggle in this area.

Tailoring: However, although you and other senior leaders continue to reinforce the importance of tailoring the acquisition process to the specific and unique characteristics of the product being acquired, the rules and policy are frequently interpreted as inflexible and prescriptive. As additional acquisition reform provisions are considered, we should look for ways to better institutionalize the expectation for tailoring, particularly as it applies to the acquisition of nondevelopmental or minimally modified COTS systems.

Workforce Development Ideas

Acquisition "Whiteboard" Sessions: I found that often when I received milestone packages through the staffing process, the acquisition strategies weren't tailored to the most effective approach to develop or acquire the system. In order to prevent frustration of the workforce and get the top level concepts right from the beginning, I began hosting "Whiteboard" sessions to ensure everyone had a common understanding of the strategy. I run these much like the military Service runs After Action Reviews by serving as a facilitator—asking shaping level questions of the program stakeholders (from the PM, legal, contracting, etc.) and allowing them to shape the strategy through their answers. The level of innovation and quality of the milestone packages has dramatically improved. I've received very positive feedback on the learning value of these sessions and encouraged my subordinates to replicate the process at lower levels.

Acquisition Categories II and III Configuration Steering Boards (CSBs): Much of the equipment we acquire is commercial or commercially based. On several occasions, we received approved requirements documents that specified requirements substantially outside commercially available features. Our engineers conduct industry Requests for Information, coordinate with commercial testing facilities, and employ analytical tools to identify requirements that are driving cost and risk. We then organize a CSB with the appropriate one-star level operational community proponent, along with virtual representation from the Service staff to review the data analysis. In each case, we've been able to temper the requirements to only the critical capabilities, thereby reducing programs' costs and technical risks while allowing them to move forward without risking lost funding or schedule delays.

Junior Employee Shadowing Program: Each PM within the PEO nominates high potential GS12/13 employees to shadow me for 2 weeks. These employees can attend all meetings that the PEO participates in and get a good sense of how to think critically about the unique facets of each program and how these considerations shape acquisition strategy, contract type, contract incentives, and source selection approaches. To date, I have had 24 shadow participants, and I have already seen evidence of grassroots movement inside their home organizations in taking more innovative approaches to acquisition strategies.

Topical Town Hall Meetings: I have held town hall meetings quarterly, and I always highlight a number of innovative accomplishments in acquisition from several of our individual PMs. As an overarching theme, I've suggested that our acquisition professionals should treat every decision they make as if it was their own money. I've continued to encourage them to challenge requirements and approaches that don't make sense based on their personal experiences both in acquisition and in their daily lives.

Conclusion

As with the Program Manager Assessments, I have responded to each of the PEOs individually. In addition, I have asked some of the writers to work on follow-up actions to explore solutions to the problems they raised, or to implement their specific suggestions. My last article and email to the workforce talked about how real acquisition reform has to come from within and it has to take the form of continuous improvement on many fronts. This is one more example of what that looks like in practice.

What Really Matters In Defense Acquisition

Reprinted from Defense AT&L: *January-February 2014*

My first inclination for this issue's article was to discuss the newly released DoDI [Department of Defense Instruction] 5000.02. We recently implemented this new acquisition policy document as interim guidance. I provided a cover letter explaining why I had done a new version and outlined some of the features of this edition. I do recommend that you look at both the cover letter and the new document, but on reflection I decided to write about something else for this issue. An enormous amount of time and energy goes into designing our processes and implementing them, but at the end of the day it isn't those processes or policy documents like 5000.02 that really drive our results. What really matters in defense acquisition is our people and their professionalism and leadership—so I thought I would start the new year by writing about that.

This past year we've gone through a lot, and all of our acquisition professionals have been asked to put up with more than any workforce should have to endure. We've had continuing budget turmoil and uncertainty, furloughs, continuing resolutions, late-breaking sequestration, and most recently a government shutdown. We're also living under pay freezes and the prospect of further budget reductions and staff reductions. I want to thank the whole workforce for the way you have all coped with these challenges. While other senior leaders and I have been asking you to improve our productivity and achieve ever greater results for our warfighters and the taxpayer, you've also had to work in very challenging circumstances. You've come through, and it has inspired me and your other senior leaders to see the way you've dealt with all these challenges in stride. Thank you. Thank you personally, but also on behalf of the Secretary and all the senior leaders in the Department. Thank you also for our soldiers, sailors, airmen and marines who benefit from your great work as they put themselves at risk for our country.

Recently, I joined Dr. Carter in one of his last official acts as Deputy Secretary in presenting the Packard Awards to this year's recipients. As I write this, I'm looking forward to going out to the Defense Acquisition University to present the USD(AT&L) [Under Secretary of Defense] awards for professionalism and developing the workforce to some of our outstanding performers. I'm sorry that we can't recognize more of our exceptional performers—there are so many of you, and you all deserve to be recognized for what you do. During the last few weeks, I also have had occasion to note the departure of some of our most capable people who are retiring or will soon retire from government service. We lose a lot of terrific people every year of course, and these individuals are just examples of the many fine professionals working in defense acquisition, technology and logistics. I decided that for this article I would note the contributions of some of these people with whom over the last few years I've had the chance to work. They are just examples, but they are especially powerful examples of what one can accomplish during a career in defense acquisition.

I'll start with Charlie Williams, the recently retired Director of the Defense Contract Management Agency (DCMA). Charlie led DCMA for the past several years. He started federal service in 1982 in Air Logistics Command in a Mid-Level Management Training Program. Charlie then rose through a series of contracting, program analysis and contract management positions with the Air Force both in the field and at Air Force Headquarters. He became Air Force Deputy Assistant Secretary for Contracting before taking the reins at DCMA. At DCMA, Charlie led the rebuilding of the organization after severe reductions in the 1990s. He kept his team together during the Base Realignment and Closure move from D.C. to Richmond, and he led the effort to ensure that our contracts in support of operations in Afghanistan and Iraq were executed properly.

Next I'll mention Maj Gen Tim Crosby, the soon-to-retire Army Program Executive Officer (PEO) for Aviation. Tim has led Army aviation programs since 2008. He was commissioned after graduating from the Citadel and started out as a field artillery officer. He moved quickly into aviation as a pilot before following his interest in research and development and flight testing. In acquisition, he worked in logistics, training and simulation, and test and evaluation before becoming a Product Manager, first for the CH-47 F and later Program Manager for the Army's Armed Scout. His long tenure at PEO Aviation is marked by strong leadership in support of our deployed forces and in building the capability of the Afghan Air Force. Tim embraced the Better Buying Power principles and was implementing them well before Dr. Carter and I gave them a name.

Rear Admiral Jim Murdoch retired recently after serving as the Navy's first PEO for Littoral Combat Ships (LCS). Jim entered the Navy with an ROTC commission after graduating from Rensselaer Polytechnic Institute in mechanical engineering. He moved between surface combatant assignments and acquisition positions. His acquisition assignments included program management for surface weapons and launchers and responsibility for integrated warfare systems as well as program manager for the Littoral

Combat Ships. In 2011, Jim was handpicked by Sean Stackley to lead the new Program Executive Office for LCS sea-frames and mission modules. He stabilized and fully integrated one of the Navy's most complex acquisition endeavors.

Finally, Scott Correll, our retiring Air Force PEO for Space Launch, also started his career as an intern. From the Pacer Intern Contracting Program at Robbins Air Force Base, where he began as a cost analyst and contract negotiator on the F-4 and F-15, Scott rose through the contracting, supply chain management and program management fields. Scott's diverse positions include leadership positions at Military Sealift Command and TRANSCOM. I was able to take Scott in to meet Secretary Hagel recently so the Secretary could thank him personally for saving the Department billions of dollars in space launch costs—quite an achievement for our taxpayers and warfighters.

The people I mention above have accomplished a great deal for their country during their careers. They've also had the opportunity to do exciting and fulfilling work. People who achieve this sort of success over their careers are what give us the best equipped military in the world. All of these people have a lot to be proud of. All of you have a lot to be proud of. I'm looking forward to 2014 with the hope that things will improve—and there are some signs that they will. But mostly I'm just looking forward to another year of working with this terrific team. Thank you again for all that you do.

Chapter Three
Managing Technical Complexity

"I don't mind a reasonable amount of trouble."
—Dashiell Hammett

Right after he became Secretary of Defense, Leon Panetta asked me a simple question. He asked me why we couldn't build other defense products as quickly as we had acquired Mine Resistant Ambush Protection vehicles or MRAPs, the armored trucks we bought on a very aggressive schedule in the tens of thousands to protect our troops in Iraq and Afghanistan from Improvised Explosive Devices. My answer was one word, "complexity." MRAPs basically are trucks assembled from pre-existing automotive components (transmissions, engines, drive trains, etc.) with a lot of armor and hull shapes designed to deflect blast and to protect the occupants. MRAPs provide effective protection and they have saved countless lives, but they were designed to deal with an improvised threat used in a counterinsurgency or counterterrorism campaign, not for high-end peer competitors. They are not representative of the weapons we usually acquire. This chapter takes up the problem of managing complexity, specifically the technical complexity that characterizes many of the products that the DoD acquires.

Most of our weapons systems are designed to give us a competitive advantage over the most capable systems any potential adversary has or will have in the foreseeable future. Some of our potential adversaries, China and Russia, are aggressively acquiring systems that are being designed specifically to defeat the most advanced U.S. systems. In pursuit of the dominant capability our warfighters expect and deserve, and that our nation needs, we often embed new cutting-edge advanced technology into our systems. For most weapons systems, complex and specialized software, often with millions of lines of code, is essential to achieving the required functionality. Our weapons also need to be cyber secure, highly reliable, and maintainable on any battlefield, sustainable at reasonable cost, and effective in a full range of climates and operational environments. All of this adds complexity, cost and risk to new designs. Our acquisition professionals' most challenging task is to manage that complexity and that risk effectively.

The first article in this section discusses "The Optimal Program Structure." This was one of the first articles I wrote for the workforce and it was intended to make a critical point: Our programs should be structured around the product that we are acquiring and the circumstances associated with that product. There is no one optimal program structure, so the title is a little misleading, but for every product there is an optimal structure for that product. I always start all discussions about program decisions by reviewing the design of the product the DoD is acquiring. Once the product and a few other driving factors like operational urgency are understood, we can then turn to the subject of how the program to design and produce that product should be structured. Building that structure is called "tailoring" and it is the antithesis of the idea that all product development programs should be structured in the same way or have identical content.

The range of products that the DoD acquires is vast, and the idea that a "one size fits all" approach should be mandated or expected is simply wrong. When I rewrote DoDI 5000.02, our fundamental acquisition policy document, I included multiple possible starting point models for program structures, and I inserted the word "tailoring" dozens of times in the text just to make this point. Because of the complexity we deal with, the second release of Better Buying Power focused on the need for critical thinking over a checklist or cookbook approach to acquisition planning and management. This article also makes the point that risk and mitigating actions taken to reduce risk, are fundamental drivers on program structure.

Risk means uncertainty, and the real prospect of things not going as we would desire. Risk is an integral part of new product development. Designing a new weapon system is a creative process. It is building something that has never been built before, and it is achieving levels of capability never reached before—by as wide a margin as possible. Our political system seems to demand perfection in program execution so that there is never a cost overrun or a schedule slip and all requirements are met. This is simply unrealistic if the United States intends to remain the dominant military power on the planet. We do know how to remove the risk from our programs: All it takes is to buy existing systems from other nations. There are times when that is a reasonable approach, but not for the systems we need so that our warfighters can dominate future battlefields against our most capable potential adversaries.

Chapter Three: Managing Technical Complexity

While risk is inherent in the creation of new weapons systems, it must still be managed. Managing risk is not a passive activity. A PEO once sent me an e-mail indicating that he was waiting to see what happened with regard to some known risks on one of his programs. For background, the DoD uses a somewhat formal standard process to identify specific risks, to categorize them, and to track program events and risk mitigation plans that are designed to reduce the risk over time. The DoD is good (maybe too good) at creating standard processes, and our framework for addressing risk is fine as far as it goes, but having a tracking system in place and waiting to see what happens isn't what we should expect from our Program Managers and their staffs. I sent the following reply to the PEO:

From: Kendall, Frank III HON OSD OUSD ATL (US)
Sent: Wednesday, April 13, 2016 3:38 PM
To:
Subject: RE: 2016 Program Executive Officer (PEO) Assessment

Thanks, Generally I agree with your assessment. I've gotten to know many elements of your portfolio pretty well.

One comment just so you are aware of what is becoming a pet peeve of mine. There are a couple of formulations of this that I've seen fairly often over the last few years. When a program goes in the ditch, what I hear from the PM or PEO is "schedule is being adjusted to reduce risk" or "because risks that were accepted were realized the program is being restructured."

Frankly I find this a little irritating. It seems like an attempt to say that we all agreed to roll the dice, and gee look what happened, guess we'll have to make some adjustments. I feel that this is basically a way to duck responsibility. The fact is that a program plan which was submitted for approval and justified as being executable wasn't executed. End of story. The reasons can be anything from poor planning to poor performance, to acts of God, but the formulation that "risk was realized" strikes me as a way to "spin" failure as something else. Of course there are some things we can't control, but our job is to manage risk, to take action to mitigate it, and to adjust immediately when we see problems emerging. We are not, or should not be, spectators to our programs waiting to see what happens. I wrote a whole article about this. Our job is to be on top of events and steer them to get where we need to go as efficiently as possible. Program management is not a spectator sport.

Frank

Frank Kendall
USD(AT&L)
RM 3E1010 Pentagon
703 697 7021

* * * *

Risk management is addressed in the second article in this chapter. It amplifies the point I made in the e-mail above and discusses some of the proactive steps a Program Manager can take, ahead of time, to reduce the potential consequences of a risk.

One of our tools for addressing and understanding risk is something called a "Technology Readiness Level," or TRL. TRLs provide a shorthand numerical scale to assess a technology's maturity. The next article in this chapter is titled (with a nod to the TV program "Star Trek"), "The Trouble with TRLs." I have a strong dislike for TRLs, or perhaps more accurately I have no respect for them. TRLs originated with NASA and were introduced to the DoD about two decades ago. They do provide a useful shorthand or benchmark for the state of maturity of a technology—as examples, is it theoretical or has it been tested in a laboratory, or in an operational setting, or is it in a fielded system? As such they are useful benchmarks to begin a discussion of the risk associated with a technology.

What has happened over time, however, is that TRL ratings alone have been viewed as dispositive and used as a substitute for that deeper discussion. The problem with a TRL rating is that it conveys no real information about the degree of difficulty associated with completing maturation and putting the technology into a design for production. Understanding that degree of difficulty tells us how much risk remains to be addressed before we can presume the technology is ready to be used in a product. As Bill LaPlante, former Air Force Assistant Secretary for Acquisition, once told me, "TRLs are what we tell nontechnical management to make them feel good. Engineers know enough to ask about the actual work that remains to be done." This in a nutshell is the reason that, as part of Better Buying Power 3.0, I have encouraged the military Services to place technically qualified people in charge of development programs. It's hard to manage something you don't understand, and development of new defense systems is the management of engineering and technical risk.

Chapter Three: Managing Technical Complexity

The next article in this chapter, written for a developmental test professional association publication, discusses the role of test and evaluation, particularly developmental test and evaluation, in a defense acquisition program. During the last several years, the DoD has rebuilt its developmental test organization within the Office of the Secretary of Defense. We have also worked hard to more effectively integrate all testing, both developmental and operational, to achieve maximum efficiency for programs as a whole. Developmental test spans all the testing activities from program inception up until fielding. The separately conducted Operational Test events support final independent determinations about whether a program is effective, suitable, and survivable or not prior to proceeding to full rate production. Developmental testing provides the information that guides program decisions, determines if risks are being addressed successfully, confirms performance or identifies problems that must be corrected. Within a program, the developmental test events must be fully integrated into the program plan and structured to support the Program Manager and Chief Engineer as they address the complexity and risk associated with the program. Developmental testers are and should be an integral part of the Program Manager's program team.

The final article in this chapter discusses a sometime neglected area, but a crucial one—manufacturing. It makes the point that we cannot neglect manufacturing technology as a critical enabler in fielding advanced technology weapon systems. Recognizing the importance of manufacturing technology, the Obama administration undertook a major initiative to open approximately 15 national Manufacturing Innovation Institutes (MIIs). The DoD was the government's leader in establishing the vast majority of the several MIIs. My office led this effort, and a number of others, to further the state of the art and to improve our manufacturing capability and capacity.

Throughout the Obama administration, we tracked the manufacturing industrial base, particularly as it was impacted by budget cuts. In some instances, we stepped in to preserve or create a needed capability. The ability to produce a design, and to do it economically, is a critical consideration in program management and new product development. Years ago when I was working on my MBA, I was exposed to a case study in which the brilliant artist who was designing beautiful and novel consumer products failed to understand the limitations that existing manufacturing processes imposed on his ideas. We made exactly the same mistake with the disastrous A-12 combat reconnaissance aircraft program in the 1980s and '90s.

If there is one "takeaway" from this section, it should be that, in the creation of a complex weapon system, perfection should not be expected; setbacks and unforeseen problems will always be the norm—if we are to remain the world's dominant military power. Managing any complex weapons system development includes trade-offs between cost, schedule, and performance. Sometimes urgent need overcomes all other considerations, as it did with the acquisition of MRAPs, but more often the customer, our military operator, wants to acquire a system that meets the Service's full set of needs, or, in DoD parlance, its requirements. Those requirements bring complexity also, but as discussed in another chapter, they are often demanded by the operational user, who understandably desires a high quality product that can be kept in the inventory for 30 or 40 years. It's useful in that regard to contrast the MRAP program with another Army protected wheeled vehicle program, the Joint Lightweight Tactical Vehicle or JLTV.

The original MRAP vehicles were built for use in Iraq's relatively flat terrain. They were large vehicles with simple suspension systems. A few years later, it became clear that these vehicles were not suited for use in Afghanistan's rougher and more constrained terrain. A separate program—the MRAP-All Terrain Vehicle (MRAP-ATV or MATV)—was initiated, and several thousand smaller vehicles, with more dynamic suspensions and other features, were acquired. As ground operations wound down, the DoD eliminated from its inventory the vast majority of the roughly 30,000 MRAPs of all types. However, the DoD is acquiring a large number of new design JLTV vehicles that have come through the more standard acquisition process. JLTVs were designed from the start to meet the full range of Army and Marine Corps requirements, including the ability to operate with high reliability in a wide variety of terrain and climates.

Which approach to acquisition is the best? The answer is "it depends." When lives were at stake and time was of the essence, it was right to initiate a rapid acquisition program focused only on critical needs that used only off-the-shelf components. Without this pressing need, the Army and Marine Corps are now acquiring a much more capable and versatile vehicle in JLTV that will remain in our inventory for decades. Both approaches, and many others, have a place in our suite of acquisition program options.

CHAPTER THREE: MANAGING TECHNICAL COMPLEXITY

The Optimal Program Structure

Reprinted from Defense AT&L: *July-August 2012*

Not too long ago, I was asked during a Q&A session with one of the courses at the Defense Acquisition University what I thought was the optimal program structure. The question itself suggests a misunderstanding of how programs should be structured, and more importantly, it may be an example of a type of behavior that I've seen too much of in the past 2 years since I came back to government service.

The answer to the question is either: (A) There is none, or (B) There are an infinite number. There is no one best way to structure a program. Every program has its own best structure, and that structure is dependent on all the many variables that contribute to program success or failure. To paraphrase and invert Tolstoy, happy programs are each happy in their own way, and unhappy programs tend to be unhappy in the same ways.

As I went around the country a year ago to discuss the Better Buying Power initiatives with the workforce, one thing I tried to emphasize repeatedly was that the BBP policies were not set in stone. All were subject to waiver. The first responsibility of the key leaders in the acquisition workforce is to think. One of the many reasons that our key leaders have to be true professionals who are fully prepared to do their jobs by virtue of education, training, and experience is that creative, informed thought is necessary to optimize the structure of a program. The behavior I'm afraid I've seen too much of is the tendency to default to a "school solution" standard program structure. I've seen programs twisted into knots just to include all the milestones in the standard program template. I'm guessing that there are two reasons our leaders would do this: first, because they don't know any better, and second, because they believe it's the only way to get their program approved and through the "system." Neither of these leads to good outcomes, and neither is what I expect from our acquisition professionals.

So how does one determine how to best structure a program? Whether you are a PM, or a chief engineer, or a contracting officer, or a life cycle support manager, you have to start in the same place. You begin with a deep understanding of the nature of the product you intend to acquire. The form of the program has to follow the function the program will perform: developing and acquiring a specific product. The nature of the product should be the most significant determiner of program structure. How mature is the technology that will be included in the product? What will have to be done to mature that technology, and how much risk is involved? In addition to the technology that is included, how complicated will the design be? Is it like other designs that we have experience with, or is it novel? How difficult are the integration aspects of building the product? Is the manufacturing technology also mature, or will work have to be done to advance it prior to production? These questions on a large scale will begin the process of determining if a technology development phase is needed prior to the start of engineering and manufacturing development. They will also affect the duration of these phases, if used, and the number of test articles and types of testing that will have to be performed to verify the performance of the design.

Beyond a deep understanding of the product itself and the risk inherent in developing and producing it, one must consider a range of other factors that will influence program structure. How urgently is the product needed? How prepared is industry to design and produce the product? How much uncertainty is there about the proper balance of cost and capability? What are the customer's priorities for performance? What resource constraints will affect program risk (not just financial resources, but also availability of competitors, time, and expertise in and out of government)? Is cost or schedule most important and what are the best ways to control them on this program? What is the right balance of risk and incentives to provide to the contractors to get the results the government wants?

We are not in an easy business. This is in fact rocket science in many cases. As I look at programs coming through the acquisition process, my fundamental concern is that each program be structured in a way that optimizes that program's chances of success. There is no one solution. What I'm looking for fundamentally is the evidence that the program's leaders have thought carefully about all of the factors that I've mentioned—and many others. I look for that evidence in the nature of the product the program is acquiring and in the structure the program's leaders have chosen to use. The thinking (and the supporting data) that went into determining that specific and often unique structure is what I expect to see in an acquisition strategy, and it is what I expect our leaders to be able to explain when they present their program plans.

CHAPTER THREE: MANAGING TECHNICAL COMPLEXITY

Risk and Risk Mitigation—Don't Be a Spectator

Reprinted from Defense AT&L: *January-February 2015*

As I have watched programs come through for Milestone Decisions and other reviews, I have gained the impression that our processes for risk management may have focused too much on the process and not enough on the substance of identifying and controlling risk. I think I may be seeing risk identification—categorization in the "risk matrix" showing likelihood and consequence and with risk burn-down schedules tied to program events. From my perspective, this by itself isn't risk management; it is risk watching. We need to do what we can to manage and control risk, not just observe it.

All programs, but particularly all development programs, involve risk. There is risk in doing anything for the first time, and all new product developments involve doing something for the first time. The Department of Defense (DoD) has a good tool that lays out in detail the process of identifying, evaluating, categorizing and planning for risk in programs. Recently updated to version 7.0 by our Chief Systems Engineer, Dr. Steve Welby, it is called the Department of Defense Risk Management Guide for Defense Acquisition Programs and is available online at https://acc.dau.mil/rm-guidebook. I don't want to duplicate that material here, but I would like to make some comments on the substance of risk identification and risk mitigation and how it drives—or should drive—program structure and content.

I think of every development program primarily as a problem of risk management. Each program has what I call a risk profile that changes over time. Think of the risk profile as a graph of the amount of uncertainty about a program's outcomes. As we progress through the phases of a program—defining requirements, conducting trade studies, defining concepts and preliminary designs, completing detailed designs, building prototypes and conducting tests—what we really are doing is removing uncertainty from the program. That uncertainty encompasses the performance of the product, its cost and how much time is needed to develop and produce the product. We can be surprised at any point in this process. Some surprises can be handled in stride, and some may lead to major setbacks and a restructuring or even cancellation of the program. It is our job to anticipate those surprises, assess their likelihood and their impacts and, most of all, do something either to prevent them or, if they do occur, to limit their impacts. All this effort is risk management.

As managers, we can take a number of proactive measures to mitigate risk. These measures all tend to have one thing in common: They are not free. In our resource-constrained world, we can't do everything possible to mitigate risk. The things we can do cover a wide spectrum: We can carry competitors through risk reduction or even development for production, we can pursue multiple technical approaches to the same goal, we can provide alternative lower-performance solutions that also carry lower risks, we can stretch schedule by slowing or delaying some program activities until risk is reduced and we can provide strong incentives to industry to achieve our most difficult program challenges.

Our task as managers involves optimization—what are the highest-payoff risk-mitigation investments we can make with the resources available? I expect our managers to demonstrate that they have analyzed this problem and made good judgments about how best to use the resources they have to mitigate the program's risk. This activity starts when the program plan is just beginning.

The most important decisions to control risk are made in the earliest stages of program planning. Very early in our planning, we determine the basic program structure, whether we will have a dedicated risk reduction phase, what basic contract types we will use, our criteria for entering design for production and for entering production itself, and how much time and money we will need to execute the program. Once these decisions are in place, the rest is details—important but much less consequential. As I've written before, these decisions should be guided not by an arbitrary process or best practice but by the nature of the specific product we intend to design and build.

What we call "requirements" determines a great deal—almost everything—about the risks we need to manage. Do the requirements call for a product like a Mine-Resistant Ambush Protected vehicle, which is basically a heavy truck built from existing off-the-shelf components? Or do they call for a Joint Strike Fighter built from all new design subsystems and much greater capability and complexity than anything we have ever built? In the first case, we probably can go directly into detailed design for production. In the second case, we need to spend years maturing the highest risk elements of the design, and it would be wise to build prototypes to reduce integration and performance risk before our performance requirements are made final and we start designing for production.

The contracting approach, fixed price or cost plus, is driven by risk considerations. We need to be careful about the illusion that all risk can be transferred to industry. This is never the case, even in a firm fixed-price contract. The risk that the contractor will not deliver the product is always borne by

CHAPTER THREE: MANAGING TECHNICAL COMPLEXITY

the government. We are the ones who need the product. Industry's risk is always limited to the costs a firm can absorb—a very finite parameter. There certainly are cases where we should use fixed-price contracts for product development (the Air Force's new KC-46 refueling and transport tanker is an example), but we should limit such contracts to situations where we have good reason to believe industry can perform as expected and where the risk is not more than the contractor can reasonably bear.

As a risk-mitigation measure, cost-plus development has a very attractive feature from the risk-management perspective—its flexibility. In a fixed-price environment, the government should have defined the deliverables clearly and should not make changes or direct the contractor about how to do the work. In a fixed-price world, we have chosen to transfer that responsibility to the contractor. In a cost-plus environment, the government can be (and should be) involved in cost-effectiveness trades that affect requirements and in decisions about investments in risk-mitigation measures. These decisions affect cost and schedule, and in a cost-plus environment the government has the flexibility to make those trade-offs without being required to renegotiate or modify the contract.

At certain points in programs, we make decisions to commit both time and funding to achieving certain goals. Sometimes the commitments include several years of work and require spending billions of dollars. These are the milestones and decision points we are all familiar with in the acquisition process. These milestones and decision points are critical risk-management events. At each of these points, we need a thorough understanding of the risks we face and a clear plan to manage those risks. Understanding these risks is rooted in a deep understanding of the nature of the product we are building.

The nature of the product should determine whether a dedicated technology maturation and risk-reduction phase is needed and what will have to be accomplished in that phase. Although they can be useful indicators, we can't rely solely on metrics like Technology Readiness Levels (TRLs) to make these decisions for us. A bureaucrat can determine if something meets the definition of TRL 6 or not. It takes a competent engineer (in the right discipline) to determine if a technology is too immature and risky to be incorporated into a design for production. The nature of the product also should determine whether system-level prototypes are necessary to reduce integration risk prior to making the commitment to design for production. We did not need those prototypes on the new Marine 1 helicopter. We did need them on the F-22 and the F-35 fighter aircraft.

One risk-mitigation rule of thumb for program planning is to do the hard things first. In the Comanche helicopter program during the 1990s, the Army didn't have enough funding to mature both the mission equipment package and the airframe. The choice was made to build prototype airframes—the lower-risk and less ambitious part of the program. This was done (over my objections at the time), because it was believed that, without flying prototypes, the program risked cancellation for political reasons. In other words, political risk trumped development risk. It didn't work, and the program ultimately was canceled anyway. I do not advocate this approach; there are other ways to deal with political risk. In general, we should do the hardest things as early as we can in acquisition program planning. Eat your spinach first; it makes the rest of the meal taste much better.

Preferably, we should do the hardest (most risky) things in a Technology Maturation Risk Reduction (TMRR) phase where the risk can be reduced with a lower financial commitment and with less severe consequences. Once Engineering and Manufacturing Development (EMD) begins, a program quickly has a marching army moving forward in a broad synchronized plan of work. When something goes wrong, that marching army often will mark time while it waits for the problem to be solved—an expensive proposition. We recently had a problem with the F-35 engine that led first to grounding the fleet and then to a restricted flight envelope. All this delayed the test program, and the effects rippled through much of the EMD effort. It would have been much better to have found this problem before it could disrupt the entire flight test program.

Within either a TMRR or EMD phase, we should structure workflow to reduce or realize as early as possible the likelier and more consequential risks. Risk should influence program planning details. We can use internal "knowledge points" to inform commitments within phases. Our chief developmental tester, Dave Brown, emphasizes "shifting left" in test planning. The benefits of this are that technical performance uncertainty is reduced as early as possible and that the consequences of realized risks are less severe in terms of lost work, rework or program disruption.

The major commitment to enter production should be driven primarily by achieving confidence in the stability of the product's design, at least as regards any major changes. The key risk to manage here is that of discovering major design changes are required after the production line is up and running. This always is a trade-off; time to market does matter and our warfighters need the product we are developing. How much overlap is acceptable in development and production (concurrency) is a judgment call, but it is driven by an assessment of the risks of a major design problem that will require correction—and the consequences of such a discovery.

We recently had a fatigue failure in an F-35 bulkhead, a major structural member. We are in our eighth year of production. Fortunately, in this case,

Chapter Three: Managing Technical Complexity

a reasonable cost fix seems viable, and we should be able to modify at modest cost the aircraft we already have built. I say "should be" because the fix will take time to verify through testing, and there remains some risk that the fix will be ineffective.

For all our major commitments, but particularly for exiting TMRR and for entering production, I demand specific accomplishments as criteria and I put them in Acquisition Decision Memoranda. The pressures are very high in our system to move forward, to spend the money appropriated and to preserve the appearance of progress. I recommend that this practice of setting specific criteria for work package initiation (or other resource, workscope expansion or contractual commitments) be used internally throughout our programs. By setting these criteria objectively and in the absence of the pressure of the moment, I believe we can make better decisions about program commitments and better control the risks we face.

Delaying a commitment has impacts now; gambling that things will work out has impacts in the future. It often is tempting for managers under cost and schedule pressures to accept risk and continue as planned. We are paid to get these judgments right—and to have the courage to make the harder decision when we believe it is the right decision.

A source of risk nearly all programs face is uncertainty about external dependencies, often in the form of interfaces with other programs that may not themselves be defined or stable. In other cases, a companion program (user equipment for the satellite Global Positioning System, for example) may be needed to make the system itself viable or useful, but that program experiences its own risks that affect schedule and performance.

We often expect program managers to coordinate with each other, but in many cases this isn't enough. Controlling potential cyber vulnerabilities across program interfaces is a good example of an area in which we have problems. No affected program manager may be willing to change or have any incentive to adjust his or her program to bring it into synchronization with the other programs. If there is a negative cost or schedule impact, the question always is, "Who will change and who will bear the cost of any needed adjustments?" I'm of the view that the DoD could do a better job at managing this type of risk. We can do so by establishing an appropriate technical authority with directive control over interfaces and program synchronization.

The sources of some of our greatest risks can go unnoticed and unchallenged. Gary Bliss, director of my Program Assessment and Root Cause Analysis Office, has introduced the concept of "framing assumptions" into our lexicon. One example of a framing assumption, again on the F-35, was that modeling and simulation were so good that actual physical testing wasn't necessary to verify performance prior to the start of production. In the case of the Littoral Combat Ship, the assumption was that commercial construction standards were adequate to guide the design. Gary's point, and it's a good one, is that programs often get into trouble when framing assumptions prove invalid. However, these assumptions are so ingrained and established in our thinking that they are not challenged or fully appreciated as risks until reality rears its ugly head in a very visible way. This type of risk can be mitigated by acknowledging that the assumptions exist and by providing avenues for us to become aware of sources of evidence that the assumptions may not be valid. Our human tendency is to reject evidence that doesn't agree with our preconceptions.

Gary found several cases where program management failed to recognize as early as it should have that core framing assumptions were false. The best way to manage this source of uncertainty is to take the time and effort during early program planning to identify a program's framing assumptions, to understand that they are a source of risk and then to actively reexamine them for validity as more information becomes available. Again, "knowledge points" can be helpful, but we shouldn't merely be passive about this. In our planning, we should create knowledge points as early as possible. If we do so, we can respond to any problems that emerge sooner rather than later.

I'll conclude by reiterating two key points: Risk management is not a passive activity, and proactive risk-management investments are not free. Those investments, however, can be the most important resource allocations we make in our programs. As managers, we need to attack risk the way we've been attacking cost. Understand risk thoroughly, and then go after the risk items with the highest combined likelihoods and consequences and bring them under control. Allocate your scarce resources so you achieve the highest possible return for your investments in risk reduction. Do this most of all at the very start of program planning. The course set then will determine the direction of the balance of the program and whether it succeeds or fails.

CHAPTER THREE: MANAGING TECHNICAL COMPLEXITY

The Trouble With TRLs (With Thanks to Gene Roddenberry and David Gerrold)

Reprinted from Defense AT&L: *September-October 2013*

For a long time now, the Defense Department has been using Technology Readiness Levels (TRLs) as a tool to assess the risk of including a new or advanced technology in one of our products. There is nothing wrong with TRLs except that they are only one input for a risk assessment and provide at best a crude indicator of the risk of using a technology in a product. In many cases, TRLs tell us virtually nothing about whether we need to take additional action to reduce risk and what it will take to reduce a specific risk to an acceptable level. Let me give you three real-life examples I've seen over the last few years:

Example No. 1: An offeror on a missile program wants to incorporate a new infrared imaging array in a missile seeker. The technology will provide a significant performance enhancement. It employs a new material or perhaps just a larger array with a proven material. The offeror has produced several test arrays and incorporated them in laboratory test articles and in a prototype seeker that has been flown in a test article against a representative target. We would seem to have a technology that has reached the benchmark TRL 6; it has been tested in a prototype in a relevant end-to-end environment. What could be wrong? For a seeker material of this type, a critical question is its affordability as well as producibility, which usually is a function of the manufacturing processes' yield percentage. Demonstrating that we can build a few test articles simply does not tell us enough about the viability of the technology for large-scale production and therefore about the wisdom of its inclusion in the design for an Engineering and Manufacturing Development (EMD) program.

Example No. 2: To support amphibious operations, a new ramp design is needed for a staging vessel that will be used to transfer ground combat vehicles from an amphibious ship to the staging vessel before they are loaded onto landing craft and deployed to shore. The intended ramp design is novel, but it does not include any new materials or design features that would expand the state of the art in any fundamental way. It is similar to other commercial and military designs but will be required to work in higher sea states than other similar structures. Subscale models have been built and tested in tank tests, and extensive modeling and simulation work has been done to verify the design. This "technology" (or design) doesn't meet the TRL 6 benchmark because it has not been tested in a relevant end-to-end environment. Should the program office be required to build a full-scale test article prior to entering EMD for the staging vessel? There is no way to know from the facts I have provided. Resolving this issue requires expert judgment about the degree to which the new design departs from proven capability, the risk of relying on model testing and simulation, as well as about the cost of designing, building and testing a pre-EMD prototype.

Example No. 3: New mathematical algorithms have been devised to fuse data from multiple onboard and offboard Intelligence, Surveillance and Reconnaissance (ISR) sources in a networked Command and Control (C2) system to be used on a new tactical strike platform. The success of these algorithms in substantially reducing the data processing loads on the C2 system will determine the viability of the design concept because of limitations on available power, cooling and volume on the aircraft. What must be accomplished prior to EMD to mitigate the risks of relying on these algorithms in the EMD design? If someone told you this technology was TRL 6, would that be enough to convince you that the risk was mitigated adequately? I hope not.

One of the hardest and most important aspects of our jobs in developing and delivering new capabilities to the warfighter is risk management. A problem I've seen repeatedly is defaulting to a TRL assessment as a substitute for informed professional risk assessment and well thought-out mitigation plans, including specific knowledge points and decision criteria or exit/ entrance criteria for the next phase of development. TRLs do not end the conversation about risk. TRLs may start the risk conversation, and they may provide a convenient shorthand benchmark, but they do not answer the question of whether the total risk of proceeding is acceptable, or define what work needs to be done to make the risk acceptable.

Some time ago I revised the technology assessment process that we require prior to major acquisition decisions, particularly the commitment to enter EMD, to place more responsibility on our Program Managers. I expect Program Managers to have a thorough and deep understanding of the technical risks associated with their programs and of the mitigation steps and resources required to reduce that risk. Technical risk considerations drive any number of program decisions, including: (1) the feasibility of requirements, (2) the need to conduct a Technology Demonstration (TD) phase, (3) the need for and value of competitive prototypes, (4) the specific accomplishments needed before entering EMD or initial production, and (5) the appropriate contract type. All this is Program Manager's business, requiring judgment that goes well beyond any formulaic assessment of TRLs.

We also can't assume that industry will take the needed steps to identify and reduce risk. A recent study of TD prototyping programs that I commissioned revealed that industry isn't necessarily trying to reduce risk as its highest priority. When there is a competition, we can expect industry's first priority is to win the competition. We have to make sure that winning the competition is synonymous with doing what the government needs done to identify risk and drive it down. The study showed that in many, in fact the majority, of the cases, industry was achieving an asserted TRL 6 benchmark for the government but not reducing the risk in the product that the vendor intended to build in EMD. This isn't something we should blame industry for; we write the rules and we enforce them.

We will never have, and should not expect to have, risk-free programs. Our warfighters have the best equipment in the world because we take the risks inherent in doing things that have never been done before. Our technological superiority rests on this foundation. As acquisition professionals, we have to manage risk so we strike the right balance between stretching for new and better capabilities and limiting our goals to ones that are attainable and will be reached efficiently at acceptable cost. TRLs are just one of the tools we use to accomplish this task, and we should not rely on them for more than they can provide or think of them as a substitute for the professional judgments we have to make.

Perspectives on Developmental Test and Evaluation

Reprinted from ITEA Journal: *March 2013*

During my first tour in the Pentagon in Acquisition, Technology, and Logistics (AT&L) from 1986 to 1994, I was responsible initially for strategic defense systems and then for tactical warfare programs. During this time, I had the opportunity to work with a Developmental Test and Evaluation (DT&E) organization that was very professional and led by an outstanding civil servant, Pete Adolph. Somewhere along the way, as priorities and personalities changed in the Office of the Secretary of Defense (OSD), the DT&E organization atrophied and all but disappeared. For the last few years, under the auspices of the Weapons System Acquisition Reform Act, we have been strengthening the DT&E organization within OSD. Ed Greer, who retired from public service recently, has rebuilt the DT&E organization to the point that it is now performing a role much closer to the one I remember from the 80s and 90s. As Defense Acquisition Executive, I rely heavily on the DT&E office and staff for sound advice on the adequacy of the test programs being proposed for major programs and on the implications of developmental test results for investment decisions, particularly for entry into low rate production. Developmental testing is a core activity in our acquisition programs, however, not just an OSD oversight function. In this article I discuss the role DT&E plays in our programs, some important principles I believe should be applied to developmental testing, and some common problems I have encountered that relate to the effectiveness of DT&E.

Role of developmental testing

The purpose of developmental testing is simple: to provide data to program leadership so that good decisions can be made as early as possible. I have a sign outside my office displaying a quote from W. Edwards Deming: "In God we trust, all others must bring data." It is our developmental testers who "bring the data" needed to make sound decisions during product development. Programs are organized in various ways, but whatever the specific organizational model, testing is the source of the crucial information that provides feedback to program management, chief engineers, lead system engineers, integrated product teams, and military users on whether their designs meet requirements or not. The spectrum of testing types and venues that is captured in compliance matrices for system specifications runs the gamut of laboratory testing and field testing. All of these sources of information can be valuable, but integrating them into a test program and an overall program plan and schedule that meet the needs of developmental testers' customers requires a high degree of professionalism and a deep understanding of how test results can influence design and program decisions. In my experience, a well-structured test plan makes all the difference in whether a program is efficiently executed or not. There are two layers of DT&E organizational roles and relationships; both are important in determining DT&E's contributions to program success.

The first layer of DT&E organization exists within the program office. I have seen several organizational models for DT&E offices within Department of Defense (DoD) programs, and any of them can work given professional leadership, well-defined lines of authority, and responsibility, and commitment to working together as a team. The DT&E office or organization within a program usually reports to the program manager, to the chief engineer, or to the lead systems engineer. In some cases, the DT&E staff can be matrix staff allocated from centralized functional test organizations, and in other cases, the testing staff can be organic staff members of the program office. Whatever the model, the role of the test organization is to support the program's leadership by providing timely, accurate, and relevant information to enable efficient and effective program decisions.

The second layer of DT&E organization exists within the Service or Military Department at a higher level than the program office. Here too there are various models, and any of them can be successful. Some Services have centralized DT&E support within test organizations that include operational test as well as DT&E. Others have created DT&E organizations at the system command level. These organizations tend to be focused on ensuring the acquisition and evaluation of the specific data needed to support major decisions, such as initiating production or proceeding to Operational Test and Evaluation (OT&E). This layer of DT&E organization, with some degree of independence from the standard acquisition chain of command of program executive officer and program manager, and even in some cases the acquisition executive, can be effective, but it also runs the risk of diluting the authority and accountability of the acquisition chain of command. In my own OSD AT&L organization, I consider the DT&E organization, which we have rebuilt over the last few years, to have a staff function that supports my acquisition decisions and also provides expertise and other support to the Services. When there are differences of opinion between the OSD DT&E organization and the Service acquisition chain of command, I expect them to be brought to my attention for resolution.

Precepts of effective DT&E

The following "precepts" are based on my own experience and are generated largely from a program or engineering management perspective. They are in no particular order and are intended merely as food for thought by anyone involved in DT&E or any customers or stakeholders in the DT&E functional area.

1. Contribute to program efficiency and effective execution: DT&E is a support function that enables sound design and program decisions, and DT&E leadership should be an integral part of the program planning team. DT&E should be part of program planning from the outset. Much of product development can be thought of as risk management, where design and technical risks are addressed and resolved in an iterative process over time. The way DT&E is structured to contribute to this process can make all the difference in the efficiency (think waste avoidance) with which a product is developed. DT&E leadership should be fully integrated into the program management and system engineering functions. Formal "design of experiments" techniques are being used widely now to ensure that tests are structured to extract meaningful information as efficiently as possible, and I applaud this development. Testing isn't free, however, and we need to balance the desire for thorough testing against the resources in time and money required to conduct the testing. This can only be accomplished through a cooperative effort that fully involves DT&E professionals in the program planning process.

2. Provide relevant information as early as possible: Once a program enters Engineering and Manufacturing Development (EMD), the commitment to design for production unleashes a marching army of interdependent engineers that needs to keep moving in a tight formation through the development process. Any serious design problems that surface late in the development process can stop this marching army in its tracks at great expense while the problem is addressed and resolved. The later a problem is identified and the solution determined, the greater the redesign burden and cost. To avoid this problem, information on the performance of the design in key areas needs to be made available as early as it can be provided and from the most reliable source of information available. As good as our design tools have become, there is still no substitute for physical testing, particularly for our more complex and novel designs. For key program technical risks, the early use of prototypes (full or subsystem level) and developmental testing during technology demonstration risk reduction activities prior to the commitment to EMD can make all the difference between a successful EMD and one that experiences massive overruns. Again, DT&E isn't free, and like any program, it needs to be conducted as efficiently as possible, but the real benefit of an effectively structured test program is in the cost avoidance it can provide by discovering problems as early as possible.

Chapter Three: Managing Technical Complexity

3. Integrate DT&E planning across the product life cycle: DT&E is not just about production representative prototype testing in a controlled environment prior to the decision to proceed to OT&E. It encompasses the total program of testing, including, for example, hardware in the loop testing in system integration laboratories, environmental stress screening at the subsystem level, and software testing in emulators. Whenever data are needed to support risk reduction, design validation, and requirements verification, there is a role for DT&E in collecting those data and evaluating them on a continuum over a program's life. This spans all phases of a program's life cycle. Increasingly, the Department is keeping systems longer and upgrading them in lieu of pursuing new designs. Effective DT&E is as central to these efforts as it is to new product development programs. Well-structured developmental testing should be integral to all phases of a product's life cycle.

4. Focus on support to internal program decisions and verification of compliance with requirements: DT&E does not exist in a vacuum and is not a separate function; its purpose is to support program management and technical leadership as it works to develop and field a product that meets user requirements. Programs move through a series of development activities that must be successfully completed and verified through testing, often as a condition of proceeding to the next phase of the program. Sometimes this is the next software build; sometimes it is a higher level of integration, and sometimes it is a decision to commit to initial production. DT&E also provides an indication of the readiness of a program to proceed to OT&E. For any of these decision points, DT&E provides crucial information to support the decisions, and the adequacy of that information is central to controlling program risk and ensuring contractual compliance. Careful planning and well-defined decision criteria are necessary prerequisites, but the discipline to enforce those criteria is what often sets successful programs apart.

5. Use DT&E to improve the efficiency and validity of OT&E: OT&E is conducted with more independence from the program office and the acquisition chain of command than DT&E and with less involvement by the contractor supplying the product, but the two test regimes should work together to complement each other and avoid unnecessary expenses as much as possible. Under Mike Gilmore's and Ed Greer's professional leadership, there has been a very cooperative relationship between the DT&E and OT&E organizations at the Department level. This relationship should continue and be mirrored at all levels. While the OT&E community works hard to preserve and ensure its independence, I am encouraged by the willingness of that community to use the data that DT&E can provide to augment and complement data provided by OT&E. We will never have the resources to do as much testing

as we would like, and achieving statistically meaningful testing is sometimes prohibitively expensive. By working together, the DT&E and OT&E communities in OSD and the Services can achieve more valid results, anchor each other's efforts, and do so at less cost.

How we get into trouble in DT&E— Some of the ways at least

There are times when DT&E doesn't fulfill its purpose, and a program ends up with one type or another of acquisition problem. This can take the form of cost overruns and schedule slips, or worse, a product that simply isn't viable, despite having been approved for development and even initial production and after years of effort and expense. The following paragraphs provide some of the types of problems I have encountered most frequently over the last 40 years.

In the technology demonstration or risk reduction phase, we permit the use of test articles that may not be adequately representative of the actual product design. In these cases, the testing that is conducted may be more intended to sell a product than to reduce that product's risks. Motivated by a specific example I encountered (a program that was up for a Milestone B decision), I recently asked a former deputy director of the Defense Advanced Research Projects Agency (DARPA) to review a number of programs that had been through technology demonstration programs, which included DT&E of competitive prototypes. The results were troubling. In the majority of the cases, the design that was demonstrated had little or no correlation to the design that was going to be developed in EMD. The DT&E that was done in the risk reduction phase was not providing data to reduce the risk of the target design. It was providing data intended to sell the government on the prospective bidder. The lesson I derived from this was that the combined government management team (program management, engineering leadership, and developmental testers) was not insisting on the relevance and validity of the test program. We can't blame industry for trying to win the EMD contract; we have to blame ourselves for not understanding industry's motivation and insisting on meaningful testing that actually addresses the risks in the intended design.

We use ill-defined user requirements that have not been translated into testable technical specifications. As a result, we cannot plan the time and resources for appropriate testing in the early stages of a development program, and we cannot hold the contractor responsible for not meeting our expectations. The government generally has to define its requirements and ensure that they are converted into testable requirements that our contractors can demonstrate they have satisfied in DT&E. If we fail in this responsibility and provide vaguely defined requirements to industry, we have no one but ourselves to blame when our expectations are not met. The largest program I ever worked on had extensive user requirements that were never properly defined to the prime contractor or converted by that contractor or the government into quantifiable and testable technical requirements. When the program eventually died of its own weight, years after it had started and after billions of dollars of cost, the prime contractor and the customer were still debating over how to interpret the requirements and how to test for compliance.

We have to resist the tendency to assume DT&E efficiencies that exceed previous experience in response to financial pressure. Most programs come under financial pressure at some point; often before the program even enters EMD. It is far too easy to assume away the need for an adequate number of test articles, or an adequate amount of test time in order to meet a budget number or a schedule that has been dictated for some reason. Usually in my experience, program leadership, including the DT&E leadership, accepts the constraints that have been provided and gambles on unprecedented test performance and efficiencies. The usual result is increased inefficiency, not the opposite. We don't want to over schedule or buy unneeded test assets, but my experience is that the far more common errors are unwarranted optimism and acceptance of excessive risk rather than excessive conservatism or risk aversion. If we have solid reasons to conclude that we can improve the efficiency of DT&E (and we should always be looking for sources of efficiencies), then we should take those efficiencies into account in our planning, but hope is still not a method.

We sometimes fail to conduct adequate DT&E prior to the decision to start production. About a year ago, I called a particular decision to enter production on an aircraft program without flight testing "acquisition malpractice." If a product enters production before the design is stable, the resulting waste in cost increases and schedule slips can be dramatic, and the program is much more likely to be canceled. I stress solid, well-defined DT&E results as an important prerequisite for this decision because the pressure to enter production can be overwhelming, and doing so prematurely has major consequences. The Service often feels that it will "lose the money" that has been requested a year or more earlier from the Congress if the production contract is not awarded. Industry wants to make the sale, and the user is anxious to get the new product. The decision to enter production is all but irreversible, and to make this commitment for a new design without the knowledge obtained from adequate DT&E entails high risk. That said, there is a balance to be struck. A well-structured DT&E program will provide confidence in the stability of the design as early as possible. Some degree of concurrency between development (including

DT&E) and production is usually appropriate. The degree of concurrency that is acceptable depends on several factors, but in every case there should be a well-defined basis rooted in data provided by DT&E to support this critical decision.

We assume untested design fixes to problems discovered in DT&E will be successful, in order to preserve schedule. It is always a judgment call, but in general, design changes have to be verified through DT&E just as much as the original design needs to be verified. Where I have seen this most often is when we are about to initiate or have already initiated low rate production. I recently slowed the rate of production of DoD's biggest program so that we could test design fixes adequately prior to increasing the rate of production. I seriously considered stopping production completely, but made the judgment call to continue at a low rate while the test program verified the design fixes. The cost of stopping and restarting would have been very high, so I limited our exposure but didn't take it to zero. We don't want to be in this position if we can avoid it.

We sometimes over-focus on DT&E as preparation for OT&E. No one wants to fail operational testing, and one of the things we can learn from the last stages of DT&E is whether or not a program has a high probability of a successful OT. This doesn't mean, however, that we should do two rounds of OT&E with the first being called DT&E. In general OT&E is not intended to be a place to discover unanticipated problems, but we shouldn't be so risk averse that we add what amounts to an extra phase of testing out of concern for failing operational test. DT&E should be focused on verifying that the contractor has met the requirements. We should do an effective job of linking those requirements and the DT&E that verifies compliance to the operational performance that we intend to demonstrate in OT&E. If we have done this effectively, the last stage of DT&E shouldn't have to be a full dress rehearsal for OT&E.

The bottom line

Developmental testers are critical professionals who make a major contribution to DoD's programs. They bring a unique body of knowledge to the table that is essential to effective program planning and execution. Again, it is largely the DT&E community that "brings [the] data" the sign outside my door emphasizes. Working with program and engineering leadership as key members of the management team, developmental testers provide the information that makes program success possible and much more probable.

Editor's Note: The *ITEA Journal* article above is reprinted here with the permission of the International Test and Evaluation Association.

CHAPTER THREE: MANAGING TECHNICAL COMPLEXITY

Manufacturing Innovation and Technological Superiority

Reprinted from Defense AT&L: *September-October 2016*

At the end of the Cold War, I was serving as the Deputy Director of Defense Research and Engineering for Tactical Warfare Programs in the Office of the Secretary of Defense (OSD). For years I had studied the intelligence reports on Soviet weapon systems and worked on ways the United States could achieve or maintain a military advantage over those systems. We knew the Russians had some of the best scientists and engineers in the world working on their designs. They also had aggressive modernization cycles in areas they considered important; their multiple competing design bureaus turned out new designs for armored vehicles, missiles and tactical aircraft on a predictable schedule at intervals of about 5 years.

After the Cold War ended, I was anxious to get a close look at the Soviet weapons systems we had been working to defeat. I soon had two opportunities to examine the newest Soviet equipment up close. One was a display at Andrews Air Force Base in Maryland of all the equipment that we acquired to test once the wall came down and the Russians were desperate for any source of cash. The other was at the Farnborough International Airshow in England, where the Russians were offering to sell their most modern systems to anyone who would buy them. What struck me most when I examined the former Soviet equipment was how primitive their production technology was compared to U.S. manufacturing technology.

Those brilliant scientists and engineers had lacked the modern materials and manufacturing technology to keep pace with the West. It was clear that the performance and reliability of their weapons systems had been severely limited by their limitations in areas like precision machining; the ability to fabricate multilayer printed circuit boards; and their inability to produce integrated circuits.

I recall in particular the presence of Bakelite, a distinct early plastic thermosetting insulating material, which the United States hadn't used since the 1950s, being everywhere in Soviet 1980s-era aircraft. One of the greatest constraints on the Soviet designers, and on the performance and cost of their weapons systems had been manufacturing technology.

Manufacturing technology doesn't just affect weapons systems and technological superiority—it also drives national economic performance. The first and second industrial revolutions were largely about manufacturing technology. The English advantages in mechanized textile manufacturing in the early 1800s drove the performance of the British economy, just as Carnegie's steel production in the late 19th century and Ford's mass production technology early in the 20th drove the growth of the U.S. economy. More recently, ever smaller and more efficient silicon-based integrated circuits that can be economically manufactured in massive quantities are driving economic growth around the world.

Recognizing the importance of manufacturing technology to both national security and our economy, the President initiated a program to establish Manufacturing Innovation Institutes (MIIs) that would create incubators for advanced manufacturing technology in key technological areas. The Department of Defense (DoD) has been a national leader in establishing these institutions. With the Acting Secretary of Commerce and the National Economic Advisor, I opened the first one—which is dedicated to advancing additive manufacturing (3D printing) technology—in Youngstown, Ohio, in 2012. Since then, several more MIIs have been opened, two by the Department of Energy and six by the DoD. Several more are on the way. The technologies of interest are determined by an expert interagency body with industry input. Focus areas include lightweight alloys, digitization of design to manufacturing processes and flexible electronics. All of these new institutions depend on collaboration between federal and local government, industry and academia. Government funding is combined with other sources of funds to get these institutions up and running, but they will have to be self-sufficient in a few years when government funding will cease. We don't know if every MII will flourish; we will let time and the requirement to be self-sufficient sort that out. Four years in we do know that some of the MIIs we have established are off to a good start, with continuing interest from industry, significant advances in manufacturing technology and successful products to their credit.

I would like to recognize some key DoD leaders who have organized and led the competitive process to set up the MIIs. First Brett Lambert, then Elana Broitman, and now Andre Gudger, as leaders of the DoD's Manufacturing and Industrial Base Policy organization, have been the senior leaders responsible for the DoD's MIIs. A remarkable team, led by Adele Ratcliff (whose article in this edition of *Defense AT&L* magazine provides much more detail on the MIIs), has done the heavy lifting required to make each of the MIIs a reality. Each of the Military Departments also has played a strong role—conducting the actual competitions and working with the selected consortium to get the MIIs up and running. All of these dedicated professionals deserve our appreciation for creating these new national assets.

Chapter Three: Managing Technical Complexity

While the MIIs are important, they are only one source of the technologies that will make building our future generations of weapons possible and affordable. Industry investments are focused on staying competitive in an ever-more-competitive world, and help to keep the United States competitive against potential adversaries.

I have been encouraging defense companies to invest more in research and development, and one of the areas of greatest promise is on technologies that will lower the production costs and improve the performance of our weapons systems. Industry is responding. One example is the "blueprint for affordability" initiative in which Lockheed Martin and major F-35 suppliers have agreed to undertake to reduce F-35 production costs. Through a creative "win-win" agreement, Lockheed Martin and the major suppliers for the F-35—Northrop Grumman and BAE—are all making investments that will reduce government cost and achieve a higher return for the industry participants. Pratt & Whitney has a similar program for the F-135 engine. In another example, Boeing has invested significantly in its ground-breaking proprietary manufacturing processes that are expected to pay strong dividends in both military and commercial aircraft manufacturing. Industry understands that manufacturing technology is the key to competitiveness.

For more than 50 years, the DoD Manufacturing Technology Program, or ManTech, has been used by the DoD to sustain our lead in defense-essential manufacturing capability. The ManTech Program, executed through dedicated teams in the Services, agencies, and within the OSD, develops technologies and processes that impact all phases of acquisition and reduce both acquisition and total ownership costs by developing, maturing, and transitioning key manufacturing technologies. ManTech not only provides the crucial link between technology invention and development and industrial applications, but also matures and validates emerging manufacturing technologies to support feasible implementation in industry and DoD facilities like depots and shipyards.

Direct investments by the government have often been the genesis of new manufacturing technology and a catalyst to spur more investment by industry. When I was vice president of engineering at Raytheon in the 1990s, I was able, with the CEO's strong support, to protect our corporate investment in the technology needed to produce gallium arsenide radio frequency components, a key enabler for a range of important national security projects and a major competitive advantage for the company. More recently, government support, together with industry investments, for Gallium Nitride components is giving the United States the opportunity to produce systems like the Next Generation Jammer, the Advanced Missile Defense Radar and others.

For the acquisition professionals managing our new product development programs, manufacturing technology and the risk associated with bringing new technology on line, should be major parts of program planning. Our policy encourages the use of Manufacturing Readiness Levels as one way to assess the maturity and risk associated with producing specific designs. As I hope you know by now, I'm not a fan of readiness levels—they convey no real information about the actual risk or the difficulty of maturing a technology to where it can be used in a product or in manufacturing a product—but they do provide a place to start a conversation about that risk. Managing the risk associated with manufacturing is as important as managing the technological risk associated with performance. This isn't a new problem. When I was working on my MBA in the 1970s, we did a case study on how to manage creative designers who failed to appreciate the difficulty associated with actually producing their ingenious designs. While a new idea might work in theory, if it can't be built at an affordable cost it doesn't have much value. As we build risk reduction plans and proactively manage the risks associated with new capabilities we cannot afford to neglect the importance of having mature manufacturing processes.

Given the importance of manufacturing technology, we must protect that technology just as we protect the actual designs and performance characteristics of our weapon systems. As I work with our international partners, one thing is almost a constant—the desire to acquire advanced manufacturing expertise in order to build more competitive manufacturing capacity and create jobs. Our competitors as well as our friends understand the importance of manufacturing technology, and they have no reticence about using every available means to acquire that technology—especially cyber theft. As we build Program Protection Plans, we must include the steps we will take to protect critical manufacturing technology—throughout the supply chain.

This issue of *Defense AT&L* magazine is focused on manufacturing, the various MIIs and on our programs, such as ManTech, established to invest in critical manufacturing technology. As we plan and execute our research efforts and our development programs, we all should be conscious of the importance of advancing the state of the art in manufacturing, of managing the risks associated with manufacturing, and of protecting the manufacturing technologies that we need to maintain our technological superiority over our most capable potential opponents. You can be certain that potential adversaries are working very hard to avoid the disadvantage embedded in the Soviet weapon systems I was so anxious to investigate at the end of the Cold War.

Chapter Four
Working With Industry

"We're all in this game together."

—William Styron

This chapter addresses the most important relationship in defense acquisition—that between the DoD and the for-profit firms that provide almost all of the products and services that the DoD acquires. The DoD does business with a wide spectrum of companies, but a mere handful are the source of most of our major weapons systems. We often refer to these firms and the specialized supply chain that contributes parts and subsystems to them, as the Defense Industrial Base, or DIB. Most of this chapter addresses that specialized industrial base. A much larger group of businesses provides a range of products and services that are less unique, specialized, or complex than the major systems we acquire. These firms are commercial and often have a broad set of customers. Information technology firms are a good example. For these companies, the DoD often is a small fraction of their business base. Still another type of firm, small business, also is important, as small firms provide a disproportionate share of the innovation in our economy and are a source of much of our economic growth.

The first article in this chapter discusses our relationship with industry in general and the balance the government has to strike as it simultaneously tries to protect the taxpayer's investment in defense, treat industry fairly, and obtain the high quality products our warfighters need and deserve. The government relationship with industry is defined largely by our contracts, but it is also defined by the attitude toward industry that we bring to the table, and the expectations we communicate by everything that we do. We need to recognize that profit isn't optional for industry, and that industry can only absorb so much risk, but we also need to protect the taxpayer. The government isn't a commercial buyer spending its own money. It has a special obligation to be good stewards of the funds we spend in defense of the nation. The relationship should be in a word "businesslike" and professional—neither too adversarial nor too familiar. At the end of the day, we need "win-win" business arrangements that motivate industry to work for the government and that provide high quality products and services to the DoD.

Over the years, a number of ideas have been suggested to "solve" the problem of cost overruns in defense weapons programs, usually overruns in the product development phase where a new design is created and tested. One particular idea resurfaces periodically, probably because its simplicity has some seductive appeal. That idea is the notion that fixed-price contracts will, first, motivate industry to bid more realistically and, second, provide a stronger motivation to control costs. In the extremes, fixed-price contracts bind industry to deliver the contracted product without the government having to pay for any cost increases, and cost-plus contracts have the opposite structure with the government paying for any cost increase but retaining the freedom to modify the product as the knowledge increases during development. We are not limited to these extremes, however. We have a broad range of contract structures we can use that balance the risk that has to be absorbed between industry and the government. This range is needed because of the wide variety of situations the government and industry have to work through successfully. For new product development programs involving complex weapons systems, the use of fixed-price contracts should be approached with great caution. The second article in this chapter explains what should be considered prior to making that decision, in order to treat industry fairly and have a reasonable chance of success.

Another frequently advocated approach to dealing with industry is to use commercial practices instead of the highly regulatory approach used in much of defense contracting. Like fixed-price contracts, the use of commercial practices definitely has a place in defense acquisition—but it is also not a panacea. The defense market isn't a commercial market. As a practical matter, there is only one customer—and that customer is spending taxpayers' money, not his own. The products being acquired often are highly specialized and complex, with long and very expensive lead times to production and sales. The DoD also is not a high-volume buyer, and sales to DoD are subject to the vagaries of a highly unpredictable political environment. Nevertheless, commercial practices often do apply to the products and services the DoD buys, and we need to be alert to these opportunities. The next article discusses commercial sources and commercial practices and describes some specific instances in which commercial approaches have been used successfully in defense acquisition.

Profit isn't optional for businesses. One thing I have always enjoyed about working in industry is that the metric for success isn't a mystery; everyone in a firm knows what success for the firm looks like. That motivator, profit, provides the DoD with its most powerful tool for eliciting better products

Chapter Four: Working with Industry

and better performance on contracts with industry. We can be certain that, when we offer the possibility of earning a profit, industry will try to obtain that profit. We need to make sure this behavior aligns well with what the government is trying to accomplish. The next piece in this chapter discusses the use of profit and financial incentives in the range of activities that DoD contracts for from industry, including development, production, and logistic services acquisition. The way we structure the potential profit drives how industry bids to us and how source selections occur as well as how industry performs once a contract is awarded. One source selection criteria, Lowest Priced and Technically Acceptable, or LPTA, has been criticized by industry as being overused; the situations in which LPTA is acceptable or preferred are also addressed in this article.

How do we get industry to offer the government better than minimally acceptable products? For decades, our source selections for weapons systems have been about offering the lowest cost product that met our "threshold" requirements. The DoD has provided "objective" levels of performance as part of our weapon system requirements definitions, but it hasn't provided any incentive to industry to achieve those higher performance levels. This practice has been changed, and with great success. The idea was simple enough: Tell industry how much more (in dollars) we are willing to pay for better performance, and then give credit for offering a better product in source selection. This is done by discounting the bid price by the extra value being offered for the purpose of source selection—or, in other words, by using a "value adjusted" price for the purpose of source selection. The next article in this chapter explains this technique in more detail and provides examples of its use during the last few years.

Our privately owned, for-profit, defense industrial base is a precious national asset. Many other nations have used public or government-owned enterprises to supply military equipment and, for the most part, this has not worked well. The profit motive is a strong incentive and it does work. The defense industrial base also is very specialized. It produces high-cost, complex, specialized, even unique products in low volumes to one principal customer in a highly regulated business environment.

Over the last several decades, the defense industrial base in the United States has slowly responded to market pressures to consolidate into fewer and fewer firms. That trend was arrested in the late 1990s when it had clearly gone too far. Competition, at all levels of the supply chain, depends on the existence of enough competitors to create a viable market. Recently one of the largest defense primes succeeded in acquiring a major new market position in a class of defense products it had not previously produced. That merger motivated me to release the following statement:

* * * *

Statement on Consolidation in the Defense Industry

DELIVERED BY USD AT&L ON SEPT 30, 2015

The Department of Defense (DoD) is concerned about the continuing march toward greater consolidation in the defense industry at the prime contractor level. While the Lockheed Sikorsky transaction does not trigger anti-trust concerns of having a negative impact on competition and we understand and agree with the basis upon which the Department of Justice (DOJ) decided not to issue a request for additional information about the transaction, we believe that these types of acquisitions still give rise to significant policy concerns.

Since 2011, DoD's policy has been that it would not look favorably on mergers of top tier defense firms. Lockheed's acquisition of Sikorsky does not constitute a merger of two top tier defense firms and it does not violate that policy. However, this acquisition does result in a further reduction in the number of weapon system prime contractors in the Defense Industrial Base. Over the past few decades, there has been a dramatic reduction in the number of weapon system prime contractors producing major defense programs for the DoD. This transaction is the most significant change at the weapon system prime level since the large scale consolidation that followed the end of the cold war. This acquisition moves a high percentage of the market share for an entire line of products – military helicopters – into the largest defense prime contractor, a contractor that already holds a dominant position in high performance aircraft due to the F-35 winner take all approach adopted over a decade ago. Mergers such as this, combined with significant financial resources of the largest defense companies, strategically position the acquiring companies to dominate large parts of the defense industry.

With size comes power, and the Department's experience with large defense contractors is that they are not hesitant to use this power for corporate advantage. The trend toward fewer and larger prime contractors has the potential to affect innovation, limit the supply base, pose entry barriers to small, medium and large businesses, and ultimately reduce competition—resulting in higher prices to be paid by the American taxpayer in order to support our warfighters.

The reality is that the defense market at the prime contract level has very high barriers to entry. Our prime contractors provide very complex and specialized products in relatively small numbers to one principal customer. The Department will continue to work closely with the Department of Justice and the Federal Trade Commission to ensure that mergers do not reduce competition. In addition, the Department is convinced that we should work with the Congress to explore additional legal tools and policy to preserve the diversity and spirit of innovation that have been central to the health and strength of our unique, strategic defense industrial base, particularly at the prime contractor level.

If the trend to smaller and smaller numbers of weapon system prime contractors continues, one can foresee a future in which the Department has at most two or three very large suppliers for all the major weapons systems that we acquire. The Department would not consider this to be a positive development and the American public should not either.

* * * *

Shortly thereafter, the Department of Justice, after consulting with DoD, released the following:

* * * *

JOINT STATEMENT OF THE DEPARTMENT OF JUSTICE AND THE FEDERAL TRADE COMMISSION ON PRESERVING COMPETITION IN THE DEFENSE INDUSTRY

The Department of Justice (DOJ) and the Federal Trade Commission (FTC) ("the Agencies") are issuing this joint statement to explain our standard of review under the antitrust statutes of proposed transactions within the defense industry. The Agencies are responsible for reviewing mergers in the defense industry under Section 7 of the Clayton Act, which prohibits mergers whose effect "may be substantially to lessen competition, or to tend to create a monopoly." The Department of Defense (DoD) is responsible for ensuring our nation's security and is in a unique position to assess the impact of potential defense industry consolidation on its ability to fulfill its mission. The Agencies rely on DoD's expertise, often as the only purchaser, to evaluate the potential competitive impact of mergers, teaming agreements, and other joint business arrangements between firms in the defense industry. When assessing proposed consolidation in this sector, the overriding goal of the Agencies in enforcing the antitrust laws is to maintain competition going forward for the products and services purchased by DoD. Competition ensures that DoD has a variety of sourcing alternatives and the most innovative technology to protect American soldiers, sailors, marines, and air crews, all at the lowest cost for the American taxpayer. The Agencies analyze mergers pursuant to the analytical framework set forth in the DOJ/FTC 2010 Horizontal Merger Guidelines. The unifying theme of the Guidelines is that mergers should not be permitted to create, enhance, or entrench market power or to facilitate its exercise. A merger can produce these harmful outcomes if it is likely to enhance the ability of one or more firms to raise price, lower output, reduce innovation, or otherwise harm customers as a result of diminished competitive constraints or incentives. The Guidelines "reflect the congressional intent [in Section 7 of the Clayton Act] that merger enforcement should interdict competitive problems in their incipiency and that certainty about the anticompetitive effect is seldom possible and not required fora merger to be illegal." The Guidelines are necessarily general, as they apply to all industries. They areal so sufficiently flexible to address DoD concerns that reductions in current or future competitors can adversely affect competition in the defense industry and thus, national security. The Agencies also consider particular aspects of the defense industry, such as high barriers to entry, the importance of investment in research and development (R&D), and the need for surge capacity, a skilled workforce, and robust subcontractor base. In light of our substantial experience applying the Guidelines to defense industry mergers and acquisitions, the Agencies are able to focus on issues that are central to, and often dispositive in, assessing the competitive effects of such mergers. In the defense industry, the Agencies are especially focused on ensuring that defense mergers will not adversely affect short- and long-term innovation crucial to our national security and that a sufficient number of competitors, including both prime and subcontractors, remain to ensure that current, planned, and future procurement competition is robust. Many sectors of the defense industry are already highly concentrated. Others appear to be on a similar trajectory. In those markets, the Clayton Act's incipiency standard is a particularly important aspect of the Agencies' analysis. As part of an investigation, the Agencies will consider any procompetitive aspects of a proposed transaction, including economies of scale, decreased production costs, and enhanced R&D capabilities. However, if a transaction threatens to harm innovation, reduce the number of competitive options needed by DoD, or otherwise lessen competition, and therefore has the potential to adversely affect our national security, the Agencies will not hesitate to take appropriate enforcement action, including a suit to block the transaction. As the 1994 Defense Science Board Task Force on Antitrust Aspects of Defense Industry Consolidation report states, "the antitrust agencies should continue to determine the ultimate question of whether a merger of defense contractors should be challenged on the ground that it violates the antitrust laws." The Agencies are committed to "giving DoD's assessment substantial weight in areas where DoD has special expertise and information, such as national security issues." Our mission when reviewing defense industry mergers is to ensure that our military continues to receive the most effective and innovative products at competitive prices over both the short- and long-term, thereby protecting both our troops and our nation's taxpayers.

* * * *

Profit is an important motivator for industry. It does work to obtain better products for our warfighters at reasonable cost for our taxpayers, but we also will have to remember that business firms will pursue their own and their shareholders' interests, as they should. It's up to the government to do what it can to ensure that the structure of the for-profit industrial base on which we depend continues to provide the products we need—at a reasonable cost.

Our Relationship With Industry

Reprinted from Defense AT&L: *November-December 2013*

As we enter what promises to be a difficult time for both defense acquisition professionals and the industrial base that we rely upon, I thought it might be useful to share a few thoughts on our relationship with industry. I want to provide some basic guidance for working with our industry partners at any time, but especially when those firms we depend on are experiencing a declining market, as they are now. At any time, we need to be aware of industry's perspective if we are going to work effectively together. I left government in 1994 after a career in uniform and as a civil servant. One of the reasons I left was that I felt I needed some time in industry to round out my background. I spent about 15 years in industry, some of it with major defense corporations, some of it as a private consultant working with defense firms of various sizes, and some of it as a partner in a small business working with defense companies ranging from start-ups to major corporations. Many, probably most, Department of Defense (DoD) acquisition people have not worked in industry and have not experienced that perspective firsthand. Industry's perspective is pretty straightforward. One of the things I enjoyed about industry was that there was never any confusion or disagreement about the metric we used to measure our own performance. In short, we were trying to make money: If certain actions made us more money, they were considered good; if they made us less money, they were not good. That's an oversimplification, of course. In actuality, the equation for industry is much more complex than this would suggest, but in the long run the principle I just articulated governs. If a firm is going to stay in business, profit is required. It doesn't stop there; business leaders also have an obligation to their shareholders to maximize the return the company achieves. Our fundamental obligation, on the other hand, is to obtain as much value as we can for our warfighters and the American taxpayer. Industry's goal and ours would appear to be in tension, and to a degree they are. We are not, however, in a purely adversarial relationship with industry. Neither are we in one with completely common interests. As we try to maximize the value we receive from industry, we also have an obligation to treat industry fairly and reasonably. Here are some thoughts about how we should behave in this complex relationship:

- Give industry the opportunity to make a reasonable profit. How much is "reasonable" is subject to some disagreement, but generally it should be commensurate with the risks being accepted by industry and with the rate of

Chapter Four: Working with Industry

return a going concern doing similar work would obtain in a free market. As I indicated above, profit isn't optional for a business, and firms won't support the DoD unless they have the opportunity to make an acceptable return.

- Don't ask companies to take on more risk than they can absorb. Defense firms generally will respond to any Request for Proposals (RFPs) the department puts out for bid that they think they have a shot at winning. We in government need to understand the risks associated with the performance we are asking for and structure the business deal so risk is allocated reasonably between the government and industry. This issue tends to dominate the decision between a fixed-price and a cost-plus contract vehicle. Firms can absorb some risk, but that capacity is limited. Before we can set the boundaries and terms of a business deal, we need to understand both the magnitude of the risk involved in providing a product or service successfully and a company's capacity to absorb risk.

- Tie profitability to performance. Profit is not an entitlement; it should be earned. Our industry partners tend to be smart people. If we give industry a financial incentive to provide the department with better services, or a better product, or anything else that we value, and if we structure that reward so it is attainable with reasonable effort, then we can expect to see the behavior we have motivated. In some business deals, this incentive is built in. A fixed-price contract always rewards effective cost control by the supplier, but the government may not share in that reward—unless we structure the contract so that we do. Incentives can and should cut both ways; poor performance should lead to poor returns. In general, I believe we can be more creative and more effective at structuring incentives that tie profit to performance. By doing so, we can create win-win opportunities for industry and government that reward the results that provide value for the warfighter and the taxpayer.

- Don't ask industry to make investments without the opportunity for a reasonable return. On occasion, I have seen government managers solicit or encourage investments from industry without a realistic prospect of a return on that investment. This can take several forms: internal research and development spending, participation in government-sponsored but unfunded demonstrations, development of proposals or option bids when there is no serious prospect of future business, or cost sharing in a technology project that isn't going to lead anywhere. This kind of behavior often occurs as part of an effort to obtain more support for a program that is on the margins within a Service's budget. Putting industry in this position is not fair to industry, and it wastes resources that could have been used more productively. It also destroys trust between industry and government when promised business opportunities do not materialize.

- Communicate as fully with industry as the rules allow. For some reason, we seem to have become "gun shy" about talking to industry. That's the wrong approach. The more we communicate our intent and priorities to industry, and the more we listen to industry concerns, the better. Up until the time a final RFP for a specific effort is released to industry, we should not overly restrict our contacts. We do have an obligation to treat all firms in the same manner—but that doesn't mean we can't have conversations with individual firms, as long as the same opportunity is available to others who want to take advantage of it. We can expect that a lot of what we hear from companies will be self-serving. At the same time, however, companies may have legitimate concerns about how we are doing business and superior ideas about how to acquire the product or service we are contemplating. We need to be as open as we can be, and we need to listen.

- Competition works—use it whenever you can. The wonderful thing about competition is that it is a self-policing mechanism. Companies are motivated to do whatever they can to reduce cost and provide a better product or service in order to win business. We also generally can rely on industry to protect itself and only sign a business deal that delivers an acceptable profit, or at least does so within the firm's risk tolerance and consistent with any broader business situation.

- Treat industry fairly, and keep your word. It is interesting that the commercial world has no requirement for one firm to treat another fairly. (Try to imagine a "protest" of a commercial contract award because the buyer's source selection process wasn't equally fair to all possible bidders.) Because we are an arm of the U.S. government and we expend public funds, we are held to that standard. It's also the right thing to do ethically, and it is necessary if we want to have constructive relationships with industry. My experience is that industry does not entirely trust government people. Our source selections are opaque to industry, and no industry capture-team leader ever told his boss that he lost because he wrote a bad proposal. If we act just once in a way that is not consistent with our values or betrays a commitment we have made, then we have sacrificed whatever trust we have built. We can spend our credibility only once and then it is gone.

- Protect the government's interests and insist on value for the taxpayer's money. I put this last for a reason. This is the other side of the coin. Industry can be counted on to try to maximize the metric that I mentioned, profitability. Most of the time, but not always, industry will do so within the "rules of the game." The "rules of the game" are defined largely by law and by the terms of the contracts we sign. The business deals codified by our contracts have to be fair, but they also have to be structured so that the government obtains what it wants at a reasonable price and industry is

Chapter Four: Working with Industry

motivated to improve its productivity. Once we have the business deal in place, we have to ensure that the product or service we've acquired is delivered as agreed. If not, we have a duty to act to protect the warfighter's and the taxpayer's interests.

Nothing I've written here should be a surprise. These are principles we should all be very familiar with already. As we continue, at least for the next few months, or maybe years, to experience shrinking budgets and environments that place great stress on both DoD and industry, I believe we should make a special effort to keep them in mind. Like everything else we do, this requires a deep understanding of the products and services we are acquiring, of the business deals we enter and of the industry partners with which we do business.

Use of Fixed-Price Incentive Firm (FPIF) Contracts in Development and Production

Reprinted from Defense AT&L: *March-April 2013*

The choice of appropriate contract types is very situationally dependent, and a number of factors must be taken into account to determine the best contract type to use. From the perspective of both industry and the government, it makes a good deal of difference whether the Defense Department asks for Cost type, Fixed-Price Incentive (FPI), or Firm Fixed Price (FFP) proposals. In the original Better Buying Power (BBP) initiatives, although Dr. Carter and I encouraged greater use of FPI, we also included the caveat "where appropriate." BBP 2.0 modifies this guidance to stress using appropriate contract types while continuing to encourage use of FPI for early production.

I would like to be more explicit about what "appropriate" means and how I believe we should analyze a given situation. In particular, I will address both Engineering and Manufacturing Development (EMD) and production situations.

During the early 1990s, I had a lot of painful experience with fixed-price development. The A-12 was a notorious case that ended badly. On another fixed-price major program in development during the same time frame, the program manager was relieved for finding creative but illegal ways to provide cash to the prime contractor who lacked the resources to complete development. FFP development tends to create situations where neither the government nor the contractor has the flexibility needed to make adjustments as they learn more about what is feasible and affordable as well as what needs to be done to achieve a design that meets requirements during a product's design and testing phases. Any fixed-price contract is basically a government "hands off" contract. In simplistic terms, the government sets the requirements and the price and waits for delivery of a specification-compliant product. While we can get reports and track progress, we have very little flexibility to respond to cases where the contract requirements may be particularly difficult to achieve.

Most sophisticated weapons systems development programs deal with maturing designs and challenging integration problems. As a result, the government often will and should provide technical guidance and make

Chapter Four: Working with Industry

trade-off decisions during development. In EMD, we often do want to work closely with the prime contractor to achieve the best outcome for the government. While it certainly is possible to negotiate changes in a fixed-price contract environment, the nature of development is such that informed decisions need to be made quickly and in close cooperation with our industry partners. The focus in a fixed-price environment is squarely on the financial aspects of the contract structure and not on flexibly balancing financial and technical outcomes.

Risk is inherent in development, particularly for systems that push the state of the art. Even with strong risk reduction measures in Technology Demonstration phases and with competitive risk reduction prototypes, there still is often a good deal of risk in EMD. By going to EMD contract award after Preliminary Design Review, as we routinely do now, we have partially reduced the risks—but again, only partially. Our average EMD program for a Major Defense Acquisition Program (MDAP) over the last 20 years has overrun by a little under 30 percent. Industry can only bear so much of that risk, and in a government fixed-price contract, industry cannot just stop work and walk away. A commercial firm doing development of a product on its own nickel has complete freedom to stop work whenever the business case changes. Firms on government contracts do not, at least not without some liabilty.

For good reasons, I am conservative about the use of fixed-price development, but it is appropriate in some cases. Here are the considerations I look for before I will approve a fixed-price or FPI EMD program:

- Firm requirements: Cost vs. performance trades are essentially complete. In essence, we have a very clear understanding of what we want the contractor to build, and we are confident that the conditions exist to permit the design of an affordable product that the user will be able to afford and is committed to acquiring.

- Low technical risk: Design content is established and the components are mature technologies. There are no significant unresolved design issues, no major integration risk, the external interfaces are well defined, and no serious risk exists of unknowns surfacing in developmental testing and causing major redesign.

- Qualified suppliers: Bidders will be firms that have experience with this kind of product and can be expected to bid rationally and perform to plan.

- Financial capacity to absorb overruns: Sometimes overruns will happen despite everyone's best efforts. We still want responsible contractors who have the capacity to continue and deliver the product despite potential overruns that may not have been foreseeable.

- Motivation to continue: A business case must be provided via a prospective reasonable return from production that will motivate suppliers to continue performance in the event of an unanticipated overrun. It is unrealistic to believe contractors will simply accept large losses. They will not.

As an example, the Air Force Tanker program met all of these criteria.

Early or low-rate production have similar considerations, but here is where greater use of FPI contract vehicles makes the most sense as an alternative to cost-plus vehicles. Over the last 20 years, the average overrun for MDAPs in early production has been a little less than 10 percent. This is a reasonable risk level to share with industry in an FPI contract arrangement. I expect our program managers and contracting officers to have meaningful, detailed discussions about the risks in contract performance over target cost. Determining a ceiling price is all about the fair recognition of risk in contract performance. Unlike an FFP contract, there needs to be a fair sharing of the risk—and the rewards—of performance.

To be comfortable with a fixed-price vehicle for early production, I would look for the following:
- Firm requirements (as explained)
- Design proven through developmental testing
- Established manufacturing processes
- Qualified suppliers
- Suppliers with the resources to absorb some degree of overrun
- Adequate business case for suppliers to continue work if they get in trouble

It should be noted that some of the items on this list reflect the "responsibility determination" that should be part of every contract we sign. However, the decision I am talking about here is not the decision to award a contract or accept a proposal for consideration but rather the decision about what type of contract to employ.

The above apply to FPIF procurements for which proposals are solicited at or near the end of EMD after we have been through Critical Design Review, built production representative prototypes, and completed some significant fraction of developmental test (DT). This is very different from a case in which we are only at Milestone (MS) B when we ask for low-rate initial production (LRIP) options. In that case, designs are not usually firmly established, production representative prototypes have not been built, and DT has not yet been done. So when we ask for FPIF proposals as options at MS B, we have already failed criterion 2 at least. In those cases, we ought to have a low risk of completing EMD without major design changes that would affect cost. Again, the Air Force Tanker program serves as an example. Another example where this can be done is a Navy auxiliary, where the shipyards have a great deal of experience with similar designs and with the design process for that class of ships.

FPIF LRIP can have a number of advantages, including better insight into contractor costs and an opportunity to share in contractor cost reductions. While it is attractive to secure FPIF prices at the time we award EMD contracts, as we usually still have competition at that point, we need to balance the benefit with the risk. Optimism tends to prevail early in programs, both for government and industry, and we need to be realistic about the risks that remain before EMD has even begun. It also is an illusion to believe we can routinely transfer all the risk in our programs to industry. Industry has a finite capacity to absorb that risk and knows how to hire lawyers to help it avoid large losses.

We can and should increase the use of FPIF contracting, but we need to approach with some caution FPIF contracting for EMD and for options on LRIP lots that are still years away from execution. During the transition to production, after successful DT has established that the design is stable and that production processes are under control, FPIF becomes a very attractive bridge to an FFP contracting regime.

Finally, there also may be times during the mature production phase of a program when the use of FPI contracts would be preferred. Typically, mature production programs are well established in terms of requirements, design content, and production processes at both the prime contractor and subcontract level. This environment should provide for accurate pricing, and FFP contracts would seemingly be appropriate. However, if we have reasons to conclude there may be a poor correlation between negotiated and actual outcomes, the use of an FPI contract would be more appropriate. In that case, we would share the degree of uncertainty with the contractor.

There could be several reasons why the correlation between negotiated and actual outcomes may be poor—e.g., ineffective estimating techniques, unreliable actual cost predictions at either the prime and/or subcontract level, incomplete audit findings, or diminishing manufacturing sources for some components. In addition, there may be times (e.g., multiyear contracts) where the period of performance is long enough that it places too much uncertainty and risk on either party. The key is understanding the pricing environment. If we have well-prepared contractor/subcontractor proposals, an environment where we have a solid actual cost history, and we have done the necessary analysis to ensure we have the price right, the use of FFP contracts is fine. If the environment is uncertain, the use of an FPI contract may make sense.

Again, BBP 2.0 stresses use of the appropriate contract types. Unfortunately, sorting this out is not always easy. It is hoped that this discussion will be helpful as we all wrestle with the problem of getting the best answer to the question of what type of contract to use in a given situation, whether it is an MDAP or an Acquisition Category III product, and at any phase of the product life cycle.

DoD Use of Commercial Acquisition Practices
When They Apply and When They Do Not

Reprinted from Defense AT&L: *September-October 2015*

The Department of Defense (DoD) generally buys major weapon systems through the defense acquisition system, a process that is highly tailorable but still built around the assumption that the DoD will compensate suppliers for product development, contract through Defense Federal Acquisition Regulations and be heavily involved in all aspects of the product life cycle. A number of organizations—including the Defense Business Board, some think tanks and some in Congress—have encouraged or recommended greater use of commercial practices. There are indeed times when using more commercial practices makes sense, and we should be alert to those opportunities—in any aspect of defense procurement.

There are three aspects of "going commercial" that I would like to address—first, purchases based on the fact that an item is offered as a commercial product; next, the need to access cutting-edge commercial technologies; and, finally, those cases where we can take advantage of private investments to develop products we might traditionally have purchased through the normal multi-milestone acquisition system.

Our policies and regulations try to strike the right balance between taking the steps needed to protect the taxpayer from overpaying while simultaneously avoiding discouraging commercial firms from doing business with DoD by asking for more information than they are willing to provide. For purely commercial items widely and competitively sold on the open market, this is easy. For thousands of items, from office furniture to cleaning supplies to laptop computers, the DoD pays commercial prices (subject to negotiated adjustments for quantity-based discounts, etc.) without inquiring as to the costs to produce the products. Other items are more clearly and purely military products, such as a replacement part for a howitzer or a low observable fighter component. The gray area between these extremes represents a problem in first determining that a product can be considered commercial, and, then, if there is no competition for setting the price for that product, obtaining adequate information from the supplier and other sources to determine that the price charged is fair and reasonable. We are working to expedite these processes, make them more predictable, and provide technical support to the procuring officials who must make these difficult determinations. I'm afraid that we will never be perfect at this, given the vast number of items the DoD procures and our limited resources, but we must and will improve our performance while preserving a reasonable balance.

It is clear that in many areas of technology the commercial market place is moving faster than the normal acquisition timeline for complex weapon systems. Examples include information technology, micro-electronics, some sensor technologies, some radio frequency devices and some software products. In most cases, these technologies will enter our weapon systems through one of our more traditional prime contractors. Our prime contractors and even second- and lower-tier suppliers are looking for a competitive advantage, and, when commercial technologies can provide that advantage, they will embed them in their products.

Competition among primes can give us access to current commercial technologies early in a program, but we often move to a sole-source situation when we down-select for Engineering and Manufacturing Development (EMD), reducing the incentives for inserting state-of-the-art commercial technologies. We can sustain these incentives by insisting on modular designs and open systems, both emphasized under the Better Buying Power initiatives. As part of this process, we also must manage intellectual property so we don't experience "vendor lock" in which we cannot compete upgrades without going through the original contractor.

Assistant Secretary of the Air Force (Acquisition) Bill LaPlante's initiative to "own the technical baseline" includes the concept of proactive management of configuration control and of interfaces so that the DoD preserves the option to introduce technology at rates more consistent with the pace of relevant commercial technology improvements.

The DoD also is taking other steps to improve our access to commercial technology. These include opening the Defense Innovation Unit–Experimental (DIU-X), in Silicon Valley, investments through In-Q-Tel and increased emphasis on the productivity of programs like the Small Business Innovative Research program. The DoD also is evaluating the congressionally sponsored Rapid Innovation Fund (RIF) and will make a decision this year as to whether to include a request for funds for a Reduction in Force in the Fiscal Year 2017 President's Budget. All these steps are designed to open the DoD to more timely and broad commercial technology insertion.

The last of the three "going commercial" topics I would like to cover involves situations in which the DoD substitutes a more commercial acquisition model for the ones depicted and described in DoD Instruction (DoDI)

5000.02. In some cases, industry, traditional defense contractors and others will invest to bring a product to the DoD market, without DoD shouldering the direct cost of product development. The critical motivation for these independent businesses decisions is the prospect of reasonable returns on the corporate investment.

Cost Sharing

Sometimes, especially when there is a mixed DoD and commercial market for the product, a cost-sharing arrangement may be appropriate in a public-private "partnership" for development. DoD acquisition professionals need to be alert to these opportunities and prepared to analyze them and act on them where they benefit the government. When we do this, we may need to be innovative and think "outside the box" about business arrangements and contract structures. In these cases, the structure and processes in DoDI 5000.02 may be highly tailored or even abandoned. I'll illustrate this concept with a few real-life examples.

As we moved down the path of DoD-funded research and development for tactical radios under the Joint Tactical Radio Systems program, we discovered that in parallel with the DoD-funded programs of record, some companies had invested their own money to develop and test products that used more advanced technologies than the Programs of Record. These essentially commercial product development efforts offered the prospect of cheaper and higher performance systems, without a DoD-funded development program. As a result of this, we changed the acquisition strategy to allow open competitions and stressed "best value" source selections so we could take advantage of the most cost-effective radios available.

Our "system" had a little trouble adjusting its planning to this type of acquisition. The Developmental Testing people wanted to perform a standard series of developmental tests, even though the development was complete. Operational Test people wanted to test each competitor—before source selection. Program oversight people wanted to do Milestone (MS) A and B certifications, even though there was no reason to have an MS A or B.

What we needed, and where we ended up, was a competitive source-selection process for production assets that included an assessment of bidder-provided test data, laboratory qualification testing, and structured comparative field testing to verify the offered products met DoD requirements. There were minimum requirements that had to be met; once that was established, a bidder would be in a "best value" evaluation for source selection for production. It was a little surprising to me how wedded our workforce, in both the Service and the Office of the Secretary of Defense, was to the standard way of doing business—even when it didn't really apply to the situation.

The next example involves space launch. The DoD is working to bring competition into this market. That opportunity exists because multiple firms have been investing development funds in space launch capabilities for both commercial and DoD customers. We acquire space launch as a service; there is no compelling reason for DoD to own launch systems. What we need is highly reliable assured access to space for national security payloads, which can be acquired as a service. For some time, we have been working to certify a commercial launch company to provide national security launches. That milestone recently was achieved for the first "new entrant" into national security launches in many years. The DoD did not fund the development of the new entrant's launch system, but it did provide support through a Cooperative Research and Development Agreement for the certification process.

More recently, the need to remove our space launch dependency on imported Russian rocket engines has caused the DoD to evaluate options for acquiring a new source of reliable competitive launch services. Through market research, we know there are options for private investment in new launch capabilities but that industry's willingness to develop the needed products may depend on some level of DoD funding. The DoD intends to ask for industry bids in a very open-ended framework for whatever financial contribution would be necessary to "close the business case" on the guaranteed provision of future space launch services. This novel acquisition approach will work only if the combined commercial, other government customer, and military launch demand function can provide enough anticipated launch opportunities to justify industry investment. This effort is a work in progress, and we don't know if it will prove successful. If it does succeed, it will provide for the continuing viability of two competitive sources of space launch services—without the need for DoD funding and executing a new standard DoD development program for a launch or propulsion system.

Another example from the space area is the Mobile Ground User Equipment (MGUE) for GPS III. These GPS receiver electronics "chips" will be ubiquitous in DoD equipment and munitions. The technology also will be relevant to commercial GPS receivers that will be embedded in millions of commercial devices. Here, also, the DoD has been proceeding with a standard DoD-funded development program with multiple vendors developing MGUE risk reduction prototypes leading up to an EMD program phase. The combined market for this capability is so great that the competitors proceeded with EMD on their own, without waiting for a DoD MS B or contract award. They did this so successfully that the EMD phase of the program was canceled in favor of a commercial approach that limits the

Chapter Four: Working with Industry

DoD's activities to compliance testing of the MGUE devices and integration of those devices into pilot platform programs.

The final example I'll cite is the Marine Corps decision to defer the program to acquire a new design amphibious assault vehicle in favor of a near-term option to acquire a modified nondevelopmental item (NDI). The Marine Corps concluded, I believe correctly, that the technology was not mature enough to support the Corps' desired performance levels and that a new product would be unaffordable. As a result, the Marine Corps opted to first evaluate and then pursue a competitively selected near-NDI alternative. This is more military than commercial off-the-shelf, but the principle remains the same. This program does include some modest DoD-funded development to, for example, integrate U.S. communications equipment and test for compliance with requirements, but it is a highly tailored program designed to move to production as quickly as possible and with minimal DoD costs.

The Common Thread

What all these examples have in common is the DoD's recognition that an alternative path—outside the normal DoDI 5000.02 route—was available and made sense from both a business and an operational perspective. Once such an opportunity is recognized, a more commercial approach can be adopted, but this requires some novel thinking and open-mindedness on the part of the DoD acquisition team. We cannot "go commercial" for all of our acquisitions or even most of our weapons systems. The normal process works best for the standard low-volume, highly specialized, cutting-edge and uniquely military products that populate the DoD inventory. The business case simply isn't there for industry to develop and offer these types of products without DoD development funding. In all standard DoD acquisitions, however, we need to proactively look for ways to embed or insert the most current commercial technologies. Where commercial approaches are justified, we need to spot and capitalize on the opportunity.

Tying Profit to Performance— A Valuable Tool, But Use With Good Judgment

Reprinted from Defense AT&L: *May-June 2015*

One thing I enjoyed about working in industry was that everyone in the private sector understood the definition of success: It was profit. If something made a profit for a business, it was good. If something did not make a profit for a business, then it was not good. Profit is the fundamental reason that businesses exist: to make money for their owners or shareholders. Without profit, businesses die.

From industry's point of view, more profit is always better. Not being profitable makes a company unsustainable and will lead to bankruptcy. Declining profits make it harder for businesses to raise capital or to invest for their futures. These facts make profit the most powerful tool the Department of Defense (DoD) has to obtain better performance from industry. It is important, however, to recognize that this also implies that over-aggressive use of this tool can seriously damage the institutions we depend upon for products and services.

Sometimes—through some combination of incompetence, poor management, the realization of risk, or external factors—defense companies will lose money and even go out of business. That is the nature of capitalism. We do not have an obligation to protect defense companies from themselves, but we do have an obligation to treat them fairly and to try to balance our use of profit as a motivator for better performance with an understanding of the possible implications for those we expect and hope to do business with over the long term.

As we continue to work through a period of uncertain and declining budgets, we need to be especially careful. A recent study by the Institute for Defense Analyses shows very clearly that cost increases correlate strongly with tight budgets. Historically, programs initiated during tight budget periods had 3 times higher acquisition cost growth for production than those started during less constrained resource periods. We're working now to understand what causes this strong correlation, but one likely factor is that tight money motivates everyone to take more risk. A shrinking market and fewer bidding opportunities put pressure on industry to bid more aggressively. Government budgeters and programmers are motivated to take risk also, or to buy into optimistic assumptions or speculative management fads as alternatives to having to kill needed programs. Industry may be incentivized to sign up for a low target—knowing that they might otherwise be out of that market permanently—and hoping that budget instability and/or changing requirements will provide a recovery opportunity. We can't entirely prevent industry from making high-risk bids in competition, but we should do what we can to ensure realism in our budgets and executable business arrangements that give industry a fair opportunity to make a reasonable profit.

The profit margins that DoD pays vary, but in the aggregate they are fairly stable. Large defense companies, in particular, have very little risk. Their markets are fairly predictable and stable. The government pays upfront for most product research and development costs, and provides excellent cash flow through progress payments, minimizing the cost of capital. Most development programs are also cost reimbursable, which significantly limits the risk to industry. Substantial barriers for new companies to enter the defense market also limit competitive risks. While there usually is competition early in product life cycles, many products end up as sole-source awards by the time they enter production. The primary defense market customer, DoD, is highly regulated, is not allowed to arbitrarily award contracts, and is subject to independent legal review if a bidder believes it has not been treated fairly. At the end of the day, it's not a bad business to be in, and we don't want to change these fundamental premises of government contracting. We do, however, want to get as much for the taxpayer and the warfighter as we can with the available resources. That means we must tie performance to profitability.

As we have tried to incentivize and improve industry's performance under the Better Buying Power (BBP) initiatives of the last several years, we have consistently followed two principles. First, BBP is not a "war on profit"—we are not trying to reduce profit as a way to reduce costs. We want to continue to give our industry suppliers a reasonable return. Second, we will use profit to motivate better performance, both as a carrot and a stick. In the balance of this article, I want to focus on this second principle.

How do we use profit effectively to obtain better results for the taxpayer and the warfighter? I'm going to address some specific cases I think are important: product development, early production, lowest price technically acceptable, commercial and commercial-like items, logistic support, and support services.

First, I would like to address the use of profit as an incentive in general. Before we solicit anything from industry, we need to think carefully about what the government really needs or desires and how we can effectively tie getting what we need to profit opportunities for industry. In product acquisitions, we need to decide whether higher performance or cost or schedule or some combination of these parameters matters to us. Often they are not independent, and we have to think about how those interdependencies are related to profit-related incentives. In services acquisitions, we often want a certain quality of performance; we may or may not be willing to pay more for higher quality performance of the service, or we may only be interested in controlling cost at a set level of performance. As we emphasized in BBP 2.0, we have to start by thinking, in this case thinking carefully about what matters to us and about the extent to which fee or incentive structures can add motivation to behavior that achieves those government objectives and that wouldn't exist without the incentives.

We can use the full range of contract types to motivate performance. For products, we sometimes place the highest value on the schedule, sometimes on the cost, and sometimes on increased performance levels. Our contracts often inherently include a high degree of profit motivation without any special incentive provisions. For example, a firm-fixed-price contract provides a strong financial incentive to control costs.

However, we also need to think about how incentives that affect profit will play out over the life of the contract and the life cycle of the program. It is not just the immediate contract that we care about. We need to think through profit incentives not only under the expected scenario but under any alternative scenarios that may develop, including the realization of any foreseeable risks. A cost-plus development contract that has reached a point where nothing is left to be gained or lost in fee by completing the effort doesn't include much incentive.

We also need to think carefully about unintended consequences. Industry may look at the situation very differently than we do. We can assume industry will try to maximize its profit—by whatever means we make available. We also can assume industry will examine all the available scenarios—including ones we have not intended. That means we need to anticipate industry's behavior and make sure that we align industry objectives with the performance we intend. In general, we also can expect industry to argue for incentives that come sooner in the period of performance and are easier to achieve. Usually that is not what we should be rewarding.

We also must recognize there is no motivational value in incentive fees or profits that are impossible to earn—or conversely that are very easy to achieve. The bottom line is that this isn't simple, and, as in much of what we do as acquisition professionals, careful thought and sound judgment based on experience play major roles. One of the items I am most interested in when I read a program's Acquisition Strategy or a request for proposal is

CHAPTER FOUR: WORKING WITH INDUSTRY

the incentive structure and how it ties profit to performance. I particularly look for why the program manager and the contracting officer chose the proposed approach. Now I'd like to discuss some specific cases.

Product development: On our major competitive development contracts, industry has been receiving final margins of about 5 percent or 6 percent—about half the levels seen in production. (Note that this isn't where we start out; the reality of the risk in development programs leads to this result. Also note that margins on sole-source development contracts are significantly higher.) Industry accepts this lower outcome because of two things. First, competitive pressures force industry to bid aggressively and take risks in the development phases. Second, winning subsequent production contracts, with their higher margins and decades of follow-on work, makes it worthwhile to accept lower returns in development. Most often, the inherent risk of development makes a cost-plus vehicle appropriate, and profit then is tied to the incentive fee structure we provide. If the situation still is competitive after award, winning the future engineering and manufacturing development or production contract provides all the motivation to perform we are likely to need. However, in a sole-source situation, we need to structure profit potential to affect desired outcomes.

The data from recent sole-source contracts show that formulaic incentive structures with share ratios above and below a target price are effective in controlling costs on the immediate contract. Often, however, performance on the current contract is not what concerns us the most. We may want lower cost in follow-on production or sustainment, or we may want higher performance in the final product, or some combination of parameters. This is where we need to be very thoughtful and creative about how we use profit to motivate desired behaviors and outcomes.

Early production: Usually when we award these contracts, we have a relatively mature design and a specified performance we intend to achieve, so cost control tends to dominate our use of the profit incentive. We generally use formulaic incentive share ratio structures during this phase. In the first iteration of BBP, we encouraged consideration of 120 percent ceilings and 50-50 share ratios, as a starting point, adjusting these structures to the situation at hand. The key to effective incentive contracting is to motivate the contractor to reduce costs as quickly as possible.

In the past, we have not done as good a job as we should have done in establishing realistic target costs. When we negotiate challenging but achievable target costs, we create an incentive arrangement that allows industry to earn a higher share of any underruns in early production. DoD should reap the benefits in future lots through lower prices. In addition, industry has more at stake here than the government: As we move up or down share lines, industry gains or loses what it cares most about—profit—at a much higher rate than the DoD gains or loses what it cares about—cost. For this reason, we should provide share ratios above and below target prices that give industry greater incentives (e.g., more favorable share ratios for industry below target and less favorable ones above target) to control cost.

Lowest price technically acceptable (LPTA): Industry has expressed concern for some time about the effect of this source-selection criterion on selections and profitability. I recently provided some policy guidance on this subject (see the March-April 2015 issue of this magazine). DoD's policy is to use LPTA only when there is (1) an objectively measurable standard of performance, and (2) there is no desire for any performance above some defined level of acceptability in that standard. In all other cases, we should use another form of best-value source selection. If LPTA is used properly in competitive source selections, it will give us the performance we desire and constrain profit levels to those necessary for businesses to be viable. That is what competitive markets do. While we aren't trying to artificially force profit down to reduce cost, we also shouldn't pay higher margins than those determined by competitive market forces for this type of work and standard of performance.

Commercial and commercial-like items: This is a particularly difficult area in which to achieve the right balance. Our policy is simple: If a supplier sells us a commercial item and the supplier can demonstrate that it sells that item in substantial quantities to commercial customers, we will pay what other commercial customers pay for similar quantities. When we buy truly commercial items, we compare prices, try to get volume discounts, and let the market set the price (often using tools like reverse auctions). When we buy a commercial item, the reasonableness of the price we pay is important to us—not the profit level a commercial company may make when selling that item. We must understand that the risk posture of a commercial company selling commercial items in a competitive marketplace is dramatically different than that of the traditional defense contractors with which we deal.

When we purchase items that may be sold commercially, or which are close in design to items sold commercially (sometimes referred to as "commercial of a type"), but for which there is really no competitive market to establish prices and margins, we have an obligation to ensure that we obtain fair and reasonable prices for the taxpayers whose money we spend. Examples include aircraft parts that are similar in design, but possibly not identical, to the parts used on commercial aircraft. In those cases, we have processes in place for our buyers to establish whether the item is commercial, and if it is, the fairness and reasonableness of the price. If an item is commercial, we only inquire about costs (and profit margins) when we have exhausted the other available means of determining price reasonableness.

Logistics support: We started emphasizing Performance Based Logistics (PBL) in BBP 2.0 as a way to reduce costs and improve outcomes on product support contracts. As we went through the difficult fiscal year 2013 sequestration scenario, our use of these types of arrangements actually declined. Today I am tracking the use of PBL through quarterly reviews at the Business Senior Integration Group. PBL is an effective tool that ties profit to performance in a way that has been demonstrated to be a win-win for DoD and industry. PBL is harder to implement and execute than other business arrangements, but the payoff is well established by the historical results; PBL profit incentives work to enhance performance and reduce cost.

Support services: In these contracts, we often buy some form of administrative or technical support to carry out routine functions that are not inherently governmental. There may be metrics of performance to which we can tie profitability—and, if they are available, we should use them. Often, however, services are about the productivity and basic skill sets of individuals working on location alongside DoD military or civilian employees. At one point, we routinely used time-and-materials or firm-fixed-price contract vehicles for these types of support services. A preferred approach is often the use of cost-plus-fixed-fee arrangements to pay actual costs coupled with DoD contract manager oversight with discretion over the acceptability of assigned contractors. In these cases, quality can be controlled by rejecting contractor staff members who are not performing up to contract standards. Since profitability will depend on providing acceptable staff to bill for, the incentive to do so is high.

Conclusion

Industry can be counted upon to try to maximize profitability on behalf of its shareholders and/or owners—that's capitalism. Our job is to protect the interests of the taxpayers and the warfighter while treating industry fairly and in a manner that won't drive businesses away from working for DoD. To achieve these complex objectives, we should strive to ensure that we create business deals that provide industry an opportunity to earn fair and reasonable fees/profits, while protecting the government's interests. Industry will respond to profit incentives if they are achievable with realistic effort. We will benefit if profit incentives provide effective motivation to industry and are tied to the goals we value.

There is plenty of room for creativity in this area because our business situations vary widely. It is up to each of us to determine how profit incentives should be structured so that reasonable profit margins can be earned with reasonable performance levels, superior performance results in higher margins, and inferior performance has the opposite effect.

CHAPTER FOUR: WORKING WITH INDUSTRY

Getting "Best Value" for the Warfighter and the Taxpayer

Reprinted from Defense AT&L: March-April 2015

We use the phrase "best value" fairly often, usually to describe the type of source-selection process or evaluation criteria we will use in a competitive acquisition. Under the Better Buying Power initiatives, we have emphasized using a more monetized and less subjective definition of best value. As a way to spur innovation, we also have emphasized communicating the "value function" to the offerors so they can bid more intelligently.

Some reluctance and understandable concern arose about the unintended consequences of trying to define best value in monetary terms. In fact, this decision can't be avoided. I would like to explain why it is unavoidable, provide some examples of using this approach, and discuss how we can avoid those unintended consequences some of us worry about. I'll also touch on the proper use of Lowest Price, Technically Acceptable (LPTA)—which is a form of monetized best value, but with a very restrictive definition and range of applicability.

A "traditional" best-value source-selection process combines disparate metrics in to one overall evaluation. In a recent example that I reviewed, four separate and unrelated metrics were proposed for the source selection: risk (high, medium or low), cost ($), performance (a composite scaled metric) and degree of small business utilization (with its own scale). Think how this would have played out in the source-selection decision making.

Setting aside the small business metric, assume that there was a slightly more expensive and higher-risk but much higher-performing offeror and a slightly less expensive and lower-risk but significantly lower-performing offeror. The Source Selection Authority would have to decide whether the increased price and risk of the higher offeror was worth the difference in performance. That acquisition official, not our customer (the warfighter), would have needed to make the "best value" determination as a subjective judgment by weighing cost against the other two metrics. In effect, that individual in the acquisition chain would make the precise cost versus performance and risk judgment we intend when we recommend monetizing the value of performance and including it in the evaluated price.

The likely bias for an acquisition official making the source selection is to take the lowest-price offer; it's much easier to defend than the subjective judgment that the higher-cost offeror was worth the difference in price. Is this the best way for us to do "best value" source selections? To the extent we can do so, we are better off defining "best value" by a single parameter we can readily compare. The easiest way to express that parameter is in dollars—using value-based adjusted price for evaluation purposes (e.g., bid price with predefined dollarized reductions for performance above threshold).

I believe there are some very good reasons to take the approach of monetizing performance metrics. First of all, it forces our customers—the operators who set requirements—to consider how much they are willing to pay for higher performance. Our normal practice in the requirements process is to define two levels of performance—threshold and objective. Unless we provide industry an incentive to do otherwise, we can expect it to bid the threshold levels of performance and no more. The simple reason is that we usually don't give industry any competitive incentive to offer higher performance. The lower threshold levels of performance almost always are the lowest-cost levels of performance.

Getting the requirements community to consider what it would be willing to pay for different levels of performance also has an important side benefit: It forces that user community to recognize that its requirements are not free and to engage the acquisition community on prioritizing those requirements. We must work as a team to be effective. Involving our customers in decisions about best value before releasing the final Request for Proposals (RFPs) builds our mutual understanding of the real-life trade-offs needed in almost any product or service acquisition. Monetizing best value to industry also provides benefits that accrue to the government. By not providing industry with a business reason to offer higher performance, we create a disincentive for innovation. We want industry to be in a position to make informed judgments about what level of performance to offer. The easiest way to accomplish this is to tell industry exactly, in dollars and cents, what higher levels of performance are worth to us. Industry then can compare its costs of meeting higher performance levels to our willingness to pay and decide what performance to offer.

We also should provide this information as early as possible, so industry has time to react to the information, including, when possible, time to develop new technologies that are integratable into their offerings. In addition, communicating this information to industry allows uncompetitive firms to avoid wasting company funds (allowable Bid and Proposal costs in overhead that the government reimburses) on proposals that have no chance of success. We have to define best value if we want industry to offer it to us.

There is a side benefit to monetizing best value criteria in that the objective source-selection criterion are harder to contest successfully. I don't believe we should design our source-selection criteria or acquisition strategies around minimizing the likelihood of a protest, whether it is a successful or an unsuccessful protest. But I don't mind having that feature as a byproduct of our approach. Avoiding successful protests is about setting down the rules for source selection, following them religiously, documenting the decisions we make so we can explain them if challenged, and maintaining the process integrity. All our source selections, of any type, should be conducted in this manner. At the end of the day, however, no one should be able to argue with the government about the monetary value we place on a specific feature or level of performance before we conduct a source selection (as long as we have a reasonable rationale for our choices and aren't being arbitrary). This judgment also is easier to defend if it is transparent and communicated to offerors well before we start the source-selection process.

About 15 years ago, while in industry, I tried for months to get the Air Force to provide some allowance, some competitive credit, for my company's AIM 9X air-to-air missile's above-threshold performance. We had a novel design with exceptional off bore-sight capability, well above the threshold requirement. I didn't succeed and we lost the competition, but the Air Force also lost the opportunity to acquire an innovative design with superior performance. I find it hard to believe that performance had no value whatsoever to the Air Force. In any event, we received no credit in the source selection for offering what we were certain was a better product. We have been using the technique of monetizing performance differences in source selections under Better Buying Power 2.0 and will continue this emphasis under BBP 3.0, but the practice didn't start with BBP.

One early use was in the second KC-46 Tanker competition. There was a successful protest by the losing offeror in the first competitive best-value source selection conducted in 2008. In the second competition in 2009, we moved to much more objective source-selection criteria, using evaluated price as the primary metric. In addition to folding fuel costs and operational efficiency into the evaluated price, we allowed for consideration of a long list of "desired but not required" features, but only if the evaluated prices were within 1 percent for the two offerors before we considered these features. Essentially, we bound the value of all these objective features as being worth no more to us than 1 percent of evaluated price. Notice that this had nothing to do with the cost of those features.

Value or worth to the buyer has nothing to do with cost; it is only about what we would be willing to pay for something. The tanker situation is analogous to buying a car and deciding what options to include. All those options, the "fully loaded" version of the tanker if you will, were only worth a 1 percent price differential to us. Having this information allowed industry to be a smarter offeror and propose a product more in line with our "value function."

More recently I had an experience with the acquisition strategy for a tactical radio program where the program manager intended to use a LPTA approach. He was asking for threshold performance and didn't plan to provide any credit to higher performance in the evaluation criteria.

I asked him hypothetically if he would want to buy a radio with twice the range and twice the message completion rate for 1 percent more. The answer, of course, was yes. We changed the evaluation criteria. Sometimes LPTA makes sense but it doesn't make sense if we are willing, as we usually are, to pay a little more for a much better product. LPTA may be an easier way to do a solicitation and a source selection, but that shouldn't be our metric. The warfighter and the taxpayer deserve better from us. LPTA is appropriate when we have well-defined standards of performance and we do not place any value on, and are therefore unwilling to pay for, higher performance.

LPTA is used in many acquisitions for services. As discussed above, it may be appropriate—if there is no value to the government in performance beyond well-defined thresholds.

The arguments against monetizing best value include a concern recently expressed by an Army program executive officer: Industry is likely to game the system to try to win. He was right, of course. We want "best value." Industry wants to win. Nevertheless, I don't find this to be a strong argument against monetizing best value. I do find it to be a strong argument for getting it right and making sure we align our source-selection criteria with what we want (what we value). If we have properly defined what is important to us and what we are willing to pay for that "best value," industry will position itself to meet our best-value proposition.

There are various possible ways to meet our best-value proposition—and from industry's point of view, that's not gaming us; that's doing what it takes to win. Our concern should be with getting the "best value" criteria right. We need to monetize best value in a way that doesn't permit an unintended consequence imposed on us by a crafty proposal team. I have worked on a reasonable number of proposals from the industry side and I know the concern has some validity. When we set source-selection criteria, we need to do our own red-teaming process to ensure we don't produce unintended and negative consequences. Basically, this is just a matter of running through the range of possible approaches to bidding to see if we have neglected an excursion that has an unintended and negative effect.

You can count on industry to do the same.

Chapter Four: Working with Industry

I have also heard the concern that industry may inflate its pricing to come just under what we are willing to pay, even if the cost is substantially lower. In a competitive acquisition, we should be able to count on the fact there will be other bidders to prevent this behavior. Offerors have to beat the competition, regardless of the government's willingness to pay. Incidentally knowing our published budget figures also provides industry with a strong indication of what we could pay for the product. In any case, we must use either competition or, in a sole-source environment, discussions about actual costs to ensure we get a reasonable price for the warfighter and the taxpayer. Monetizing best value doesn't change those processes.

In development contracts, we often are concerned about risk, and it's fair to ask whether it is possible to monetize risk considerations. We can set subjective risk scales for evaluation purposes and do so routinely, using High, Medium, and Low—or a more finally grained alternative. Translating these comparisons into relative monetary value takes some thought, but it can be done. One has to be careful because risk valuations can be very nonlinear. For example, "low-risk" and "medium-risk" offerors might have fairly small differences in "value," but a high-risk offeror could (and probably should) have prohibitively high cost adjustments to overcome. We would expect both low- and medium-risk offers to be obtainable but with cost and schedule impact differences. A high-risk offer has a finite probability of being outside the realm of the possible.

A better way to handle risk factors is to create thresholds or "gates" as opposed to comparative assessments. If an offer has acceptable risk, it is considered responsive and evaluated for cost and performance. If an offer has high risk, it is eliminated from the competition. This is one of the many areas in which we have to use professional judgment and a real understanding of the actual risks involved in order to make a good decision.

It is argued that this approach is more difficult and time consuming. A former senior official once told me that "convenience" was the biggest determiner of an acquisition strategy. I certainly hope that is not so. We do have finite capacity, but we owe our customers our best efforts in every acquisition. I am not persuaded that monetizing best value is prohibitively difficult. It is a new approach for many in the requirements community, and they won't be comfortable with it until they have more experience.

My first attempt to use this approach was on the Combat Rescue Helicopter program. It took several attempts to get the user community to stop bringing me cost estimates for various levels of performance. Ultimately, the users concluded that the cost premium the Air Force was willing to pay for objective performance was only about 10 percent. This information caused one company to drop out of the competition. I'm not troubled by that result. It would have been a waste of time for that company to prepare an offer. It does take a little more effort up front to define best value in monetary terms. However, the source-selection process is made simpler, and, more importantly, we can get better results for our customers. That is the metric that should matter most to us.

As we build our teamwork with both the warfighters who set requirements and with industry which tries to win business by meeting those requirements, I believe there will be more acceptance and support for monetizing best value. It is in everyone's interest and well worth the effort.

Chapter Five
Responding to External Forces and Events
Congressional Direction, Financial Management Policy, Funding Cuts, Changing Threats, and Military Customers

> "So we beat on, boats against the current,
> borne back ceaselessly into the past."
>
> —F. Scott Fitzgerald, "The Great Gatsby"

The list of external forces and actors affecting defense acquisitions is long. By external, I mean external to the community of defense acquisition practitioners. The list includes the Congress; other executive branch operations, such as financial management; potential adversaries; and our customers—military operators and their leaders. These and others create constraints and an environment that exerts forces to which the defense acquisition enterprise must react. This chapter deals with some of these forces and their impacts on defense acquisition.

The Congress almost continuously makes legislative changes that affect defense acquisition, often under the rubric of "acquisition reform." These efforts wax and wane, but they recur with higher intensity every few years, often as a result of dissatisfaction with the performance of the "acquisition system." Some of these efforts have produced very positive results—the Weapon Systems Acquisition Reform Act of 2009 or the Improve Act of 2011 are good examples. Others have had mixed results or worse.

In my view, the best results are obtained when Congress works closely with the DoD and there is an informed discussion of any proposed changes before they are implemented. One example of a process that fosters this is the initiative of the last few years by the House Armed Services Committee, led by Chairman Mac Thornberry, to file proposed legislation for the purpose of obtaining feedback before a final bill is drafted. Another example was the outreach in 2014 by Senators John McCain and Carl Levin to obtain acquisition reform suggestions from a wide range of involved and concerned individuals. I was one of those individuals. I submitted the recommendations included in the following letter:

THE UNDER SECRETARY OF DEFENSE
3010 DEFENSE PENTAGON
WASHINGTON, DC 20301-3010

ACQUISITION,
TECHNOLOGY
AND LOGISTICS

JUN 1 3 2014

The Honorable John McCain
Ranking Minority Member
Permanent Subcommittee on Investigations
Committee on Homeland Security
 and Government Affairs
United States Senate
Washington, DC 20510

Dear Senator McCain:

    Thank you for your April 16, 2014, letter regarding improvements in defense acquisition. I look forward to seeing the ideas put forth in response to your request. Enclosed for your use, and hopefully for inclusion in your assembled compendium, is an article I recently wrote for our defense acquisition workforce on the status of the Better Buying Power (BBP) acquisition improvement initiatives that I am implementing within the Department of Defense. The current version of BBP contains over 30 specific initiatives spread over several major focus areas. Under our "continuous improvement" approach to improving acquisition system performance, the Department is also considering the next steps to improve efficiency and productivity. Your compendium will be helpful to that process.

    I agree with your view that acquisition improvement, as opposed to acquisition reform, should be our goal. We have seen enough attempts at acquisition reform to know that there is no easy or simple way to dramatically improve acquisition outcomes. The Weapon System Acquisition Reform Act took major steps in the right direction. However, now we are at a point where our focus should be on the professionalism and incentives of people in government and industry who make thousands of individual acquisition decisions each day, rather than on "rule sets" or organizational responsibilities. When, as mentioned in your letter, "inefficient, outdated, and (at times) imprudent practices" occur, they are manifested in those thousands of individual daily decisions.

    As the Defense Acquisition Executive, I offer the following actions that Congress could take to help the Department, and over 150,000 acquisition workforce professionals, be more effective and productive as we acquire products and services for our Warfighters:

1. <u>End the threat of sequestration</u>. Nothing is causing more inefficiency in the Department than the continuing uncertainty about future budgets. The threat of sequestration makes sound planning impossible and causes inefficient execution as our managers try to cope with unpredictable program profiles for both development and production.

Chapter Five: Responding to External Forces and Events

2. <u>Continue to fund the Defense Acquisition Workforce Development Fund (DAWDF)</u>. The Department has made excellent use of this fund to bring new acquisition professionals onto the team. Increasingly we are using DAWDF funds to provide much needed training and practical experience to all our acquisition career fields, including program management, engineering, and contracting. DAWDF is a valuable resource that is providing a high return on investment.

3. <u>Work with the Department to simplify the rules we already have</u>. We do not need more rules, in fact I believe we have too many already. I have a team working with congressional staff on a legislative proposal that is intended to provide a simpler and more easily understood and implementable set of requirements for our program managers – without sacrificing the good intent behind the original legislation. Our managers are faced with a vast and confusing array of overlapping statutory requirements that is in need of simplification. I look forward to working with Congress and for your continued support for this activity.

4. <u>Avoid highly restrictive rules which particularly limit our ability to make the best decisions about risk management actions or business arrangements</u>. The Department acquires a huge range of products and services with widely varying risk profiles, degrees of urgency, and business situations. We need the flexibility to tailor how we do business to the situation. No best practice is universally applicable. I have seen far too many program plans in the last 4 years where our managers have tried to force fit a program into what they thought was the approved "school solution" way of doing business. There is no one type of contract, or one set of decision points, or one set of risk mitigation techniques that applies to all programs.

5. <u>Reduce the counter-productive incentive to obligate funds on a fixed schedule</u>. For 4 years I have worked to train and encourage our acquisition workforce to take time to get good business deals for the Taxpayer by conducting appropriate upfront analysis, and by doing the systems engineering and planning necessary for successful programs. At the same time our program managers live in a world in which they are punished for not obligating the funds they control on set schedules. We should have realistic plans to execute our budgets, but when a manager has sound reasons to delay obligation, that behavior should not be punished. I have worked successfully with the Under Secretary of Defense (Comptroller) to provide a more balanced approach to how we handle obligation reviews within the Department, and we would like to work closely with Congress in striking a similar balance on this matter.

6. <u>Allow, or even require, Services and Agencies to hold a management reserve to be applied when problems arise in development programs</u>. Development of new products inherently involves risk. Even with the best of risk reduction or mitigation actions as a prerequisite, developing any cutting edge technology-based new product embodies cost and schedule risk. It is also <u>not</u> efficient to plan and budget for a very low risk development program profile; a modest degree of challenge to our managers and contractors coupled with well-structured incentives results in more efficient overall execution. Under our current practices, we are forced to take funding from one program

2

to address any shortfalls that emerge in another program. Large businesses do not operate this way; they plan for risk and hold reserves available to manage aggregate risks. While Congress would need to provide the Department this authority, I believe there is great value in exploring how a transparent and flexible account could address the inevitable problems that some development programs will encounter. It likely would be of great utility to the Department and would improve Warfighter and Taxpayer outcome.

7. <u>Help the Department improve professionalism of our government acquisition workforce</u>. At day's end, workforce strengthening, rather than any new set of best practices or set rules, is the most effective way to improve defense acquisition. Defense acquisition is a human endeavor that requires a high degree of professionalism in multiple disciplines for success. I have asked all Department acquisition leaders to make leaving behind a stronger, more professional workforce (military and civilian) their most important personal legacy. Our current budget environment instability, years of pay freezes, furloughs, revolving door limitations, threats of workforce reductions, a relatively inflexible civil service system, "up-or-out" career management, and the effects of over a decade of conflict all work against this goal. I would like to work with Congress to find creative ways to recruit, retain, and incentivize our professional government workforce. These are the people we depend on to structure and implement successful programs. While I also have concerns for the health of the industrial base, we have the tools we need to motivate industry using contract financial incentives. Together I believe we should explore ways in which we can do more to strengthen our government workforce. Today we have a large number of high quality acquisition professionals doing their best to support the Warfighter and protect the Taxpayer, but I believe we can do more to build on what we already have.

I close with a final comment about the complexity of defense acquisition system and what it really takes to succeed. Over the last few years I have published a quarterly article on some aspect of acquisition in the Department's Acquisition, Technology, and Logistics magazine. To give you a sense of both scope and scale of what we do, I am enclosing a list of those articles with links to them. I do not anticipate running out of topics to write about over the next few years. Over my 40-year plus career in this field I have heard, and in some cases been subject to, a lot of ideas on how to "reform" acquisition. We should not forget that we have the best equipped military in the world and we have prevailed in multiple modern conflicts with unprecedented battlefield dominance. If acquisition of military equipment were professional football we would have a dominant team, even if there is an occasional fumble or interception. A highly successful professional football team puts it all together: spotting talent; recruiting; training and conditioning; designing offenses, defenses, and special teams around the talent on the team; effective practice; careful study of individual opponents strengths and weaknesses; sound game plans and play calling; openness to innovative ideas; the ability to create surprise; a thorough 'odds of success' understanding for each option; and constant attention to thousands of details. So it is with defense acquisition. At the end of the day, it is about motivation, skills, training, experience, and leadership of the fielded team. I ask for your support of the ideas expressed above and in the enclosed. I look forward to working together to build on the professional defense acquisition team that has already contributed so much to the United States of America by enabling the most capable military in history.

3

CHAPTER FIVE: RESPONDING TO EXTERNAL FORCES AND EVENTS

> An identical letter has been sent to Senator Levin.
>
> Sincerely,
>
> *[signature]*
>
> Frank Kendall
>
> Enclosures:
> As stated
>
> 4

One of the suggestions in this letter was that the Congress refrain from writing additional rules for the DoD and instead work on reducing the current number of rules. The fact is that we already have too many rules; some of them are too rigid and limit our flexibility, and almost all of them require increased bureaucracy for implementation and to ensure compliance. Recently there has been some success in our efforts to work with the Congress to reduce bureaucratic requirements, as several of the DoD's legislative change requests have been implemented. Unfortunately, many more new requirements have also been added and the appetite to continue the effort to improve acquisition by statute does not seem to be diminishing. On a positive note, the DoD has a congressionally directed team, a commission, currently conducting a 2-year review of the publication that implements all the congressionally directed federal and defense contracting regulations, a document that spans thousands of pages and which has been continuously added to for decades. The intent is to drastically simplify the content. It is a noble endeavor and one that I hope will be successful. That success, however, will ultimately depend on Congress' willingness to repeal existing legislation.

Another issue mentioned in my letter to Senators McCain and Levin was the problem of the perverse incentives to get our budgets out the door—to spend to an arbitrary schedule. The Congress will rescind funds that are not obligated in a timely way. This puts pressure on the DoD's acquisition managers to put money on contract in order to avoid loss of the funds. Industry is well aware of this constraint, and it can put our managers in a difficult negotiating position. We should certainly not ask for money before we need it, and we should be managing our cash flow efficiently, but when the circumstances call for patience, we should not be punished for failing to obligate funds. To address this issue, I worked with the DoD's financial management leader, the Under Secretary of Defense (Comptroller) to issue the letter that appears below to provide guidance to the DoD's Program Managers and contracting professionals on how obligation rate requirements and sound business practices would be balanced. This practice has been implemented, in part through joint reviews by the Comptroller and Acquisition staffs, to good effect and it should continue.

CHAPTER FIVE: RESPONDING TO EXTERNAL FORCES AND EVENTS

OFFICE OF THE SECRETARY OF DEFENSE
1000 DEFENSE PENTAGON
WASHINGTON, DC 20301-1000

SEP 1 0 2012

MEMORANDUM FOR: SEE DISTRIBUTION

SUBJECT: Department of Defense Management of Unobligated Funds; Obligation Rate Tenets

The purpose of this memorandum is to address a long-standing Department of Defense (DoD) problem regarding the way we manage unobligated funds.

The acquisition community, starting with the Under Secretary for Acquisition, Technology and Logistics, has been stressing the importance of spending money in a way that maximizes the value the Department and the taxpayer receive. Our policy encourages managers to obligate funds when a satisfactory contract is negotiated or when they can be used most efficiently. The financial management community, starting with the Under Secretary of Defense (Comptroller), has primarily been measuring program execution against established obligation benchmarks as the basis for sourcing funds for higher Department priorities. Obviously, both goals – effective acquisition practices and use of resources for the highest Department priorities – have merit. We must strive to meet both goals while also taking into account two types of risks.

First, there are risks in focusing on obligation benchmarks. The threat that funding will be taken away or that future budgets can be reduced unless funds are obligated on schedule is a strong and perverse motivator. We risk creating incentives to enter into quick but poor business deals or to expend funds primarily to avoid reductions in future budget years. We need to rethink how we approach managing mid-year and end-of-year obligations and to change the types of behavior we reward or punish. We will continue to hold our Program/contracts teams accountable for executing to their planned schedules, but we have to stop measuring only benchmark execution as the dispositive method of determining whether funds are available for higher priorities. Such benchmarks should only be a place to start a discussion of obligation management, not a place to end that discussion.

But there are also risks in ignoring obligation benchmarks. For the past several years, Congress has used unobligated balances as a means to reduce our budgets. To avoid this result, we need to stop thinking of the transfer of funds to higher priorities as something we must avoid at any cost. We need to build a culture where maximizing the Department's buying power for both the taxpayer and the Warfighter as well as meeting the Department's highest priorities become the primary driving force behind obligation decisions. Often, these funds can be better employed elsewhere and individual programs should not fight to avoid "losing" the unobligated funds.

We believe that the following tenets should be adopted and enforced at all levels of the chain of command, and by acquisition and financial managers throughout the Department:

1. Taxpayer funds should be obligated and ultimately expended only in the taxpayers' interest and if best value is received for the money in support of the Warfighter.

2. While they can be useful indicators, obligation rates slower than established benchmarks should not be the determinative measuring stick for program execution and must not be regarded as a failure.

3. Late obligation of funds should not be presumed to imply that the funds are not needed or that future budgets should be reduced unless there is other evidence to support that conclusion.

4. Providing savings to the organization, military service, or DoD component as early in the fiscal year as possible should be encouraged and rewarded, professionally and visibly.

5. Savings will not be reallocated at any higher DoD level than necessary to fulfill shortfalls in priority requirements.

6. Managers who release unobligated funds to higher priorities will not automatically be penalized in their next year's budget with a lower allocation and may be candidates for additional funding to offset prior year reductions.

This year, the undersigned will begin implementation of a deliberate process by reviewing MDAPs and other programs that have not obligated funds consistent with normal obligation rates. We will do this together, co-led by officials designated by the undersigned, and we will follow the tenets we have listed. We will start with guidelines for the review, which will be issued soon.

We urge all financial and acquisition managers and the chain of command in each Component to follow the same guiding principles and to implement similar reviews within their organizations.

Robert F. Hale
Under Secretary of Defense
(Comptroller)

Frank Kendall
Under Secretary of Defense for
Acquisition, Technology and Logistics

Chapter Five: Responding to External Forces and Events

```
DISTRIBUTION:
SECRETARIES OF THE MILITARY DEPARTMENTS
CHAIRMAN OF THE JOINT CHIEFS OF STAFF
UNDER SECRETARIES OF DEFENSE
DEPUTY CHIEF MANAGEMENT OFFICER
COMMANDERS OF THE COMBATANT COMMANDS
DIRECTOR, COST ASSESSMENT AND PROGRAM EVALUATION
DIRECTOR, OPERATIONAL TEST AND EVALUATION
GENERAL COUNSEL OF THE DEPARTMENT OF DEFENSE
INSPECTOR GENERAL OF THE DEPARTMENT OF DEFENSE
ASSISTANT SECRETARIES OF DEFENSE
DEPARTMENT OF DEFENSE CHIEF INFORMATION OFFICER
ASSISTANTS TO THE SECRETARY OF DEFENSE
DIRECTOR, ADMINISTRATION AND MANAGEMENT
DIRECTOR, NET ASSESSMENT
DIRECTORS OF THE DEFENSE AGENCIES
DIRECTORS OF THE DOD FIELD ACTIVITIES
```

For the past few years, the DoD—in fact, most of the federal government—has been operating under the threat that our annual budgets will be determined by a process called sequestration. Sequestration is an external force that is unprecedented and severe in its consequences. This budget mechanism was originally implemented in statute as a motivator to a congressional "super-committee" that was tasked to reach a political budget compromise. Sequestration was intended to be the unacceptable default that would motivate the super-committee to succeed. It failed, and in 2013 sequestration was implemented, causing the DoD to cut more than $30 billion from its operating budget halfway through the year. As I write in 2017, sequestration is still a threat hanging over the DoD. Without statutory relief, it will remain the default budget mechanism through 2021.

In early 2013, on the eve of the implementation of sequestration, I published the first article in this chapter, laying out some of my plans for acquisition improvement, including the second version of the Better Buying Power initiatives. With the general election over, I believed that the next few years would be difficult, but I also believed that I would have a few relatively uninterrupted years to provide consistent acquisition policy guidance and management to the DoD. Sequestration was about to make this much more difficult.

The DoD had not anticipated, and did not adequately prepare for sequestration in 2013. In addition to the large reductions we had to absorb, we also had the problem that the law provided virtually no flexibility as to where the funds would be cut. In addition, the fiscal year was already approximately half completed before sequestration was initiated. Because the cuts were widely distributed, the impact was not dramatic or obvious—but it was severe. The DoD was forced to furlough most civilian employees to make up some of the shortfall in operational funds. The workforce members felt betrayed by a process and a government that had let them down. (Later in the year, we also endured a government shutdown as well.) Secretary Panetta and the entire DoD leadership did everything we could to mitigate the impact. In July 2013, I issued the following guidance to the acquisition workforce:

* * * *

From: Kendall III, Frank HON OSD OUSD ATL
Sent: Tuesday, July 09, 2013 4:54 PM
Cc: AT&L Personnel
Subject: Guidance During FY13 Sequestration and Furloughs

OUSD AT&L OFFICE OF ADMINISTRATION BROADCAST
AUDIENCE: ALL AT&L PERSONNEL
DATE: July 9, 2013

To the Defense Acquisition Workforce,

As we continue to execute a sequestered FY13 and enter a period of furloughs for most DoD civilian employees, I'd like to give you some basic guidance as to how we should do our jobs during this period.

Firstly and most importantly, we have an obligation, now and always, to

Chapter Five: Responding to External Forces and Events

extract as much value as we can for our taxpayers and the warfighters we support with the resources that are made available to us. Nothing in the current situation changes that, despite the fact that everything, and I mean everything, about sequestration, including: idle operators who should be training, facilities that are being allowed to deteriorate, equipment that isn't being maintained, research and development that is extended unnecessarily, disrupted test plans, and production that is at less economical quantities creates inefficiency and lowers our capabilities. It does not, however, change our fundamental duty to be as efficient and productive as we can be under any circumstances. We all know that the effects of sequestration are real, even if they are not dramatic and highly visible because of the way the cuts are distributed across the Department. We all know that this is no way to conduct business—but these are the cards we have been dealt and we have to play them to the best of our ability. Our taxpayers and the warfighters deserve no less.

Next we have to follow the rules—statutory and regulatory—to the best of our ability. We are in uncharted territory to some degree, so you are likely to have to consult with your chain of command and appropriate government legal authorities to determine the exact constraints you have to operate under. Unfortunately the rules were generally not written with this situation in mind; it is after all unprecedented. Many of the rules allow for exception and waivers. When that is the case and the effect of following the rules leads to even more inefficiency and waste, you should seek an exception or a waiver or an interpretation that allow you to do the right thing and avoid unnecessary waste.

Finally most of our work involves contractors and we have an obligation to treat contractors fairly and reasonably under all circumstances including these. We should honor contracts we have in place where the requirement is still needed. Where the requirement has changed due to funding cuts, furloughs of government employees or for some other reason, we should modify the contract to address the change in requirements provided it will result in savings to the government. In either circumstance we need to deal with our contractors equitably and with full transparency.

This is a painful time for all of us. The pain comes in different forms; operators are losing the chance to train and their equipment is not being kept ready, many contractors are losing their jobs entirely, and government employees are experiencing furloughs. As we make our way through this uncharted territory please keep in mind our core responsibility is to get as much for the resources we have as possible. We don't need to make sequestration look any worse than it is; that will take care of itself. This isn't about everyone experiencing the same pain in the same way—that isn't possible. It's about doing our best to perform our duty.

Frank Kendall
Under Secretary of Defense
Acquisition, Technology, and Logistics

* * * *

At about the same time I published the next article in this chapter. It deals with my expectations for the period lying ahead of the DoD. I noted that the period we were in was "the most difficult defense planning and management situation I have ever seen." The acquisition workforce, indeed the whole of DoD, responded to the challenge with remarkable professionalism and dedication. Morale may not have been high, but I will always be proud of how the Department soldiered on during all the trauma and dysfunction we experienced in 2013. We need to ensure this does not happen again.

The next two articles in this chapter deal with my concerns about the impact of developments by potential adversaries on America's military technological superiority. For years I have been giving speeches about this concern. After the Cold War and our astonishingly successful campaign in the First Gulf War in 1991, we entered a period of unprecedented military dominance in conventional warfare. The capabilities we demonstrated in 1991—stealth, precision munitions, networked forces, wide-area surveillance systems—have been serving us well for the past quarter-century. Unfortunately, all military advantages, including this one, are transient. Our potential adversaries have had a quarter-century to analyze and respond to the way America fights—and they have done so.

The first of these two articles deals with the need to protect the future, to invest in the research and development needed to move new weapons systems through the new product pipeline and into the hands of our military operators. It lays out the reasons why investment in research and development should not be neglected, even in times of tight budgets when there are many competing demands for resources. In brief, our technological superiority is not assured, research and development is not a variable cost, and time is not a recoverable asset. We ignore these tenets at our peril.

The second of these articles explains with more specificity why I decided in 2014 to issue and implement a third version of Better Buying Power. This version retained many of the initiatives from the earlier versions that had emphasized cost control and professionalism, but added emphasis on actions that could be taken to increase innovation and move technically and militarily higher quality products to our warfighters more effectively.

CHAPTER FIVE: RESPONDING TO EXTERNAL FORCES AND EVENTS

Defense acquisition also must deal with the external impact of political change, including general elections every 4 years. Political appointees often change with even higher frequency. One of my goals has been to remain in office long enough to provide consistent policy direction and effect real change. I have seen other leaders scramble to achieve all their goals during their last few months in their positions, and I wanted to avoid that.

The theme I chose for the 2016 election year was "sustaining momentum." In other words, let's keep doing what we've been doing and let's focus on doing it even more effectively. As I will discuss in the next chapter, the DoD has built up momentum in the right direction and substantially improved acquisition performance. If external factors, such as congressional reform efforts, don't disrupt that progress, the right thing to do is remain focused and to keep moving in the direction of proven results. The next article in this chapter provides a summary of the areas in which momentum has been achieved and needs to be sustained. Most of these areas of progress have their origin in Better Buying Power initiatives.

The final "outside force" I will discuss is the most important of all—the customers for defense acquisition, our military operational communities and their leadership, including the Service Chiefs. A tight relationship—in fact, a close partnership—between operational customers and acquisition professionals is an important element of acquisition success. At one time, early in my career, operators wrote requirements for weapons systems, handed them to acquisition personnel, and waited for the desired product to arrive. We are long past those days, but there remains a strong need for close and continuous cooperation and teamwork between these communities. Both have special expertise, and both need to recognize the value of that special expertise to each other as weapons systems are defined, developed, produced, and fielded. Both communities have crucial roles to play, throughout the life cycle of our defense products. To be successful, they have to work together as one team.

Recently, the Congress acted to increase the role of the Service Chiefs in acquisition. The DoD and I fully supported this provision. The Service Chiefs are responsible for defining the requirements for weapons systems, and they have overall responsibility for the Services' budgets where programs are funded. They also oversee and direct the management of Service personnel systems, which directly affect the health of the acquisition workforce. Each of these responsibilities is tightly coupled to acquisition success.

There are, however, aspects of acquisition that Service Chiefs should influence but generally not control. These include for example: acquisition strategy decisions including contract type, technical risk mitigation, technical maturity and concurrency risk, testing adequacy, and development cycle time. Most chiefs have no expertise in these areas, and history has demonstrated very clearly that, given the opportunity to do so, they will tend toward optimism and higher risk program planning. Therefore, a close working partnership between Service military leadership and Service acquisition leadership is imperative so that decisions in both areas can be fully informed. Operational urgency may dictate a higher-risk, more concurrent program. Conversely, the need for long product life cycles and low sustainment costs may dictate a more robust design with more reliability growth and testing. This chapter includes a letter that I sent to the Service Chiefs laying out my views on how they could best work with the acquisition community to improve defense acquisition in their Services.

The final article in this chapter is really intended for the Service operational leadership and also for the Service Chiefs. It is based on thinking that was stimulated by two conversations I had; one with Secretary Panetta and the other with the Chief of Staff of the Army, General Mark Milley. Both had raised the subject of why we couldn't do new weapons systems faster. My immediate reaction, and an accurate one, when Secretary Panetta asked me this in our first one-on-one meeting was "complexity." That was correct, but where does the complexity originate? The answer is that it comes from operational user community requirements.

There are two kinds of operational user requirements—first, basic military performance and, second, all the other desirable attributes or features the user wants in a weapon system that likely will be in the inventory for decades. The point of this article is that the acquisition community will respond to user requirements, and if you want something quickly (always the desire) with just basic military performance features, we can do that for you—but be careful what you ask for. Technologists and engineers, like me, love to build creative new things that are better than all preceding products at what they do. We do not particularly enjoy the myriad design details associated with manufacturability, reliability, maintainability, cyber security, full weather and environment compatibility, human interfaces, training systems, ease of field support, and many other features that are considered in a high quality product.

The article was written to clarify that there is a real trade-off between length and cost of development (time to market) and the quality of the product that will be delivered. The article includes several examples of cases in which the desire for speed has had disastrous results, but it also discusses as I did in an earlier chapter, some successes like MRAPs. Accelerated or rapid acquisition definitely has its place, but it isn't free, and it certainly isn't "acquisition magic." User communities need to understand that there is no acquisition "magic" that produces everything they want on a much shorter timeline, although plenty of people and institutions will promise that—in return for large sums of money, of course. The price of rapid acquisition is higher risk in cost, schedule and performance, and, as importantly, a reduction in quality. Sometimes that's a smart decision, and sometimes it is not.

Moving Forward

Reprinted from Defense AT&L: *January-February 2013*

I wanted to take this opportunity, with the general election now behind us, to give Defense AT&L magazine readers a sense of what we can expect during the next few years. First of all, we can expect to be challenged. Budgets are shrinking and threats to our national security are not. The department has articulated a sound strategy, and, unless there are major budget reductions to come and we are forced to make revisions, we will be charged with supporting that strategy through effective acquisition of products and services across the full spectrum of Defense Department needs. We must do everything we can to execute effectively—to extract full value from the money with which we are entrusted. Over the next several years, I will do everything I can to help you perform that challenging duty.

When I replaced Dr. Ashton Carter in an acting capacity over a year ago, I articulated six priorities: support ongoing operations, achieve affordable programs, improve efficiency, strengthen the industrial base, strengthen the acquisition workforce, and protect the future. You can expect those priorities to remain in place.

I recently introduced the "for comment" version of Better Buying Power (BBP) 2.0. BBP 2.0 is the next step in a process of continuous improvement. Like BBP 1.0, it is not intended to be a "school solution" or a checklist of ideas for you to unthinkingly "check off." BBP 2.0 is consistent with my goals and priorities, and it is designed in large part to drive critical thought in the daily execution of our work. BBP 2.0 will help improve our effectiveness in the tradecraft of acquisition. There is no single "schoolbook" answer in this business, and as we move forward on BBP 2.0 over the next year or two, we will learn from our joint experiences and make adjustments as necessary. We will identify and share new best practices, and we will reject or modify the ideas that turn out to be impractical or ineffective. You can expect future versions of BBP as together we learn about and discover what works and what doesn't.

Increasingly, we will measure our own performance and try to learn from those who are most successful at acquiring products and services for our warfighters. This winter I will publish the first edition of what I intend to be an annual AT&L publication on "The Performance of the Defense Acquisition System." For the first time in my experience, we will begin to measure the trends in our own performance and to understand, through data and

Chapter Five: Responding to External Forces and Events

analysis, the root causes of superior performance. You can expect that this report will be updated annually and that it will contain increasingly sophisticated assessments of our ability to execute programs of various types, of the productivity of Department of Defense institutions, and of the firms in the defense industrial base.

This winter, hopefully before this article goes to press, I will issue the coordination draft of the new DoDI 5000.02. This draft will update 5000.02 to be consistent with current law. It also will provide a range of models for structuring programs, and it will emphasize the need to tailor our acquisition approaches to the natural workflow and decision points for the product being developed and fielded. I will expect the principles embodied in the new 5000.02 to be used immediately while the document goes through the standard review cycle.

The process of rewriting DoDI 5000.02 has made clear to me that over the years an increasingly complex web of statutory direction has significantly complicated the lives of our key leaders, particularly our program managers. As a result, I have asked my chief of staff, Andrew Hunter, to form a team with other stakeholders, working with interested parties from Congress, to prepare a legislative proposal that would provide a single coherent and simplified body of law to guide the defense acquisition system. The goal is to have this completed and submitted to Congress within 1 year.

Finally, you can expect my continued support and dedication to giving you all of the tools you need to be effective. You, the total acquisition workforce—and I include in this grouping all of you who are involved in technology development, logistics, and sustainment activities of all types, as well as those working in the traditional product development and production activities—are the key to our success.

The next few years are not going to be easy. I expect that the Department will be stretched significantly as we attempt to retain the force structure needed to execute our national security strategy while simultaneously maintaining readiness, sustaining infrastructure, recapitalizing or modernizing aging equipment, introducing innovative technologies, preserving our industrial base, and ensuring the continuing technological superiority that our forces have every right to expect. Our success depends on your ability to execute the overall AT&L mission: supporting the warfighter and protecting the taxpayer. I look forward to meeting this challenge with you.

What Lies Ahead

Reprinted from Defense AT&L: *July-August 2013*

I usually write about acquisition policy and best practices, but given our current circumstances I felt I should provide you with some thoughts on the highly unusual and unfortunate budget situation we face.

I want to begin by thanking everyone who works in defense acquisition, technology, and logistics for all the hard work, dedication, professionalism, and, increasingly, the patience and fortitude that you display. This includes our military personnel and government employees and also our industry partners. We provide our warfighters with the best equipment in the world, and we sustain and support that equipment so our warfighters know they can count on it when they need it. We all know we aren't perfect—there is room to be more efficient, and all of us can learn from our experiences, education, and training and become more capable. Nonetheless, all of us work hard every day to provide capability to our warfighters and value to the American taxpayers who provide us with the resources for which we are stewards.

In the next few months and possibly years, our work ethic, dedication, and professionalism, and, yes, our patience and fortitude are going to be needed. I started my military career in 1966 as an ROTC cadet. A year later I entered West Point and, while I didn't serve in Vietnam, I did serve during the turmoil of the Vietnam era and in the aftermath. Later I served in the Pentagon during the final years of the Cold War as the Goldwater-Nichols Act was being implemented. I was in the Pentagon for the first few years of the transition after the fall of the Berlin Wall. After that, I experienced the defense drawdown of the 1990s from industry's perspective. In all my experience, I have never seen a situation like the one we are trying to cope with today. After Vietnam, and again after the Cold War, the Department of Defense went through a period of transition that included major changes in defense budgets and force composition. But today we are confronted with the most difficult defense planning and management situation I ever have seen.

What makes this environment so difficult in part is the uncertainty and the lack of stability in our budgets and, therefore, in our planning activities. Defense is a cyclical business—budgets do not follow a straight line but generally correlate to perceptions of national security needs. Today we are looking at sharp reductions in our budgets—not because threats to our

CHAPTER FIVE: RESPONDING TO EXTERNAL FORCES AND EVENTS

national security are diminished (in fact, the opposite is true) but because of concerns about annual deficit levels and the size of the national debt, and the resulting political gridlock about how to address these issues. The sequestration mechanism was put in place to try to force Congress out of this gridlock and to obtain a $1.2 trillion reduction in projected deficits. Former Deputy Secretary of Defense Bill Lynn said before he left the department that "the idea of sequestration was to be so crazy nobody would ever let it happen, and they did a really good job." Not good enough, apparently.

Like most people in the national security community, I did not expect sequestration to be implemented in January 2013. Technically, I was right—it was deferred a few months. But, in the larger sense, I was wrong. I won't belabor this, but after the tax bill passed in January it was clear that Congress would not reach an agreement to avert sequestration permanently before it went into effect.

During the long period leading up to sequestration, the administration and the leadership of the department, military and civilian, argued against sequestration and its devastating impact on our military. That impact is real, and everyone working in any aspect of defense acquisition reading this article knows this. Sequestration never was going to arrive with the sound of trumpets and stacks of contract termination notices and reduction-in-force announcements; it comes more like a steady rain that doesn't stop rather than like a hurricane. But the water keeps rising. Every week we compile a list of the actions being taken to absorb the cuts. Individually, they are not dramatic: training not conducted, buildings not furnished or repaired, maintenance on equipment deferred. The cuts are distributed all across the department, and there are thousands of them. In FY2013, the sequestration mechanism gave us no choice about where to absorb the nearly $40 billion of spending we have to eliminate. I refer to what we are doing now as "damage limitation." We don't have the flexibility to do much else.

We are using reprogramming requests to address our greatest readiness needs and some high-priority investment needs, but serious shortfalls will remain. Many of the things we are doing amount to a decrease in our productivity (stretched-out development programs, reduced economic production quantities) and work deferred into future budgets. Probably worst of all is the impact sequestration will have on the readiness of the force, now and into the future. As a former Army officer who lived the readiness crisis of the 1970s in a combat arms unit in West Germany, I understand the fragility of readiness and what it takes to recover once people and equipment have lost their edge.

As I write, we also are on the path to implementing furloughs that will make almost $2 billion available for our highest-priority remaining shortfalls. I want you to know that Secretary Chuck Hagel worked very hard to find a way to avoid taking this step. In the end, he felt he had no choice, and he made the difficult decision to proceed with as minimal a level of furloughs as possible. We know how difficult this will be for our workforce, particularly those in the lower pay scales. Senate-confirmed political appointees like me are not legally subject to furloughs, but many (if not all) of us, including me, will be sacrificing an equivalent share of our pay. The department's leadership will continue to look for ways to reduce this burden.

What will happen next? Our hope, and the administration's goal, is a political compromise that will resolve the impasse in the Congress and de-trigger sequestration. The next forcing function for such a deal might be the requirement to raise the debt ceiling that Congress will confront in the late summer or early fall. Even if an agreement can be reached, that will be very late to impact FY2013 spending. I'm afraid there is a good chance that the debt ceiling issue will be resolved without a grand bargain that allows Congress to remove the remaining 9 years of sequestration ($50 billion a year). As a result, sequestration may stay in place as the default mechanism determining the level of our resources.

As I write, the department is nearing the conclusion of the Strategic Choices Management Review that Secretary Hagel directed Deputy Secretary Ashton Carter and Gen. Martin Dempsey to lead. This review is assessing the implications of significantly reduced budgets for the department. The current budget options on the table include the House of Representatives' budget resolution that does not cut defense, the Senate Budget Resolution that removes about $250 billion (mostly outside the Five Year Defense Plan [FYDP]), and the President's Budget Submission, which removes about $150 billion(also mostly outside the FYDP). Sequestration of course removes $50 billion per year, starting immediately. Under the circumstances, it is only prudent to assess the implications of significant reductions. The FY2014 budget that the president submitted is consistent with the Security Strategy that we announced in 2012 and provides for the resources the administration believes are needed for national security.

The frightening scenario that may confront us looks like this: Congress remains gridlocked and the uncertainty about future budgets continues at least through FY2014. We start FY2014 under a Continuing Resolution (CR) that funds the department at the FY2013 level. The funds we now are executing in FY2013 already include cuts to the levels required by sequestration, and that is the level we would receive under a CR. In effect, sequester already would be built into an FY2014 CR. Under a CR, the department still would be constrained to keep funds in the same budget accounts, but

CHAPTER FIVE: RESPONDING TO EXTERNAL FORCES AND EVENTS

not as constrained as we were this year where essentially each budget line had to take the same reduction. In this scenario, Congress does not have to determine where the cuts occur; it can leave that politically painful task to the sequestration mechanism and the department. If past experience is any guide, Congress also may not allow the department to take some of the steps (such as Base Realignment and Closure [BRAC] and early ship retirements) it needs to take to eliminate low value added or unneeded expenses.

I think this is the worst-case scenario the acquisition community needs to be prepared to manage through, until we know more or receive other guidance. Will furloughs be necessary under this scenario? I don't know. I can promise that the department's leadership will do whatever it can to avoid them. Under this scenario, we still will not know what the department's ultimate budget levels will be. This uncertainty will make long-term planning all but impossible. We will have our share of challenges in defense acquisition.

In normal times, the resources are balanced by the department's budget among force structure (the size and composition of the force), readiness (training and maintenance), and investment (research and production of equipment to modernize and recapitalize the force structure). Each of these major spending categories depends on the other; a healthy Department of Defense keeps them in balance. When that balance is skewed for any length of time, the result is a "hollow force," such as the one I experienced in the 1970s when readiness was underfunded for a period of years. In addition to not knowing what size force to design the department around and resource, the precipitous cuts required by sequestration compound the problem. Force structure cannot be reduced overnight; it takes time to bring the force down. Because of that fact, immediate cuts fall on other parts of the budget—readiness or investment. Today we are at war, and the readiness of our deployed units and those preparing to deploy is of the highest priority. That leaves investment, which has to absorb a disproportionate part of the reductions until force structure is reduced. Remember, however, that in this scenario we lurch into FY2014 under a CR with no resolution of the long-term budgets we can expect and, therefore, no clear indication of how far our force structure should be reduced or how quickly. Finally, just to make matters worse, we also have the problem of the work we deferred in FY2013 as we were trying to absorb the sequestration cuts in the last half of the fiscal year. We will have to adjust our FY2014 plans to take this deferred work into account.

I have written this piece for two reasons. One reason is to let you know how I see the situation and what we need to be prepared for. The second is to again thank you for all that you do, and will do, for our country. I'm afraid that more is about to be asked of us. I say "us" because of my background and because my intention is to be with you through the next several years. The Defense Department's total acquisition community, and the industrial base that is part of that community, provide two of the three pillars of the department; we are not the warfighting force itself, but that force's technological superiority and rate of recapitalization, and its material readiness levels, will depend on how well we do our jobs in the difficult months that may lie ahead.

CHAPTER FIVE: RESPONDING TO EXTERNAL FORCES AND EVENTS

Protecting the Future

Reprinted from Defense AT&L: *May-June 2014*

If you've heard me speak recently or read about any of my recent congressional testimony, you may be aware that I'm fairly vocal about my concerns regarding our ability to sustain the unchallenged technological superiority our military has enjoyed for several decades. This isn't a new concern, but given the budget cuts we face and the difficult trade-offs among competing needs for force structure, readiness and investment, I decided it was time to be much more public and vocal about our current and future risks. The Secretary and the acting Deputy Secretary have been extremely supportive and are expressing the same concerns.

One of my priorities as USD(AT&L) is "Protect the Future." In October 2011, I added this item to the list of priorities I had articulated as Principal Deputy Under Secretary in 2010. "Protect the Future" spans several areas. It includes keeping alive the capabilities we developed to support the two-prolonged counterinsurgency campaigns we have waged in Iraq and Afghanistan—we may need them again. On this list are items like contingency contracting, counters to improvised explosive devices, and rapid acquisition in general. "Protect the Future" includes the protection of our science and technology accounts. It would also include protecting the gains we have made in staffing and training the acquisition workforce using the Defense Acquisition Workforce Fund. Most of all, however, I am concerned about protecting the adequacy of our research and development investments in capabilities and systems that will allow us to dominate on future battlefields and keep engineering design teams that develop advanced defense systems.

The department is dealing with an unprecedented level of uncertainty about our future budgets. It is normal to have a small gap between the requested budget and the appropriated one, but not on the order with which we have been forced to cope. The large gap between the budgets we have been requesting and what we could receive under sequestration is a planning nightmare. The president's budget this year acknowledges this disconnect. We are asking for an FY 2015 number that complies with the Bipartisan Budget Act, but the president is appropriately requesting additional funds for defense in the Opportunity, Growth and Security Initiative. In FY 2016 and beyond, our request narrows the gap between sequestration and our hopes by about half, but this still leaves us with a significant band of uncertainty. Whatever the ultimate result, we live in a world of reduced resources and a world in which we may plan based on an assumption of substantially more resources than may actually be provided.

In this environment there is a tendency to hang on to what we have—namely, force structure and programs that are already in production. There is also a strong desire to keep the readiness of our forces at acceptable levels. Having lived through the readiness crisis of the 1970s as an Army officer stationed in West Germany, I can appreciate this desire. Nevertheless I will continue to argue that we need to properly balance readiness, force structure and modernization, while preserving our research and development activities. Here are three reasons why I believe preservation of research and development is necessary.

First, technological superiority is not assured. Ever since returning to government service in the spring of 2010, I begin my day with an intelligence update. Because of my role, I tend to focus more than most senior leaders on technical intelligence. While a conflict with any specific power may be unlikely, it was immediately apparent to me 4 years ago (and nothing has changed this view except to reinforce it) that China in particular, but also Russia and other states, are developing cutting-edge military capabilities that are designed to defeat current and planned U.S. capabilities. We have had the luxury of living for a long time off technological capital largely developed during the Cold War. We demonstrated dominant operational effectiveness in the first Gulf War, which was won in a very short time with many fewer casualties than anyone expected. Our advances in stealth, precision weapons, networking and wide-area surveillance combined to give us an unprecedented level of military capability. We used these same fielded technologies in Serbia, in Afghanistan and in the invasion of Iraq. Potential adversaries saw what we had demonstrated so clearly over 20 years ago, and they took action. In the meantime, I'm afraid we have been complacent and tended to take our technological advantage for granted. We also have been focused for more than a decade of intense counterinsurgency campaigns.

What areas concern me the most? The areas we refer to loosely as A2AD for Anti-Access and Area Denial. Our ability to project power around the globe depends on an array of assets and actions that include our space-based global-positioning systems, our communications and sensors, our long-range strike, our ability to move carrier-based strike forward, our networks, forward basing (including airfields and command, control and communication as well as logistics nodes), and our ability to be dominant in the air. These are all areas in which we are being challenged with both current capabilities and capabilities still in development. This bears repeating. While a conflict with any specific power may be unlikely, I do not want to live in a world in which the United States no longer is the dominant

CHAPTER FIVE: RESPONDING TO EXTERNAL FORCES AND EVENTS

military power or in which potential adversaries may possess equipment (from any source) that would remove the advantage our warfighters have depended on for so long.

My second point is that research and development is not a variable cost. This is not an obvious point to many people, and in the past there has been a tendency to reduce research and development more or less proportionately to other budget reductions. This can be dangerous, if done in excess, because research and development costs are not related to the size of our force or the size of the inventory we intend to support. The cost of developing a new weapons system is the same no matter how many of that system we intend to produce. If we don't do the research and development for a new system, then the number of systems of that type we will have is zero. It is not variable.

Third and finally, time is not a recoverable asset. It takes a certain amount of time to develop a new system, test it and put it into production. Time lost is, for the most part, not recoverable. By taking higher risks and accepting inefficiencies and higher costs, we can reduce the "time to market" of a new weapon system. This approach was used successfully to field MRAPs for the conflicts in Iraq and Afghanistan; however, MRAPs are not complex cutting-edge weapon systems. Nominally, it takes about 10 to 15 years from conception until we have a modern complex system in the field in operationally meaningful numbers. Even during the 1940s we had to fight World War II largely with systems that were in development years before the war began. We can shorten, but not eliminate, the time required to field new cutting-edge weapons systems.

Fortunately the department's leadership understands and supports these views. As Secretary Hagel made clear, we must strike a balance between our ability to meet current global requirements, maintain a trained and sustained force that can meet near-term needs and at the same time "protect the future" by continuing our highest-priority research and development programs and the science and technology programs that feed them. The Secretary, senior leadership in the Office of the Secretary of Defense and in the Joint Staff and the Services all tried to strike the right balance as we built the Future Years Defense Program.

That brings me to our role in defense acquisition, technology and logistics. The efficiencies we continue working on under the Better Buying Power label are some of the tools we have to help sustain technological superiority. Every dollar of cost savings from a successful "should cost" initiative, every business deal we negotiate that provides better value to the government and every successful incentive structure we implement with industry will allow us to invest more in future technological superiority. We also have to become better at working with the operational requirements communities. By focusing on performance features that really matter militarily, this relationship helps ensure we provide the users with products that give them advantages they need at an affordable cost. Our technology base work also has to be strategically focused on areas that give us a significant operational advantage. Our responsibility in these still uncertain times, as always, is to deliver as much capability to the warfighter as we can with the resources entrusted to us. We will not sustain our technological superiority or "protect the future" unless we succeed.

CHAPTER FIVE: RESPONDING TO EXTERNAL FORCES AND EVENTS

Technological Superiority and Better Buying Power 3.0

Reprinted from Defense AT&L: *November-December 2014*

Each morning I start my day with a half hour or more devoted to reading the latest intelligence. I've been doing this for about four-and-a-half years now.

It took me only a few weeks from the time I came back into government in March 2010 to realize that we had a serious problem. Some of the countries that might be future adversaries, (or that could at least be counted on to sell their weapons to countries that are our adversaries) were clearly developing sophisticated weapons designed to defeat the United States' power-projection forces. Even if war with the United States were unlikely or unintended, it was quite obvious to me that the foreign investments I saw in military modernization had the objective of enabling the countries concerned to deter regional intervention by the American military.

How did we get here? This journey began after the Cold War and in particular the First Gulf War that followed shortly thereafter. At that time, I was the Director of Tactical Warfare Programs in the Office of the Under Secretary of Defense for Acquisition. For years, since the 1970s, the Department had been working on a suite of capabilities originally designed to overcome the Soviet numerical advantage in Europe. As a young Army officer, I had served in Germany in the 1970s and studied firsthand the problem that successive echelons of Soviet armor formations posed to NATO forces. Our answer to this problem was something called Follow-On-Forces-Attack (FOFA), which had grown out of the Assault Breaker technology demonstration program at the Defense Advanced Research Projects Agency. The basic idea was to combine wide-area surveillance, networked Command, Control and Communications, and precision munitions into an operational concept that would negate the Soviet numerical advantage. The concept could be summed up as "one shot, one kill." From 1989 to 1994, I was responsible for the FOFA programs. In the First Gulf War, we had a chance to demonstrate the effectiveness of this concept, and we did so.

As we started operations against Saddam Hussein, most experts predicted thousands of coalition casualties. In the event, the number was only a few hundred. The combination of sensors like the JSTARS [Joint Surveillance Target Attack Radar System] and precision munitions like Maverick and laser-guided bombs made quick work of Iraqi armor formations. Stealth also was introduced to the battlefield to great effect by the F-117.

The dramatic success of American and coalition forces in 1991 did not go unnoticed. No country paid more attention to this stunning display of military dominance than China, followed closely by Russia. The First Gulf War marked the beginning of a period of American military dominance that has lasted more than 20 years. We used the same capabilities, with some notable enhancements, in Serbia, Afghanistan, Libya and Iraq. It has been a good run, but I am concerned that, unless we act quickly, this period will end in the not-too-distant future.

When I left the Pentagon in 1994, the intelligence estimates suggested that, while China might be a concern in the future, the United States then had no reason to be worried for 15 to 20 years. It is now 2014, and I am worried. There has been more than adequate time for countries like Russia, with its energy-revenue-funded military modernization, and China, with its spectacular economic growth, to develop counters to what has been called either the Military-Technical Revolution or the Revolution in Military Affairs that the United States introduced so dramatically in 1991.

The foreign modernization programs that I refer to include investments in cyber capabilities, counter-space systems, electronic warfare programs, land-and-surface-ship attack ballistic and cruise missiles with smart seekers, anti-air weapons, advanced platforms to host these capabilities and many more. Taken together, these modernization programs are clearly designed to counter American power projection forces and to ensure that the United States does not interfere in the areas close to Russia or China. Even if our relationships with these states improve and military confrontation is avoided, the capabilities I am concerned about will still quickly proliferate to other states, such as Iran and North Korea. We cannot afford to be complacent about our technological superiority, and we cannot allow other less-sophisticated threats to distract us from the task of maintaining that superiority. This brings us to Better Buying Power 3.0.

For the last 4 years, our focus in Acquisition, Technology, and Logistics has been on improving our business outcomes. Usually, we discuss the Better Buying Power goals in terms of productivity, waste elimination, better business deals, and efficient execution of programs and services. In BBP 3.0, my goal is to shift our emphasis toward the actual products we are developing, producing, fielding and maintaining. We will continue our efforts to improve productivity, but the focus of BBP 3.0 is on the results we are achieving—particularly our ability to bring innovative and game-changing technologies into fielded capabilities for the warfighter as quickly and efficiently as possible. Our technological superiority is not assured. I

Chapter Five: Responding to External Forces and Events

also do not expect the budget climate to improve for the foreseeable future. Sequestration may well return in Fiscal Year 2016—and, even if it does not, the threat is unlikely to be removed entirely.

We are going to have to work hard to bring the innovation and technology we need to our warfighters—and we are going to have to achieve this in a very tough environment.

Our Theme for 2016—
Sustaining Momentum

Reprinted from Defense AT&L: *March-April 2016*

It's hardly a secret that we are headed toward a change in administration next year. I've been through these transitions several times, as have most acquisition professionals. During my previous experience in the Pentagon organization of the Under Secretary of Defense for Acquisition, Technology, and Logistics, I worked for a total of eight Under Secretaries in as many years, and I went through one same-party and one other-party administration change.

As some of these transitions approached, there were attempts to cram a lot of accomplishment into a very short time. This generally caused a lot of work and wasn't very successful. In my case, I have had several years to effect the improvements in defense acquisition I thought were most needed. As a result, there won't be a Better Buying Power (BBP) 4.0 this year and, while I do plan to modify Department of Defense Instruction (DoDI) 5000.02 on the margins and to make it consistent with current law, there also won't be a major acquisition policy rewrite this year, although we will be implementing the changes required in the Fiscal Year (FY) 2016 National Defense Authorization Act. We still have a lot to do in implementing the existing BBP actions, however. Also, the new DoDI on the acquisition of services has just gone into effect, so we still have work to do on implementation of that as well.

What I would most like to accomplish during the balance of this year is to sustain and build on the momentum we have achieved over the last few years. I don't know what will happen in the election, and, depending on how it turns out, I also don't know what opportunities I may have. But I do know that we have the better part of a year together in which to make more progress on the areas in which we have been working. I also know that we are improving acquisition outcomes. The evidence is clear from the most recent *Annual Report on the Performance of the Defense Acquisition System* and other data that contract costs and schedule overruns are being reduced, as well as cycle time, and that we are tying profit more effectively to performance through the use of incentive structures. I would like to discuss some of the actions that stand out as important areas in which to sustain and build on the momentum we have gained as we get ready for a new administration next year.

CHAPTER FIVE: RESPONDING TO EXTERNAL FORCES AND EVENTS

Promote Technical Excellence and Innovation: We are well into implementing BBP 3.0, but we have many actions in progress that need to be completed. My concerns about technological superiority that motivated this edition of BBP are reinforced every time I receive a daily technical intelligence update. This year's budget includes a number of advanced technology demonstrators and experimental prototypes and we need to get these provisions enacted and the projects started. Steve Welby, who has been confirmed as Assistant Secretary of Defense for Research and Engineering, and his teams completed the Long Range Research and Development Planning Program, which was very influential in the FY 2017 budget. We are strengthening the ties between operators, intelligence experts, and acquisition professionals. We will continue to manage the ongoing actions to improve our workforce's technical capacity, and to extract as much benefit as possible from all of our various Research and Development accounts and from industry's investments. Bill LaPlante has left his position as Assistant Secretary of the Air Force, but his dictum to "own the technical baseline" is an enduring imperative to all of our technical and management professionals working to bring new products to our warfighters. As I have said many times, our technological superiority is being challenged in ways we have not seen since the Cold War, and we must respond.

Continue Establishing and Enforcing Affordability Analysis and Caps: We have been doing this for more than 5 years now, and there is solid evidence that both the analysis process by Service programmers and the enforcement of caps by the acquisition chain and the requirements chain are having a beneficial impact. The use of long-term capital planning analysis was a new concept when we introduced it, but it is becoming institutionalized. We can't predict future budgets accurately, but we can do analysis now that helps us make better decisions. Enforcing the resulting caps is the most difficult aspect of having them, but if the caps are to be meaningful, they have to be enforced. We've learned from our experience, but this is still an evolving area. The caps should be set at a level that leaves some margin; they are neither cost positions nor program baselines, nor budgets. They are tools to ensure meaningful long-term capital investment planning and to guide cost versus performance trade-offs during development. I am hopeful that the Department of Defense (DoD) will continue to establish them and enforce them in subsequent administrations.

Promote Increased Use of "Should Cost" as a Management Practice: I believe that in many, but not all, cases "should cost" is now a normal part of business. It should be. Every manager should understand the cost structure under his or her control, analyze it for savings opportunities, set goals to achieve those opportunities and act on those goals. After several years of effort, the use of "should cost" has proliferated across the DoD. It is changing thought patterns and behaviors in a positive way. That implementation isn't uniform, however, and I'm afraid it hasn't been fully embraced in all cases. Some still regard this initiative as a threat to their budgets, which it is definitely not. Others seem reluctant to set significant goals for fear of being unable to attain them. The "culture of spending" isn't dead yet, and the perverse incentive of execution rate targets isn't going away. We need to continue to strike the right balance and to encourage our workforce to do the right thing for both the taxpayer and the warfighter by not wasting resources that could be saved and put to a better purpose. Of all the BBP initiatives over the years, this is the most fundamental thing we have done. Use of "should cost" targets has saved the DoD billions of dollars, and we need to continue expanding and supporting its use.

Provide Strong Incentives to Industry: As I have said and written many times, industry is easy to motivate. Corporations exist for the purpose of making money for their shareholders, so the motivation tool is obvious and effective. The trick for the DoD is to align this self-interest with the DoD's interests, and to do it in a way that will be effective at improving outcomes. We're making progress on this, but I still see some unevenness in how our managers structure incentives. It takes good critical thinking to get incentives "right" because we deal with so many different business situations. Incentives need to "thread the needle" between being easily achieved and impossible so that they do influence behavior. They also need to be meaningful financially both as carrots and sticks, without asking corporations to assume an unreasonable amount of risk. I'll continue to focus on this aspect of our acquisition strategies as programs come in for review, and I'll expect managers at all levels to do the same.

Effectively Manage Intellectual Property: Going back to BBP 1.0, we have worked hard to mature our collective understanding of how to protect the government's interests while also respecting industry's property rights. This is a complex area of law and one in which the DoD was at a longtime disadvantage relative to industry. I occasionally still wrestle with cases of "vendor lock" based on proprietary content. Hopefully, we have all but stopped the practice of just accepting industry assertions of property rights. We need to continue to grow our expertise in this area and spread the best practices associated with effective management of intellectual property.

It's perfectly legitimate for a company to expect a reasonable return on the intellectual property it has developed or acquired. In general, that return should be in the competitive advantage conveyed by superior technology or lower costs. On the other hand, the use of intellectual property by a firm to sustain a decades-long grip on the aftermarket for a product is something the DoD should and can work to prevent. We're getting better at this, but our efforts need to be sustained and broadened.

Acquire Modular Designs and Open Systems: This idea is anything but new. However, our practice has traditionally not matched our policy. It takes active technical management of design architectures and interfaces to make both open systems and modularity a reality. This is "owning the technical baseline," and the devil really is in the details. Assertions of modularity and openness are not always valid. There are also always cost impacts and design trades that work against achieving these goals. We can point to a few successes in this area over the last several years; each Military Service can take credit for programs to provide open architectures in general and modular designs on some specific platforms. The Long Range Strike Bomber is a notable example. This effort should continue and expand, but success will require a technical management workforce that is trained, experienced and empowered.

Use Monetized Performance Levels in Source Selection: We've had several notable successes with this initiative. They include the Combat Rescue Helicopter, the Joint Light Tactical Vehicle, and the Amphibious Combat Vehicle. This is a relatively new concept; it asks the requirements community to do something that it has traditionally resisted—put priorities and relative value on requirements. Industry traditionally would simply bid threshold values of performance. This initiative gives industry a reason to aim higher, as long as it can do so for a reasonable cost. By providing industry with information on how much we are willing to pay, and how much competitive source selection evaluation cost credit we will give in an evaluated price, we motivate industry to create better products for us. We also get the benefit of more objective source selections. This is a useful property in a period in which protests are more common. The fact is we have to make these best value judgments anyway. We are better off to make them rationally prior to asking for bids. I hope to see several more successful examples of this approach over the balance of the year and to see it continued indefinitely.

Improve the Acquisition of Services: With the publication of DoDI 5000.74, we marked the transition to a more structured way of looking at management of contracted services acquisitions. This is one culmination of a series of steps that date back to BBP 1.0, where we took Air Force initiatives introduced by now LTG Wendy Masiello when she was the Air Force's Program Executive Officer (PEO) for Services Acquisition and expanded them to the rest of DoD. Over the last several years, we have built on these initial steps. Despite this progress, I remain convinced that this area of spending, which is now well above the spending on products, offers the greatest potential for savings and efficiency in the DoD. My Principal Deputy, Alan Estevez, has led this effort and it is starting to pay big dividends.

As we go through this year and gain experience implementing the new DoDI, I would expect us to gain insights that will lead to some modifications, but overall I think we are the right track. This is one area in which I will ask the Service Secretaries and Chiefs to become more involved. A great deal of contracted services are acquired and managed outside the standard acquisition chain and institutions. As Gen. David Petraeus once wrote to his staff in Afghanistan, "Contracting is commanders' business." This is as true outside the operational contingency arena as it has been in Afghanistan and Iraq. However, many of our operational and institutional leaders are not focused on the management of these extensive resources. During the coming year, we can and will do more to change that.

Continue Our Annual Acquisition Assessment Activities: We have instituted three sources of annual assessments that will be continued this year. They are: the *Annual Report on the Performance of the Defense Acquisition System*, the Annual Preferred Supplier Program, and the Program Mangers' Annual Assessments. The first of these provides a growing body of statistical data and analysis on the performance of the acquisition system using a range of metrics. The third edition, released last fall, shows strong evidence of improved performance over the last several years. Each year we have added additional data and analysis to this volume and we will continue to do so this year. The second item provides public feedback to industry on the relative performance of major business units based on the Contractor Performance Assessment Reporting System (CPARS). We struggled to get this off the ground, but thanks to the Navy's pilot effort led by Sean Stackley and Elliot Branch we were finally successful. Last year, all three Military Departments published their results simultaneously. We will continue that practice this year. The third item is the Program Manager's Annual Assessments, of which I published a subset last fall. I published them (with the writers' permissions) because I was very impressed with the inputs I received and because I thought providing them to a wider audience was a great way to educate outside stakeholders on the great variety of real life problems that our program managers face, and how professionally they deal with those problems. I recently requested this year's assessments and they will be submitted by the time this piece is published. At the PEOs' request, I am also giving PEOs an opportunity to provide a similar input. I will do my best to dedicate two solid weeks to reading and responding to each of the 180 odd assessments I will receive. Last year's reports highlighted a number of problems and opportunities that needed to be addressed; and I expect the same this year. I also will request another round at the end of 2016.

Chapter Five: Responding to External Forces and Events

Build Even Greater Professionalism: The DoD has an incredibly professional workforce. When building professionalism was introduced in BBP 2.0, there were some who took that as an assertion that our workforce is not professional. Nothing is further from the truth. However, we all can become even more professional through experience, training, education and personal effort. None of us should ever be complacent; there is always more to learn and always opportunity for increased levels of expertise and broader experience. We also all have a duty to improve the professionalism of those who work with and for us. If there is one legacy each of us should strive for, it is to leave a more professional workforce behind us than we found when we arrived. We are fortunate to have the support of the Congress and Secretary of Defense Ashton Carter in this endeavor. Our Director of the Human Capital Initiative for acquisition personnel, Rene Thomas-Rizzo, has worked hard with the Under Secretary for Personnel and Readiness Brad R. Carson to include provisions in Secretary's Force of the Future initiatives that will benefit our workforce. We will work hard with the Congress and internally to see those initiatives enacted this year.

Increase the Involvement of the Service Chiefs in Acquisition: The most recent National Defense Authorization Act included provisions strengthening the Service Chiefs role in acquisition. I fully support this direction and have already met with all four Service Chiefs to discuss their role. The areas in which I think they can make the greatest contribution are in requirements, budgeting and personnel. As stated above, I also think they can do much to improve the management of acquisition activities that take place outside the acquisition chain of command. During the year we will be implementing this direction.

The BBP initiatives have spanned several major areas of emphasis, included dozens of specific initiatives, and involved more than 100 actions—in each version. There also have been any number of steps we have taken over the past several years to improve acquisition outcomes across the full range of products and services that DoD acquires. Many of them have been outside the specifics of the BBP initiatives.

Underlying all this effort are some fundamental cultural goals. One of them is to move from being a culture that focuses on spending to one that focuses on controlling costs. This may be the area in which we have made the greatest gains. Another has been to encourage a culture that values and encourages the critical thinking needed to confront the huge range of problems acquisition professionals must deal with. We are not engaged in cookbook activities where one way of doing business always works. A third goal is to achieve the widespread appreciation of, and a culture that values, professionalism inside our workforce and, perhaps more important, outside it. Our success depends entirely on the efforts of thousands of true professionals in the full range of disciplines needed for new product design, testing, production, and support. Finally, there is the resurgent importance of being a culture that values and rewards the technical excellence and innovation needed to stay ahead of the committed and capable adversaries we may face in combat. Building and sustaining these aspects of our culture is a task that should never end.

CHAPTER FIVE: RESPONDING TO EXTERNAL FORCES AND EVENTS

MEMORANDUM FOR CHIEFS OF THE MILITARY SERVICES

SUBJECT: Defense Acquisition

December 8, 2016

Dear Military Department and Service Leadership:

For literally years I have been mentally composing a letter to you on your role in Defense Acquisition and how you can help make your Service's acquisition efforts be more successful. With the recent changes in Service civilian and military leadership, as well as the changes in the FY 2016 National Defense Acquisition Act (NDAA), which I fully support and which affects your role, it seems like a good time to set my thoughts down and provide them to you. I'd like to start by talking about the aspects of defense acquisition where I think you can have the most positive impact; requirements, budget, and—most of all—the acquisition workforce. I follow that with some comments on things to avoid, some thoughts on our relationship to industry, and close with some comments on my role in defense acquisition.

I encourage you to actively manage requirements and major requirement trades at your level. All acquisition programs start with user requirements –they drive everything in the program; the risk profile and resulting reduction and mitigation phases and activities, the contracting approach and incentives, and the test program structure, just to name a few. Acquisition programs can get into trouble in a lot of ways, but if the requirements are not reasonably achievable and clearly stated so that they can be put on contract and tested, the program is likely to be headed for trouble from day one. Each Service has its own structure and authorities for determining and setting requirements. This in itself is not the source of the problems in requirements that I've observed. In my experience I have most often seen the following problems with requirements set by the Services: technical infeasibility, arbitrary levels with marginal operational benefits achieved only at high cost (most often in the area of reliability numbers, but sometimes in other performance levels), vagueness, and rigidity. Getting requirements to the right place depends on an open, constructive, and continuous interchange between operational, intelligence, and acquisition communities. You can have a major and positive influence in this area.

One of the Better Buying Power initiatives, monetizing differences in desired performance levels, has an important impact on the requirements communities. The idea behind this is simple; if we tell industry how much we are willing to pay for higher performance levels and give them monetary credit for offering higher performance levels when they bid competitively, than they are more likely to offer the performance we want—and to do so at a reasonable price. Historically we have set Threshold and Objective level requirements. Industry then bids the threshold level and ignores the objective level, which invariably is more expensive and therefore less competitive. By telling industry how much in dollars we value higher performance (meaning how much more we are prepared to pay for it—this has nothing to do with what it costs), and by giving industry an evaluated price adjustment in source selection, we provide a meaningful incentive to industry to be innovative and offer us more capability. Without this we default to threshold levels. This concept is working, but it depends on Service leadership support and the willingness of the requirements communities to prioritize and to set a value on different levels of performance.

Another aspect of getting requirements right is the willingness to adjust as changes occur and knowledge increases. Here you can play a major role in streamlining decision making and encouraging the elevation of requests for needed changes. In each Service, requirements are approved at a senior level (usually the four star level, but not the Service Chief). Once requirements have been enshrined in a four star approved document, and for Major Defense Acquisition Programs (MDAPs) blessed by the Joint Requirements Oversight Council, it can be very hard and time consuming to make needed adjustments. Part of the problem is cultural. Lower level operational community officers, usually field grade officers, are generally tasked to coordinate with the acquisition community on behalf of the operational community that set the initial requirement. These people are not predisposed to go back to their superiors to request a change in a four star approved requirement. The Service's Configuration Steering Boards are intended to provide a forum in which requirements decisions and trades can be evaluated. Under our current rules, the CSBs for MDAPs are supposed to meet at least annually. In the early stages of development this is probably not enough. My advice to you is to create a climate and mechanism by which both operational staff and acquisition staff are encouraged to surface requirements issues early so that needed trades can take place before a great deal of time and money is wasted pursuing a goal that needs to be changed.

With the technological superiority challenges DOD faces today, time is a more important consideration than ever. One of the more difficult choices we have to make in defense acquisition is whether or not to increase a requirement on a program that is well into a multi-year development because of new intelligence on the threat that system will face. Doing this can be very disruptive and increase cost and schedule significantly. Sometimes a threat change calls the very utility of the program into question. When intelligence reveals a change in the threat, Service operational leadership, in consultation with both intelligence, and acquisition leadership should make a conscious decision on how to proceed; continue as planned and upgrade the system later, change the requirements (and the design and the program) now, or cancel the program because it is obsolete already. From the acquisition community perspective this is a customer decision and the Service leadership is the customer, but it is also one in which acquisition professionals want to be involved so that the operational customer appreciates the full implications of any decision he or she makes. In my experience our Program Managers have a bias toward stability—they know that more stressing requirements mean increased risk, cost, and schedule—but we are building these systems for a reason, to provide the warfighter with the tools he needs against potential adversaries, and the acquisition community is dedicated to that result.

Service leadership generally controls the Service's budget, subject to review at the DOD level. Here I would ask simply that you ensure Service acquisition programs are adequately funded. This isn't easy when budgets are tight and it is tempting to talk yourself into "accepting risk" by under-funding acquisition programs, thereby keeping more programs on the Service's books. I would urge you to give your acquisition leadership and cost estimators a strong voice as you build your budgets. One of the most revealing studies on defense acquisition I have ever seen shows a very strong correlation between budget climate ("tight" or "accommodating") and future cost growth. Going back several decades, the evidence is clear that when budgets are tight we are more inclined to be optimistic about new program costs. This feels really good until reality intervenes, as it always does eventually. While we have been consistently improving our cost performance over the last few years, the mean is still well above zero for our programs. Development phases in particular tend to overrun, on average about 30%. Early production is better behaved, but still overruns about 10% on average. Succumbing to the wishful thinking of under-funding programs is contrary to the entire history of defense acquisition, and it compounds future problems when they inevitably arise.

I would also ask that you take into full account the long term affordability of programs as you create your Service budgets and decide on any new systems the Service will acquire. Most of the program cancellations I have observed have been because of long term affordability concerns. The most recent one was the Marine Corps Expeditionary Fighting Vehicle, which the Commandant correctly concluded could not be afforded in foreseeable Corps budgets under any circumstances. For the past five plus years I have been requiring the Services to conduct affordability analyses in order to derive affordability caps for programs. We set affordability "goals" or "targets" early in an acquisition program lifecycle and firm them up as "caps" at the time we commit to development for production and establish the program's baseline. Defining these caps is not an acquisition community responsibility; they are a Service leadership responsibility. Generally the Service programmers are responsible for the analysis and recommending caps, usually caps on unit production cost and annual sustainment cost. Those who criticize this approach do so based on the difficulty of predicting budgets for the 30 or 40 year life cycle of a new program. It is true that we can't predict budgets accurately; but is also true that conducting affordability analyses now so that we can make better decisions now about new starts and program requirements can keep us from embarking on clearly unaffordable programs, and it can help us make better informed requirements versus cost trades as the program advances and we learn more. This is nothing other than prudent long term capital investment planning, and I urge you to support it in your Service.

In the second addition of the Better Buying Power initiatives, I included a section on building the professionalism of the acquisition workforce. This section in some form should be in any Better Buying Power or other future acquisition improvement program. As senior leaders you are fully aware of the importance of good leadership and management skills. I'm not sure that you are as aware of the importance of professionalism in the acquisition workforce, which includes professionals in about a dozen fields. Those fields include management of new product development, engineering, contracting, testing, logistics, and maintenance. Each of these, and the other acquisition professions, requires special expertise, not just good leadership and general management skills, to be successful. I'm particularly concerned that our technical engineering management workforce isn't as large or capable as it should be. Supervising new product development is supervising engineering. Anyone managing a development program without an appropriate technical background is largely just deciding who to trust. In the government we generally do not hire professionals from outside; we build them over long careers. This is particularly true of our uniformed acquisition professionals, but it is also generally true of our civil servants. Senior operational leaders are professionals also, but in different fields; I doubt that any of you would consider putting someone with no relevant operational experience in charge of an air wing, or a brigade, or an aircraft carrier. I would ask that you do all you can to recognize the importance to your Service of our acquisition professionals and that you do everything you can to strengthen the professionalism of this critical part of your Service.

CHAPTER FIVE: RESPONDING TO EXTERNAL FORCES AND EVENTS

On occasion I have heard senior Service leadership talk about the gap between operational and acquisition people in their Service. Many times, I have seen evidence of the, for lack of a better word, tribal structure of each Service, and how acquisition people are viewed in that structure. At a retirement for a senior acquisition flag officer a few years ago, I heard the Service Chief complement the retiring officer's ability to bridge the gap between operations and acquisition people. In my opinion this gap is a fiction; acquisition people are fully part of the Services. They are very much members of the team and very dedicated to the team's success. All acquisition officers should have been through at least one operational tour; the operational world is well known to them. Perception is often the equivalent of reality, however, and if the operational community perceives the acquisition community as a tribe apart, that will not be lost on your acquisition professionals. As leaders of your Services, you can do a great deal to counter this perception. What you say and how you say it about the acquisition workforce sends powerful messages to that workforce, and to the rest of your Service. Spending time with acquisition organizations and people matters. Ensuring at least equivalent promotion rates and the existence of meaningful opportunities for advancement in the Service will speak very strongly to your acquisition workforce.

Throughout the Department, with great support from the Service Acquisition Executives (SAEs), we have encouraged a culture change toward cost consciousness and active cost management. As a result, over the last several years we have seen significant improvement in acquisition outcomes, particularly cost growth. The Department's most recent "Annual Report on the Performance of the Acquisition System" and other data confirms the positive trends. These improvements are the result of 1,000s of individual decisions by members or the Services' acquisition workforces. They are in part due to an increased focus by our workforce on cost control, especially under a management technique that was introduced in 2010 as a Better Buying Power initiative called "should cost." Should cost directs all our mangers to understand and assess their cost structures, to identify opportunities for savings, to set targets, and to act on those opportunities. Targets are established and documented, and managers work to achieve them. The policy is that any savings remain within the Service. Savings are not assumed or taken out of budgets until they are actually achieved—should costs are "stretch goals" and success is not assumed. This is a major cultural shift because our system tends to reward spending as opposed to saving. Managers are reviewed for execution rates, and if they aren't spending their allocated funds quickly enough they are subject to reductions. I've worked closely with the DOD Comptroller through joint reviews in order to make sure that programs are not harmed if their cash flow doesn't meet established norms. I'd ask that you support "should cost" management everywhere we contract for products and services and that you encourage your programmers to work closely with your acquisition leadership to mitigate the perverse incentive to spend no matter what that is associated with execution rate enforcement.

As we continue to experience budgetary stress and execute mandatory workforce reductions, I would ask that you protect your acquisition workforce as much as you can. During the late '90s we effectively gutted our acquisition workforce. Once this was recognized, the Department, with support from the Congress, went through a period of increasing the workforce in size and increasing its quality through training. This period came to an end in about 2012 when sequestration became law and budget cuts started in earnest. We have been fairly successful in protecting the gains we made prior to 2012, and under Better Buying Power and other initiatives we have increased our focus on developing and retaining the professionals we have. I am very concerned that the Department or individual Services may reduce their acquisition workforces in order to preserve operational force structure on the margins. I'd ask that you pay close attention to this area as you consider both civilian and military personnel reductions. In the near term I am seeing problems in the adequacy of our contracting workforce—this shows up as increased time to award and as quicker, but not better or more cost effective, forms of contracts being more widely used. This can deprive us of needed support and it leads to higher costs that dwarf the short term savings. In the longer term it can also mean not having the engineering expertise we need to manage contracts with industry. People matter most—no acquisition policy anyone can invent will compensate for lack of expertise or capability within your Service's workforce.

So far I've tried to emphasize the ways in which I think you can help your Service's acquisition efforts move in the right direction. I'd like to address the other side of the coin now, the ways in which you might unintentionally do harm. This isn't speculative. I've seen all of this too many times. Our military culture includes elements that serve us well operationally; a can do spirit, the ability to make decisions in the face of uncertainty, strong leadership, obedience to authority. When these same qualities are applied to acquisition decisions by leaders with the best of intentions, but who know little or nothing of the acquisition professions, the results can be unfortunate.

First of all avoid arbitrary mandates, especially for schedules. The greatest disaster I know of in acquisition history occurred in large part be-

Chapter Five: Responding to External Forces and Events

cause a Service Chief set a totally unrealistic schedule goal. The "can do" attitude and respect for authority led the acquisition leadership in place to take huge risk, with predictable results. When the Service Chief in question retired, four years were added to the schedule, but the damage had already been done. Your acquisition professionals, and historical data, provide a good basis for assessing the realism of schedules. The simple determiner of schedule is complexity. New product development times are driven by the work that had to be done, which is related directly to the complexity of the product. An F-35 is orders of magnitude more complex than an MRAP, or almost anything else we've ever built. Arbitrary performance levels can be problematic also. Both performance risk and technical risk were compounded when the Navy was directed to change course on the aircraft carrier USS FORD and implement higher performance, but higher risk, subsystems more quickly than the Navy's acquisition professionals thought wise. I think it is fair to say that if the honest professional judgement of competent acquisition professionals had been elicited and listened to in each of these cases, that major problems could have been avoided. Our military culture can make it very hard for subordinates to tell senior leadership things they don't want to hear. I would urge you to challenge your acquisition professionals to do better, make sure they understand your sense of urgency, but at the same time encourage them to be candid and listen to their advice about subjects they understand. An analogy I like to use is that of a patient who is told by his brain surgeon that an operation on a tumor will take several hours. Would you insist that the brain surgeon competed the operation in half the recommended time?

Don't mistake events like contract awards for real progress; signing a bad business deal isn't progress—it's a trap that will be sprung later. For years we have encouraged our program management and contracting people to take the time to get a good business deal for the government while treating industry fairly. Sometimes this leads to long negotiations. When this is the case your acquisition people will need your support as they face industry and sometimes political pressure to get a contract awarded. Once we have a signed contract that document defines our relationship to industry for the period of performance of the work; we need to get these agreements right, and sometimes that takes time. In every negotiation time favors one side or the other; we shouldn't artificially constrain our own negotiators by putting too much pressure on them to sign awards so that we can have the appearance of progress.

Please don't create additional bureaucracy to fulfill your new formal responsibilities. The NDAA requires your concurrence in programs at Milestone A (the start of any contracted risk reduction needed prior to commitment to development for production) and at Milestone B (the start of development for production) when we really commit to a program and establish the program baseline for the duration of the product lifecycle. For programs for which I am the Milestone Decision Authority (MDA) we have introduced a simple way for you to provide this concurrence in writing. For programs for which the Service Acquisition Executive (SAE) is the MDA you will need to work out a similar procedure demonstrating concurrence. We already have too much bureaucracy as it is, and I would urge you not to create more review process or organizations to help you with this new statutory requirement. In fact I would urge you to examine the existing review and staffing processes within your Services to see if it can be reduced. For the past several years (in every version of Better Buying Power), the SAEs and I have tried to reduce the unproductive bureaucracy associated with acquisition programs. We've made some progress, but I'm not happy with where we are. This is still a work in progress, but the fact is that most of the bureaucracy associated with programs exists within the Services rather than OSD, and it is something that you have control over. I would also add that staffing and review processes are not the problem with defense acquisition nor are they synonymous with it. They do add overhead to our programs, and they do distract our managers from their real work, but the problems with cost, schedule, and performance that we encounter are not because of our bureaucratic processes, which generally run parallel and concurrent with the actual contracted work. The big problem with those processes is that they sometimes fail in their fundamental purpose—to prevent programs from having major problems that could have been avoided or mitigated.

Understand the difference between risk reduction prototypes and production prototypes. They both have their purposes, but they are not the same thing. Engineers love to build risk reduction prototypes. They don't take as long or cost nearly as much as production prototypes; they include the most interesting and important technical challenges associated with the new product; they provide a gratifying physical demonstration of what a producible product could do; and they provide a basis for experimentation with how a production version would be used in practice. They also may also provide some operational capability, on a limited scale. Despite all these good things, risk reduction prototypes are not a substitute for a complete design that meets reliability and suitability requirements and provides all the features our operators need. In a crisis we do produce clones of risk reduction prototypes, but when we do so we pay a price. Global Hawk provides a good example. It took years to work off the supportability problems and the program was nearly canceled in favor of the venerable U-2, largely because of high support costs. I'm

CHAPTER FIVE: RESPONDING TO EXTERNAL FORCES AND EVENTS

a big proponent of risk reduction prototyping and experimentation; we have a number of demonstrations funded in the FY 17 budget. Please do not equate these demonstrators to production prototypes, however.

I would ask that you be wary of claims of "acquisition magic." There is no acquisition magic. We all share the frustration that programs overrun and take longer than we would like. In my forty odd years in defense acquisition I have seen a lot of versions of acquisition magic. While some of them included sound ideas that make for marginal improvements, none really change the fundamentals. They took the form of Firm Fixed Price Development, Total Quality Management, Reinventing Government, Total System Performance, Lead System Integrators, and others. We can learn lessons that are sometimes applicable from each of these, but at the end of the day new product development and transition to production remains what it has always been, a challenge that demands experience and professionalism for success and that can never be totally free of risk. Creating something new as efficiently as possible means setting reasonable achievable goals (requirements), doing the necessary risk reduction to ensure the product has a good chance of being created within reasonable cost and schedules (sometimes, but not always, including full scale risk reduction prototypes), planning and executing all the tasks needed to complete a design for production that balances many often competing features, making and testing production prototypes, correcting problems and ramping up production. All of this entails risk, and most of this is done by industry in a relationship defined by the terms of a contract under some degree of Service supervision, which brings me to the next topic I want to address; our relationship to industry and your involvement in that.

Industry is very simple to understand. One of the things I liked about working in industry is that everyone in a corporation knows what the definition of success is and how it is measured. In short, if something makes money for the firm it is good. If it doesn't it isn't. Industry tries hard to deliver products to us successfully; when industry fails it isn't because they don't care about achieving results or aren't trying. Stronger incentives can lead to better performance, but only so much. The more financial impact achieving success has, the more industry will focus its efforts, its talent, and its resources to achieve success. For example, on average development contracts yield about 6% profit. Production contracts yield about 11%. That's a strong a motivation to get through development and into production. There is nothing wrong with this system; the quasi-free market approach the United States has taken to defense acquisition has served us well. Market incentives and competition have been very effective at providing us with the best weapons systems in the world.

One of the things we have tried to do over the last few years is to provide stronger financial incentives to industry that align profit with industry performance. Industry would on the whole prefer as easy an environment as possible in which to make money, so some of our initiatives have not been popular. We have to strike the right balance here; if we squeeze industry too hard we will drive firms out of the defense industrial base. As we have sharpened our own business practices, however, industry has continued to report good margins, so at this point I'm not highly concerned. I am concerned that we have too few new products in our pipe line and I am concerned about trends in the structure of our research and development accounts and of the industrial base. There are limitations to what can be accomplished with financial incentives and you should be aware of them. Industry can only absorb so much financial risk, and if that risk is realized industry reacts very predictably—as it did in the infamous A-12 case. As a result, the SAEs and I think very carefully before we authorize fixed price development contracts. At the end of the day we are the ones who need the product, the risk that it will never be produced is always ours.

Service leadership is also often the recipient of marketing by industry. I encourage you to be open to discussions with industry; they are the source of most of the innovation contained in our weapons systems. To be successful they need to know our requirements and challenges, and we need to hear their concerns and ideas. While self-interest can safely be presumed, that doesn't mean their ideas don't have value. Many times they will be good for government and industry both, and we should be open to them. I would just make the point that a marketing pitch isn't always the whole truth. As much as industry can be considered our partners or team members (I refer to the industrial base as part of our force structure, which in effect it is), at the end of the day industry has to make money to survive and shareholders rightfully hold defense firm management accountable for success as a business above all else. I would ask that you work closely with your acquisition professionals to ensure that your Service, and the DOD, present a consistent and stable set of positions to industry.

Finally a word or two about my role in defense acquisition. I provide acquisition policy for the Department. Statute governs much of what we do, but within the limitations of statute I work with the SAEs to identify and promulgate best practices for the Department. That's what every version of Better Buying Power has tried to do; not magic, but incremental improvement based on results as measured by data. I'm also very involved in the development of the acquisition workforce, which comprises approximately 150,000 people, mostly civilian. I provide some measure

Chapter Five: Responding to External Forces and Events

of leadership for that workforce, but this is a shared responsibility with Service chains of command. For those programs for which I am the MDA, I make the major milestone decisions which commit large sums of taxpayer funds to the next phase of the products life cycle. These decisions are based on Service plans which are presented for approval. In doing this I focus on the affordability and executability of the Service's plan. I ask the basic questions about requirements firmness and clarity, technical feasibility, funding and schedule reasonableness, soundness of the contracting approach and incentives, test planning, and production and life cycle support planning needed to make the due diligence decision for the Department that the program has a reasonable chance of success. Program planning, management, and execution are Service responsibilities. If a program encounters serious problems, I work with the Service to determine the best corrective action.

I've covered a lot of ground, much of it I hope is familiar to each of you. Some Service leadership has extensive experience in acquisition, but most uniformed leaders and many civilian leaders do not. It is a complex and challenging activity, one among many, which the DOD tries to accomplish for our country. I would be happy to discuss the content of this letter and any other acquisition related topic with you at any time. You also have a standing invitation to any meeting I might hold on any of your Service's programs or acquisition activities, including Defense Acquisition Boards. We are united in our desire to improve acquisition outcomes, and I look forward to working more closely with you as we all do everything we can to improve the efficiency and effectiveness of all aspects of defense acquisition.

Sincerely,

Frank Kendall
USD (AT&L)

When and When Not to Accelerate Acquisitions

Reprinted from Defense AT&L: *November-December 2016*

Why don't we do all our acquisition programs faster? What keeps us from having all acquisition programs be "rapid" acquisitions? The short answer is that, if we choose to, we can trade quality for time. Sometimes that is smart, and sometimes it isn't.

Often, and for good reasons, we demand high quality, and that takes more time. What I mean by "quality" in this case is the suite of features we want in the equipment intended for a large fraction of the force and that we keep in our inventory for a long time—30 or 40 years, in many cases. Quality includes high reliability, maintainability, operation in a range of climates and terrains, modularity and upgradability, well-designed user interfaces, cybersecurity, robustness against responsive threats, and effective training and logistics systems. None of these things is free, and they all take time to design for and test.

For most so-called Programs of Record, we do take the time to design and build products of the quality desired by the customers, our operational communities. If you want something quick, it is generally going to be of lower quality—but that may be perfectly fine, depending on what you want. This is the operator's call; the acquisition system responds to operator requirements. As acquisition professionals, we do want a two-way continuing discussion about requirements throughout the design and development process—and beyond. That conversation is necessary because design and development always involve a voyage of discovery. And because many desired design features have to be traded off against each other and against cost, those trade-offs should be operator/customer decisions, but should still be decisions informed by acquisition professionals.

To do anything, we need money and a contract. There are vehicles that let us spend some money quickly, particularly for early stage prototypes, and there are some contract types that allow us to move out quickly, but they have limitations on scope, purpose, and amount we can spend. Lead time can be close to zero, or up to 2 years if we have to wait for a budget to be prepared, submitted and funded by Congress. We can work contracting activities (preparation of the request for proposal or even source selection) and milestone review processes (Defense Acquisition Board document

Chapter Five: Responding to External Forces and Events

preparation, as required) in parallel with the process of getting money—and usually we do so. If we already have the money, then some time is needed to have a contract. Again, for some limited purposes, this can be fast—but for major competitive awards this now takes about 18 months, close to the time it takes us to get funding from Congress. That's twice the time it used to take a couple of decades ago, and one of the actions we are working is to reduce this lead time.

If we just want a small number of prototypes for experimental purposes, and we only care about some key features and not the overall quality of the product, we can deliver in a matter of months or a few years, depending on how much new design work has to be done and the lead time for building small numbers of items or acquiring any needed subsystems from the manufacturers in the supply chain. If we want to try out a new kind of capability, to experiment, and don't care about long-term ownership quality quality-related features, then rapid prototyping is the way to go. We can do this sort of thing fast, and the technical community loves to work on projects like this. However, some quality aspects such as safety must be dealt with when we work with energetics such as munitions and rocket propellants. We can do experimental prototyping without having a program of record, so no acquisition system bureaucracy overhead need be involved in an experimental prototype program. The product you will get from an experimental prototyping program is unlikely to be one you can just replicate and field in large numbers—it wasn't designed for that. Sometimes we have liked the key features of experimental prototypes and just bought more of them. Because of their poor quality for long-term ownership and use, this has often been a disaster (see Global Hawk and the Exoatmospheric Kill Vehicle, as examples).

Next up on the quality hierarchy are assembled items that focus on one or two key performance parameters that we do want in larger quantities, but where we are willing to sacrifice some aspects of quality in order to have an important operational capability fast, usually for operational reasons or maybe because we've been surprised by a threat. Think Mine-Resistant Ambush Protected (MRAP) vehicles, which were pulled together from existing automotive components. The goal was to get more protection to the field and to get it fast. MRAPs were a big success. We saved a lot of lives. MRAPs are relatively simple designs assembled from existing components and designed for low-end threats. They lack a lot of the features needed or desired by the Army, however, and almost all of the 30,000 or so we built are going out of the inventory now that the major counterinsurgency campaigns are over.

Next on the quality scale are new designs that take into account all the things the customer wants. These are high quality products, and they take longer, but that's because we ask for more of them and have to do more work designing, building and testing. We want integrated designs that have many features desired by the customer (again requirements). Think of the Joint Light Tactical Vehicle (JLTV). The JLTV is a much higher quality product than any of the MRAPs. It will be in the Army inventory for decades, and most of the cost will be in maintenance and sustainment. The Army wants a highly reliable, maintainable design that will operate in a wide variety of terrain and in any climate. This is very different from what we did with MRAPs. JLTV is still a relatively simple design, but it has taken several years to mature the designs and pick a winner. For most of these systems, we do use the standard acquisition system milestones associated with decisions to start risk reduction (if needed), design for production and production itself. When the acquisition system's set of milestone decisions is needed, we do this in parallel with the actual work so we don't slow programs down. The decision process adds overhead, but it generally does not add time.

Highest of all in terms of quality are systems like the F-35 fighter jet. These are designs that integrate the newest technology, have the highest possible performance, and that we count on for a significant, decades-long military advantage. We want quality features like high reliability, maintainability, upgradability for tech insertion, well-designed user interfaces, cybersecurity, anti-tamper, resilience against jamming and responsive threats, and a host of other things our operators understandably desire. These systems are the Formula 1 race cars that are going to win against the best there is and do so for years, not just for one racing season. They are not Chevies. These are our highest quality and most difficult products, but these are also the ones that often make the most difference in terms of technological superiority and operational dominance. They take several years in development, and often we need to do a risk-reduction technology maturation phase before we start designing for production. That adds 3 years or more if we build risk reduction prototypes before we start designing for production. For these systems, you do have to wait about 10 years, but they are what populates most of our force. Think F-18 combat jet, Aegis missile defense, DDG-51 destroyer, the Virginia SSN submarine, F-15 and F-22 fighter jets, C-17 military transport aircraft, AMRAAM air-to-air missile, Abrams tank, Bradley fighting vehicle, Patriot missile, and Apache helicopter. Notably, every one of these high quality systems struggled to get through development and into production. Most were close to cancellation at some time in their development cycles.

The acquisition system can produce experimental prototypes quickly, but if our customers want a high quality product that we will have in the inventory in large numbers for a lot of years, that takes longer. Many of the demonstrations we have funded in the budget are experimental early prototypes. We are effectively buying options to do lower risk follow-on Engineering and Manufacturing Development phases leading to production. The ability to afford those follow-on programs, or even a subset of the concepts we will have demonstrated in the next few years, will be problematic. Unfortunately, the threats we are most worried about are not low-end threats—we are going to need high quality robust designs.

Chapter Six
Measuring Progress in Improving Acquisition

"People only ask questions when they're ready to hear the answers."

—John Irving

As I write today, cost growth in the DoD's most risky contracts is at a 30-year low. This remarkable result has been achieved after several years of consistent management and continuous improvement efforts centered on the three versions of the Better Buying Power initiatives. Figure 4 provides the data that support this statement.

Figure 4. Contract Cost Growth on Highest Risk (Major) Programs

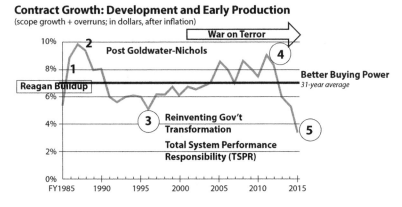

SOURCE: AT&L (2016, p. xxviii).

NOTE: This is a 5-year moving average of annual growth in development and early production contract costs for major DoD programs after inflation, including overruns and work added to the contracts. These data reflect 18,470 reports on 1,123 major contracts for 239 major programs.

This chart and many others reflecting the DoD's acquisition performance exist because of my decades of frustration with how we careened from one acquisition policy to another. One of my great frustrations has been the tendency to significantly change acquisition policy on 10- or 20-year cycles without ever determining first whether a policy was improving results or not. Developing new designs beyond the state-of-the-art weapons systems will never be free of risk, but there seems to be an expectation that all programs should execute perfectly on time and schedule. This doesn't happen, of course, so we are often dissatisfied with results, leading to a political and management practice of more or less constant change. The occasional acquisition disaster further fuels this tendency. I believe firmly that we can analyze and understand the results we are achieving and identify the policies that work and those that do not.

Several years ago, I formed a small cell of statistical analysts who have been dedicated to analyzing and reporting on the DoD's acquisition performance. We have also used the work of others, such as think tanks and the Government Accountability Office, to further our understanding. Each of the last 4 years the DoD has published a compendium of the results of this analysis. As time has gone on, we have been able to identify policies that work and policies that have no or negative effect. This record now demonstrates quite clearly that the policies we have pursued are making a positive difference in our outcomes, particularly on controlling cost. Some of those results are provided here, but I refer you to the complete volumes for a much more complete set of data and a very rich discussion of the analysis the DoD has compiled.[1]

In addition to being at a 30-year low, our cost performance improvements have not come at the expense of industry profitability. As noted earlier, profit is not optional for any business. Figure 5 summarizes the reported profit margins for the biggest defense contractors over the last several years. They have generally remained stable or even increased.

---

[1] Under Secretary of Defense for Acquisition, Technology, and Logistics. (2013). *Performance of the Defense Acquisition System*, 2013 annual report. Washington, DC: Department of Defense. http://www.dtic.mil/dtic/tr/fulltext/u2/a587235.pdf

Under Secretary of Defense for Acquisition, Technology, and Logistics. (2014). *Performance of the Defense Acquisition System*, 2014 annual report. Washington, DC: Department of Defense. http://www.dtic.mil/dtic/tr/fulltext/u2/a603782.pdf

Under Secretary of Defense for Acquisition, Technology, and Logistics. (2015). *Performance of the Defense Acquisition System*, 2015 annual report. Washington, DC: Department of Defense. http://www.dtic.mil/dtic/tr/fulltext/u2/a621941.pdf

Under Secretary of Defense for Acquisition, Technology, and Logistics. (2016). *Performance of the Defense Acquisition System*, 2016 annual report. Washington, DC: Department of Defense. http://go.usa.gov/xkf4t

Figure 5. Profits of the Six Largest DoD Primes

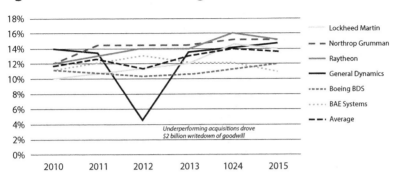

SOURCE: Company 10-K filings; AT&L (2016, p. xlviii).

NOTES: Profits are corporate fiscal year earnings before interest, taxes, depreciation and amortization (EBITDA).

Under Better Buying Power, in every version, the DoD has stressed the importance of managing cost by identifying and setting targets for cost reductions and working to obtain those savings. Figure 6 reflects the major increase in the percentage of the DoD's programs that are achieving cost savings relative to their original baselines for both programs in development and programs in production. This is a dramatic improvement.

Figure 6. Percent of Major Programs with Cost Reductions

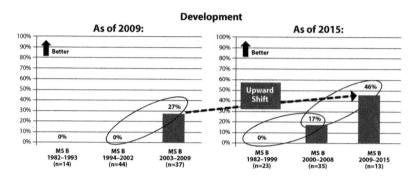

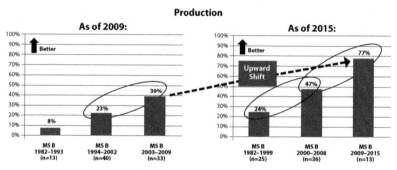

Significant positive shifts from 2009 to 2015

SOURCE: AT&L (2016, p. xxvii).

NOTE: Procurement funding growth is after adjusting for any quantity changes. The "n" gives the number of active programs in each time window.

Unfortunately, the performance of the entire acquisition enterprise is often characterized based on one or two outlier programs that have incurred large and highly visible cost and schedule overruns; the F-35 fighter jet, a very atypical program, is a good example. Figure 7 shows that over the last several years the numbers of programs having large cost increases that trigger statutory review processes known as Nunn-McCurdy reviews have also decreased consistently. We have analyzed the root causes of these large cost growth events (Table 1), and many can be traced to poor decisions to accept excessive risk in development.

Figure 7. Major Programs Crossing Critical Congressional Cost-Growth Thresholds

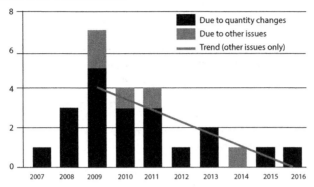

SOURCE: AT&L (2016, p. 25).

Table 1. Root Causes for Major Programs Crossing Critical Congressional Cost-Growth Thresholds or Other Major Problems

	Fraction	Count
Inception		
Unrealistic baseline estimates for cost or schedule	29%	6
Unrealistic performance expectations	10%	2
Immature technologies or excessive manufacturing or integration risk	10%	2
Other	10%	2
Execution		
Poor performance by government or contractor personnel responsible for program management	48%	10
• Systems engineering	43%	9
• Inadequate contract incentives	38%	8
• Limited situational awareness	29%	6
• Failure to act on information	29%	6
Changes in procurement quantity	19%	4
Unanticipated design, engineering, manufacturing or technology integration issues arising during program performance	14%	3
Other	19%	4
Inadequate program funding or funding instability	0%	0
Total:		21

SOURCE: AT&L (2016, p. 28).

Together with the misimpression that the DoD has a large number of high-cost-growth programs, there is also an impression that the acquisition system takes too long to develop and field new systems. Again, outliers like the F-35 are not representative of overall performance. Cycle time on major programs has, however, increased with complexity over the last few decades, but the average time from starting Engineering and Manufacturing Development (EMD) to Initial Operational Capability (IOC) over the last two decades averages about 7 years and is fairly stable (Figure 8).

Figure 8. Planned Length of Active Development Contracts for Major Programs
Average (years)

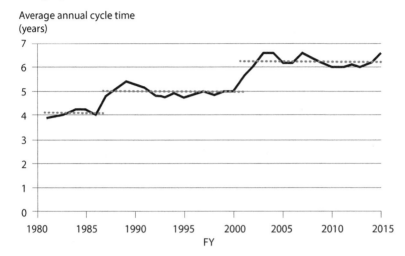

SOURCE: AT&L (2016, p. 60).

For major information systems, the cycle time has decreased significantly at the median over the last few years (Figure 9). Also, we have been reducing schedule growth on individual contracts overall since 1985 (Figure 10).

Figure 9. Planned Major Information System Development Time

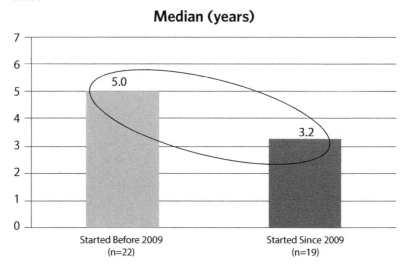

SOURCE: AT&L (2016, p. xxxviii).

Figure 10. Contract Schedule Growth on Highest Risk (Major) Programs

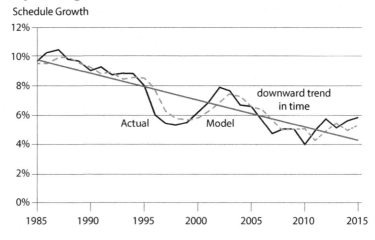

SOURCE: AT&L (2016, p. xxxviii).

CHAPTER SIX: MEASURING PROGRESS IN IMPROVING ACQUISITION

As we try to understand the factors that affect the performance of the acquisition system we need to look beyond the obvious acquisition and contracting policies. One significant, compelling result was obtained by the Institute for Defense Analysis in a study of the relationship between budget climate (tight or decreasing versus loose/obliging or increasing) and future cost growth (Figure 11). This correlation is the strongest one we have identified to explain program cost growth. The data below show that, until now at least, acquisition policy has been much less important than budget climate in explaining cost growth in programs. This fact makes the results we are currently achieving during a period of tight budgets even more significant.

Figure 11. Cost Growth on Highest Risk (Major) Programs Started in Different Budget Climates

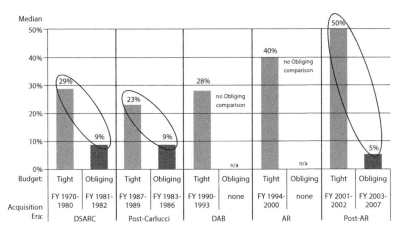

SOURCE: McNicol and Wu (2014); AT&L (2015, p. xxxiv).

The first article in this section is a progress report on the Better Buying Power initiatives written in 2014, approximately 4 years after the first version of Better Buying Power was introduced and 2 years after version 2.0 was implemented. The "core" initiatives that I believe should be in any version of Better Buying Power (under any label) are emphasized. These include the use of affordability caps, the requirement to use "should cost" management approaches, and the need for strong financial incentives tightly coupled to the government's goals. Perhaps most important among these "core" initiatives are those designed to improve the professionalism of the government workforce. Whatever progress we have made over the past several years is all due to the many actions across the vast defense acquisition workforce taken by our dedicated professionals as they go about the day-to-day business of extracting as much value as possible from every taxpayer's dollar they are trusted to spend on behalf of our warfighters and our country.

The second and final article in this section is the foreword to the fourth and most recent annual *Report on the Performance of the Defense Acquisition System*. This article summarizes some of the measurable results reflected in the annual report.

Better Buying Power— A Progress Assessment

Reprinted from Defense AT&L: *July-August 2014*

We are now four years since Dr. Carter and I began work on the first iteration of Better Buying Power, the label Dr. Carter gave to the original set of policies we promulgated as part of then Secretary Gates' efficiency initiatives in 2010. In the intervening years, I've released the second iteration, or BBP 2.0 as it's called, and I've also recently made some statements in public that BBP 3.0 may be on the horizon. Has all this made a difference? I believe it has, although I'm also certain that we have ample room for additional gains in productivity and other improved outcomes. Despite some comments I've made about BBP 3.0, the commitment to the enduring practices and policies from both the original BBP and BBP 2.0 remains. The whole concept of Better Buying Power is of a commitment to continuous incremental improvement; improvement based on experience, pragmatism and analysis of the evidence (i.e., the data). Four years on, as we to begin to consider the next steps we may decide to take, it's a reasonable time to take a look at what we have done so far.

When I introduced the second iteration of Better Buying Power, we had already made a number of adjustments (continuous evolutionary improvements) to the initiatives in the first iteration. Under 2.0, most of the BBP 1.0 initiatives continued, either under the 2.0 label or just as good best practices we may not have emphasized under BBP 2.0. Where changes were made, this was clearly articulated in 2.0. For example, the overly restrictive guidance on fixed-price incentive contract type (never intended to be as proscriptive as it may have been interpreted to be) was changed to emphasize sound decision making about the best contract type to use in a given circumstance. We also relaxed the model constraints on time to recompete service contracts that proved too restrictive. In general, BBP 2.0 moved us in an incremental way from the set of model rules or best practices that tended to characterize BBP 1.0, to a recognition that, in the complex world of defense acquisition, critical thinking by well informed and experienced acquisition professionals is the key to success—not one-size-fits-all rules. This is equally true of the acquisition of contracted services for maintenance, facility support, information technology, or anything else we acquire from industry, as it is for the various aspects of the large programs that we normally associate with defense acquisition. I won't cover every initiative in BBP 2.0, but in general here's where

I think we are in improving defense acquisition, and where I think we still need to go on these initiatives.

Achieving Affordable Programs

Over the past 4 years we have continuously increased the number of major programs with assigned affordability targets (Milestone A or before) or caps (Milestone B) as programs come through the milestone review process. I recently reviewed the status of compliance, and, in all but two or three cases, programs with caps have so far remained under their caps. The few that need to act immediately to reduce costs have estimates that are very close to their caps. I believe we have been successful in applying the caps. The affordability analysis process is also detailed in the new Department of Defense Instruction (DoDI) 5000.02, and in most cases this process is being followed by service programming communities who do the long-term budget analysis needed to derive caps on sustainment and production. For smaller programs that are a fraction of the considered capability portfolio, assigning a cap can be problematic, but it still needs to be done to instill discipline in the requirements process. Looking forward, the Department has a significant problem in the next decade affording certain portfolios—strategic deterrence, shipbuilding and tactical aircraft are examples. This situation will have to be addressed in the budget process, but I think we can say that we are making reasonable progress in the acquisition system in constraining program cost, especially for unit production cost, which is easier to control than sustainment. Nevertheless, we have challenges particularly in understanding long-term affordability caps outside the 5-year planning cycle, especially under a sequestration level budget scenario.

Controlling Cost Throughout the Acquisition Life Cycle

The implementation of "should-cost based management" is well under way, but work is still needed to instill this concept deeply in our culture and the way we do business. "Should cost" challenges every DoD manager of contracted work to identify opportunities for cost reduction, to set targets to achieve those reductions, and to work to achieve them. Managers at all levels should be taking and requiring that these steps be taken and rewarding successful realization of cost savings. I am seeing more and more of the desired behavior as time passes, but I am also still seeing cases where implementation seems to be more token than real. We also have work to do in understanding and teaching our managers the craft of doing "should cost" for our smaller programs (e.g., Acquisition Category IIIs, Services, etc.)—this remains a work in progress. Overall, "should cost," as a single measure alone, if fully implemented, will cause fundamental change in how we

Chapter Six: Measuring Progress in Improving Acquisition

manage our funds. The letter the Under Secretary of Defense (Comptroller) and I signed 2 years ago laying out our expectations for major program obligation rate reviews is still operative; the job is not to spend the budget, it is to control costs while acquiring the desired product or service and to return any excess funds for higher-priority needs. The chain of command still has to learn how to support that behavior instead of punishing it. For major program "should cost" realization, the saved funds will continue to remain with the Service or Agency, preferably for use in the program or portfolio that achieved the savings.

We are making progress at measuring and understanding the performance of the acquisition system. Last year I published the first edition of the *Annual Report on the Performance of the Defense Acquisition System*. The next report should be published at about the time that this article goes to press. Each year we will try to expand the data set with relevant information about all aspects of defense acquisition performance. We will also add analysis that will help us understand the root causes of good and poor results and that correlates the results we are seeing with our policies. We need to make decisions and track our performance via data and robust analysis, not anecdote or opinion.

Further, it isn't always easy to look in the mirror, and some government institutions or industry firms may not like what the report reveals, but the road to improvement has to begin with an understanding of where the problems lie.

I believe we are also gaining ground with regard to cooperation between the requirements and acquisition communities. My own partnership with the Vice Chairman of the Joint Chiefs of Staff and the Joint Requirements Oversight Council is intended to set the example in this area. We meet frequently to discuss issues of mutual concern and to reinforce each other's roles in the requirements and acquisition systems. The use of affordability caps and expanded use of Configuration Steering Boards or "provider forums" are also strengthening the linkage to the requirements communities. There is an ancient debate about which comes first, requirements or technology. The debate is silly; they must come together and it cannot be a one-time event in a program but continuous. Requirements that are not feasible or affordable are just so many words. A program that doesn't meet the user's needs is wasted money.

The BBP 2.0 program to increase the use of defense exportability features in initial designs is still in the pilot stage. I believe this concept is sound, but the implementation is difficult because of some of the constraints on our budgeting, appropriations and contracting systems. Support for U.S. defense exports pays large dividends for national security (improved and closer relationships), operationally (built-in interoperability and ease of cooperative training), financially (reduced U.S. cost through higher production rates), and industrially (strengthening our base). This initiative will continue on a pilot basis, but hopefully be expanded as the implementation issues are identified and worked out.

Incentivize Productivity and Innovation in Industry and Government

Our analysis of the data shows that we have more work to do in aligning profitability with performance. This year's *Annual Report on the Performance of the Acquisition System* will provide the data. In most cases we get it right—good performance leads to higher profits, and poor performance leads to lower profits. In some cases, however, there is no discernable impact of performance on margins, and in a few cases profit actually moves in the opposite direction from performance. In addition to getting the correlation right, we also need to make the correlation stronger and to tie increased rewards to real accomplishments. We want win-win business deals, but we aren't always obtaining them.

In BBP 2.0, we modified the guidance from BBP 1.0 to focus attention on professional judgments about the appropriate contract type, as opposed to emphasizing one type over others. As we analyze the data on major programs, it shows that in general we get this right, particularly with regard to choices between fixed-price and cost-plus vehicles. We are still in the process of providing updated guidance in this area. One thing is clear from the data: Where fixed price is used, there is benefit to greater use of fixed-price incentive vehicles, especially in production contracts and even beyond the initial lots of production. We are increasing the use of fixed-price incentive contracts in early production—and it is paying off.

We have begun to monetize the value of performance above threshold levels, however this practice is still in its early phases of implementation. Requirements communities usually express a "threshold" level of performance and a higher "objective" level of performance, without any indication of how much in monetary terms they value the high level of capability. It represents a difficult culture change for our operational communities to have to put a monetary value on the higher than minimum performance levels they would prefer—if the price were right. The Air Force Combat Rescue Helicopter was the first application of this practice now in the process of being applied more widely across the Department. Forcing Service requirements and budget decision makers to address the value they place on higher performance (which has nothing to do with the cost) is leading to better "best value" competitions where industry is well informed about

Chapter Six: Measuring Progress in Improving Acquisition

the Department's willingness to pay for higher performance, innovation is encouraged and source selections can be more objective.

One of the strongest industry inputs we received in formulating the BBP 2.0 policies was that the "lowest price, technically acceptable" (known as LPTA) form of source selection was being misused and overused. We have provided revised policy guidance that, like other contracting techniques, LPTA should be used with professional judgment about its applicability. This technique works well when only minimal performance is desired and contracted services or products are objectively defined. LPTA does simplify source selection, but it also limits the government's ability to acquire higher quality performance. I believe we have been successful in reducing the use of LPTA in cases where it isn't appropriate, but we are open to continued feedback from industry on this.

Instituting a superior supplier incentive program that would recognize and reward the relative performance levels of our suppliers was a BBP 1.0 initiative that we have had great difficulty implementing. I'm happy to report that the Navy pilot program has completed the evaluation of the Navy's top 25 contracted service and product suppliers. The evaluation used the Contractor Performance Assessment Rating System (or CPARS) data as its basis. Major business units within corporations were assessed separately. The Navy is providing results divided into top, middle and lower thirds. Business units or firms in the top third will be invited to propose ways to reduce unneeded administrative and overhead burdens. The Superior Supplier Program will be expanded DoD-wide over the next year. We expect this program to provide a strong incentive to industry to improve performance and tangible benefits to our highest performing suppliers. Finally, we expect to build on this Navy pilot and expand it to the other Services.

BBP 2.0 encouraged the increased use of Performance Based Logistics (PBL) contract vehicles. These vehicles reward companies for providing higher levels of reliability and availability to our warfighters. If the business deal is well written and properly executed, then PBL does provide cost savings and better results. The data shows that we have not been able to expand the use of PBL for the last 2 years and that prior to that the use was declining. Declining budgets as well as the budget uncertainty itself, and therefore contract opportunities, are part of this story, as is the fact the PBL arrangements are harder to structure and enforce than more traditional approaches. Those factors, combined with the imposition of sequestration, furloughs and a government shutdown last year are likely to have suppressed the increased use of PBL. This area will receive additional management attention going forward; we are going to increase the use of this business approach.

Another major input to BBP 2.0 received from industry concerned the large audit backlog with the Defense Contract Audit Agency (DCAA). The backlogs both delay contract close-out payments and extend the time before new awards can occur. Pat Fitzgerald, the DCAA Director, has worked very closely with the acquisition community to address this. Pat is a regular participant in the monthly Business Senior Integration Group meetings that I chair to manage BBP implementation. Under Pat's leadership, DCAA is well on the way to eliminating most of the incurred cost audit backlog and expects to effectively eliminate the areas with the most excessive backlog over the next year. This is being accomplished despite all the workforce issues the Department has been forced to deal with.

Strengthening discretionary research and development by industry was an early BBP initiative. I am concerned that industry is cutting back on internal research and development as defense budgets shrink. This is an area we have tried to strengthen under BBP. We have made good progress in providing an online forum for industry to understand the Department's technology needs and internal investments, and for industry to provide research and development results to government customers. If company R&D isn't being conducted, then these steps certainly can't substitute for doing the actual research. We will be tracking these investments carefully going forward, and I will be working with defense company chief executives and chief technology officers to review their investment plans. The wisest course for industry is to continue adequate investments in R&D so as to be positioned for the inevitable future increase in defense budgets. Now is the time for all of us to invest in research and development. This requires discipline and commitment to the long-term as opposed to short-term performance, however. Most of the chief executives I have discussed this with share this perspective; they recognize that the Department needs industry partners who are in this for the long term with the Department.

Eliminate Unproductive Processes and Bureaucracy

I would like to be able to report more success in this regard, but I am finding that bureaucratic tendencies tend to grow and to generate products for use within the bureaucracy itself, together with the fact that the comfortable habits of years and even decades are hard to break. This is all even truer, in my opinion, within the Services than it is within the Office of the Secretary of Defense (OSD). On the plus side, however, we are making progress and I have no intention of stopping this effort.

I have taken steps to reduce the frequency of reviews, particularly reviews at lower staff levels. Whenever possible we are combining OSD

Chapter Six: Measuring Progress in Improving Acquisition

and Service reviews or using senior-level in-depth reviews without preceding staff reviews and briefings. I have also instituted an annual consideration of major programs for delegation to the Services for management. Where the program risk has been significantly mitigated and/or all major Department investment commitments have already been made, I am delegating programs for Service oversight. I am also looking for opportunities to conduct pilot "skunk works" type oversight of programs which will, among other features, substitute in-depth but short on-scene reviews for the numerous formal documents with attendant staffing process that are normally required to support milestone decisions. I have also set firm and short time spans for staff review of some key documents so that issues are identified quickly and elevated rather than debated endlessly at the staff level.

Our efforts to increase the role and primacy of the acquisition chain of command are also making progress, but have additional room for improvement. A full-day workshop the Service Acquisition Executives (SAEs) and I recently conducted with all the Department's Program Executive Officers (PEOs) was very effective in communicating our priorities and in obtaining feedback on Better Buying Power and other initiatives. That feedback will be very helpful as we adjust our policies going forward. I also recently conducted a half-day workshop with our PEOs and program managers who manage and direct the Department's business systems. This is an area where I feel strongly that we can reduce some of the burdensome overhead and bureaucracy associated with these programs. I will need the support of the Congress to achieve this, however.

Time is money, and reducing cycle time, particularly long development times and extended inefficient production runs would improve the Department's productivity. I have reviewed the data on development timelines and they have increased, but not on average by outrageous amounts; the average increase in major program development time over the last few decades is about 9 months. Much of this increase seems to be driven by longer testing cycles, brought on by the growth in the number of requirements that have to be verified, and by the increased complexity and size, and therefore development time, of the software components of our programs. We are still collecting data and analyzing root causes of cycle time trends, but the most debilitating one is obvious: Budget cuts in general and sequestration cuts in particular are forcing the Department to adopt low production rates, in some cases below the theoretical minimum sustaining rate. Lowering production rates is stretching out our production cycle time and raising unit costs almost across the board.

Promote Effective Competition

Competition works. It works better than anything else to reduce and control costs. Unfortunately, the current data shows that the Department is losing ground in the percentage of contracted work being let competitively each year. The erosion is not huge, and I believe that decreasing budgets, which limit new competitive opportunities, are a major root cause. The Air Force launch program provides an example; we were moving aggressively toward introducing competition when budget cuts forced the deferral of about half the launches scheduled for competition. This is an area that I will be tracking closely and managing with the SAEs and agency heads in the coming months to try to reverse the recent trend.

Under BBP, we have recognized that for defense programs, head-to-head competition isn't always viable, so we are emphasizing other steps or measures that can be taken to create and maintain what we call "competitive environments." Simply put, I want every defense contractor to be worried that a competitor may take his work for DoD away at some point in the future. As I review programs, I ask each program manager and PEO to identify the steps they are taking to ensure the existence of a competitive environment for the efforts they are leading.

Open systems provide one opportunity to maintain competition below the prime level and to create a competitive environment for any future modifications or upgrades. Open systems and government "breakout" of components or subsystems for direct purchase are not necessarily in the interest of our primes, so careful management of interfaces and associated intellectual property, especially technical data rights, is key to achieving competition below the prime level and for future upgrades. Industry has a right to a fair price for intellectual property it has developed, but the government has many inherent rights and can consider the intellectual property implications of offerings in source selection. Our principal effort in this area has been to educate and train our workforce about how to manage this complex area. This is an effort that will bear fruit over time and in which I believe reasonable progress is being made. As we mature our practice in this area, we need to also guard against overreaching; industry cannot be forced or intimidated into surrendering valid property rights, but the government has to exercise its rights and protect its interests at the same time as it respects industry's.

Further, we in the government must have strong technical and programmatic capabilities to effectively implement open systems. The Long Range Strike Bomber program is applying modular open systems effectively in its acquisition strategy and provides a good example of how this balanced approach can work—again, if there is strong technical leadership by the government.

Chapter Six: Measuring Progress in Improving Acquisition

Small businesses provide an excellent source of competition. Due in no small part to the strong leadership of the Department's Office of Small Business Programs Director, Andre Gudger, we have made great progress over the last few years. We have improved our market research so that small business opportunities are identified and we have conducted numerous outreach events to enable small businesses to work more effectively with the Department. While much of our effort has been directed toward increasing the amount of Department work placed with small businesses, this has been done with the recognition that work allocated to small businesses will be provided through competition, and competition that involves firms without the overhead burdens of our large primes. At this time, the trends in our small business awards are positive, despite the difficulties of the last few years, and I have strong expectations for our performance this fiscal year.

The Department continues to emphasize competitive risk-reduction prototypes—when the business case supports it. This best practice isn't called for in every program; the risk profile and cost determine the advisability of paying for competitive system-level prototypes. The available data shows that when we do acquire competitive risk-reduction prototypes we have to work harder on the government side to ensure that the relevant risk associated with the actual product we will acquire and field is really reduced. BBP 2.0 reinforces this maxim, and I believe we have been correctly applying it over the last few years. This is one of many areas where simply "checking the box" of a favored acquisition technique is not adequate; real understanding of the technical risk and how it can best be mitigated is necessary. It is also necessary to understand industry's perspective on these prototypes; industry cares much more about winning the next contract than it does about reducing the risk in the product that will be developed or produced under that contract. Competitive prototypes are successful when government acquisition professionals ensure that winning and reducing risk are aligned. The data show that in many past cases they were not aligned.

Improve Tradecraft in Acquisition of Services

We have increased the level of management attention focused on acquisition of services under both BBP 1.0 and 2.0. I still see this as the greatest opportunity for productivity improvement and cost reduction available to the Department. I have assigned my Principal Deputy, Alan Estevez, to lead the Department's initiatives in this area. He is working with the Senior Service Acquisition Managers that we established under BBP 1.0 in each of the Military Departments. We have also now assigned senior managers in OSD and in each of the Military Departments for all of the several major categories in which we contract for services: knowledge-based services, research and development, facilities services, electronics and communication, equipment-related services, medical, construction, logistics management and transportation.

Our business policy and practices for services are improving. A counterpart to the often revised DoD Instruction for Programs, DoDI 5000.02, has been completed in draft and will soon be implemented. We have begun the process of creating productivity metrics for each of the service categories and in some cases for sub-areas where the categories are broad and diverse. We are also continuing efforts begun under BBP 1.0 to improve our ability to conduct effective competition for services, including more clearly defined requirements for services and the prevention of requirements creep that expands and extends the scope of existing contracts when competition would be more appropriate. Services contracting is also an area in which we are focusing our small business efforts.

Services are often acquired outside the "normal" acquisition chain by people who are not primarily acquisition specialists—they are often acquired locally in a distributed fashion across the entire DoD enterprise. Services are also often paid for with Operation and Maintenance (O&M) funds where specific efforts have much less visibility and therefore less oversight. The results achieved as a result of acquisition practices for service procurements are often not as evident to management, nor as well publicized as the results for weapon system. We are working to correct this by strengthening our business management (not just contract management) in these areas and to identify and encourage best practices, such as requirements review boards and the use of tripwires.

In summary, I believe that we have made a good start at addressing the potential improvements that are possible in contracted services, but we have more opportunity in this area than in any other.

Improve the Professionalism of the Total Acquisition Workforce

The total acquisition workforce includes people who work in all aspects of acquisition; program management, engineering, test and evaluation, contracting and contract management, logistics, quality assurance, auditing and many other specialties. All of these fields require high degrees of professionalism. I'm proud of our workforce; it is highly professional, but there isn't a single person in the workforce, including me, who can't improve his or her professional abilities.

The addition of this major category in BBP 2.0 was the most significant adjustment to BBP 1.0. The specific initiatives included several measures to enhance our professionalism. Under the Defense Acquisition Workforce

Chapter Six: Measuring Progress in Improving Acquisition

Improvement Act, the Department created three levels of acquisition proficiency. I don't believe that the standards for these levels as currently defined or implemented are adequate for the key leader acquisition positions that carry our highest levels of responsibility. We are in the process of creating and implementing higher standards for these positions. That process should conclude within the next year. As part of this initiative, we are conducting a pilot program to establish professional qualification boards. The pilot is being conducted by the Developmental Test and Evaluation community under the leadership of the Deputy Assistant Secretary of Defense for Developmental Test and Evaluation, David Brown.

These boards will help to establish a culture of excellence in our acquisition career fields and DoD-wide standards for our key leaders. We are also taking steps to better define the qualification requirements for all our acquisition specialties. These qualifications will rely more heavily on specific hands-on work experience than we have in the past. Finally, we have taken steps to more fully recognize and reward our top performers. At my level, this includes spot awards as well as our standard periodic awards. We are making a particular effort to recognize the contributions of teams as well as individuals and to recognize exceptional performance in the full range of defense acquisition activities.

People matter. If there is one legacy I would like to leave behind it is a stronger and more professional Defense Acquisition Workforce than the one I inherited from my predecessors. The tide would seem to be against me because of events like pay freezes, sequestration, furloughs, shutdowns and workforce reductions—all brought about by the current budget climate. However, if there is one thing that has impressed me during my 40-plus years in defense acquisition, most of it in government, it is the dedication, positive attitude, resilience and desire to serve the taxpayer and our Servicemen and -women well that characterizes this country's acquisition professionals. Neither the public, nor everyone in Congress, nor even all of our operational communities seems to fully appreciate the nation's acquisition workforce. This country owes a lot to you; together with our industry partners, you are the reason we have the best-equipped military in the world. I think that's a good note to close on. Thanks for all that you do.

Foreword to the 2016 Report

Reprinted from the Fourth Annual Report on the Performance of the Defense Acquisition System, *October. 24, 2016*

Eliminate all other factors, and the one which remains must be the truth.

—Sir Arthur Conan Doyle in "The Sign of the Four"

As this report is being published, I am concluding 5 years of serving as the Under Secretary of Defense for Acquisition, Logistics, and Technology. This fourth report in the series continues my long-term effort to bring data-driven decision making to acquisition policy. This report demonstrates that the Department of Defense (DoD) is making continuing progress in improving acquisition. The overall series presents strong evidence that the DoD has moved—and is moving—in the right direction with regard to the cost, schedule, and quality of the products we deliver. There is, of course, much more that can be done to improve defense acquisition, but with the 5-year moving average of cost growth on our largest and highest-risk programs at a 30-year low, it is hard to argue that we are not moving in the right direction.

Each year we add cumulative data and new analysis to the report. This year is no exception. While that data can show us ways and places to improve, I believe there is no secret to what it takes to achieve good results in defense acquisition. The short form of this is to: (1) set reasonable requirements, (2) put professionals in charge, (3) give them the resources that they need, and (4) provide strong incentives for success. Unfortunately, there is a world of complexity and difficulty in each of these four items.

Creating new—and sometimes well beyond the current state of the art—weapons systems that will give our warfighters a decisive operational advantage far into the future will never be a low-risk endeavor. That risk can be managed, however, and while we should not expect perfection, we should be able to keep the inevitable problems that will arise within reasonable bounds. We should also be able to continuously improve our performance as we learn from our experience and work to improve our ability to make sound acquisition decisions. This volume and its predecessors are dedicated to these propositions.

We open this volume with some accrued insights and an attempt to refute some popular myths about defense acquisition. Too much of our decision

Chapter Six: Measuring Progress in Improving Acquisition

making on acquisition policy has been based on cyclical and intuitive conventional wisdom and on anecdote—or just the desire, spurred by frustration, to affect change. As I've worked in this field for more than four decades, it has become clear to me that there is no "acquisition magic"—no easy solution or set of solutions that will miraculously change our results. Most attempts to direct or legislate acquisition "magic" in some form have been counterproductive and often only increased the system's bureaucracy and rigidity or led to excessive risk taking—neither of which is helpful. What we need, and always will need, is professionalism, hard work, attention to detail, and flexible policies and incentives that the data show align with the results we desire. Improving each of these is a continuous endeavor of which this volume is a part.

Conclusion

"Any fool can make a rule and every fool will mind it."
—Henry David Thoreau

I would like to end this anthology where I began Chapter 1, with the simplest formulation of how to get defense acquisition right that I've been able to conceive:
- Set reasonable requirements.
- Put professionals in charge.
- Give them the resources they need.
- Provide strong incentives for success.

If we can find a way to do these four things, we will have done almost all that is possible at the senior management level.

The first of these, setting reasonable requirements, is a job for military operational customers working in very close cooperation with acquisition professionals. Requirements should include not just performance, but also cost, urgency, and desired features. They should include well-defined priorities and, when possible, monetized value judgments to guide trade-offs and inform industry. Requirements maturation and the cooperation between operational and acquisition communities should occur over the life cycle of the product, but be particularly strong during the early stages of development when all the major decisions that will drive the design of a new product are made.

The second applies to the government acquisition workforce particularly, and to all the leaders that influence that institution. Defense acquisition is managed by a collection of professions. If you want a champion sports team or a first-in-class organization of any type, you recruit the best and you develop talent. The entire acquisition chain of command and each key acquisition leader in all of the dozen or so acquisition professions should be qualified, trained, and experienced professionals. This includes the Defense Acquisition Executive and the Service or Component Acquisition Executives. Building this professional workforce is a job for everyone who can affect the result, by action or inaction. This includes Congress, the leadership of the Department and the Services, and everyone in the chains of command of the people comprising the defense acquisition workforce. It starts with appreciating the challenges the workforce must overcome and the great difficulties they face in doing so, and it includes a host of measures that can be taken to strengthen that workforce.

The second point also addresses the authority that should be granted to those professionals. Put them in charge, let them do their jobs, and hold them accountable for the results, but be realistic about expectations. Frankly, the DoD's acquisition professionals get far too much direction in how to do their jobs from people and institutions who know next to nothing about what it takes to develop and deliver a new product. Washington seems to be full of people with theories about how to "reform" acquisition, and no experience whatsoever in actually delivering products. Along those lines, one risk of the move to increase Service Chiefs' and Secretaries' involvement in acquisition is just this. Almost without exception Service Chiefs have no experience or training in acquisition, in developing and delivering a new cutting-edge design. Also, the most recent version of the NDAA, the 2017 bill that recently became law, contains incredibly detailed language on newly devised acquisition approaches that seem to be totally divorced from the reality of new product development and all the painful lessons of earlier statutory or management experiments. One cannot manage acquisition by remote control, and statutory constraints are just that, constraints that get in the way of sound situation-based decision making by professionals. I would ask Congress to stop telling the Department's acquisition professionals how to do their jobs. Give them the flexibility they need to be successful, and then hold them accountable for the decisions they make, even if there is a delay of several years, as there often is, from the decision to its consequences becoming apparent. I, for one, am fully prepared to testify someday on the decisions I made as USD(AT&L). I'm sure I made mistakes, and if the Department can learn from those mistakes so as not to repeat them, I fully support that process.

The third applies to all the resources needed for success, but especially time and money. Programs that begin with unrealistic schedules and inadequate funding are headed for failure from day one. The major risk I see in the trifecta of the current enthusiasm for "rapid acquisition," combined with a climate of tight budgets and the delegation of more authority to the military Services, who are always motivated toward optimism, is that we will set programs up for failure, as we often have in the past. The Under Secretary for Acquisition was established to address precisely this issue. I worked on the Army's Future Combat Systems in industry (at least $10 billion and nothing delivered to the warfighter), and I was involved in oversight of the A-12 combat reconnaissance aircraft fiasco in government (several billion spent, nothing delivered to the warfighter, and a 20-year lawsuit). I know what this looks like, and I hope we have learned not to repeat these experiences, but I'm skeptical.

Conclusion

The last point, "provide strong incentives for success," is trickier than it sounds. Its application to industry is relatively clear, but not always straightforward or easy. Industry responds to financial incentives, but that is not the end of the story. Aligning those incentives so that they work effectively and consistently with the government's goals can be a delicate balancing act. I have stressed this aspect of acquisition planning, and the data reflect that we have made progress. It's important for government people, acquisition and otherwise, to realize that industry is motivated, first and foremost, to win contracts. After that they are strongly motivated to make money on those contracts. Both motivations are important, and both can lead to behavior that is or isn't in the warfighter and the taxpayer's interests.

Incentives within government are more subtle and diverse. They include organizational and personal rewards that are generally not monetary, and they include positive and negative incentives (carrots and sticks). One feature of those incentives is that they are rather limited in both directions. Providing more incentives for the behaviors we want by our government team is a leadership challenge that I and many other leaders throughout the acquisition chains of command work on constantly. We need the help of other leaders in and out of DoD. I cringe whenever I hear an operational leader complain about the acquisition community's perceived shortcomings, or a congressman reflect negatively on the government workforce. Both are strong disincentives for bright young people to join or stay in the field of government defense acquisition.

As I was rolling out one of the versions of Better Buying Power at a Washington, DC think tank, someone asked me what grade I would give the defense acquisition system. My answer was a B+ or maybe an A-. If the defense acquisition enterprise, industry and government combined, were a professional sports team, in football say, we'd be the repeat Super Bowl winners year after year. In fact we'd win almost all of our games. We'd also have a fumble, or drop a pass, or miss a tackle once in a while. More directly we deliver almost all of the products we set out to build, even the most difficult and advanced products. We have fewer overruns and schedule slips than many commercial product developers, and we easily outperform the cost and schedule performance of large public works projects. Even as criticized a program as the F-35, which was very much an outlier in many ways, is delivering a best-in-the-world product that will anchor our dominance in the air for years to come.

I close with one more article, the last I expect to publish for the DoD acquisition workforce as USD(AT&L). It is a collection of anecdotes or stories drawn from over my career. I believe in the use of data to drive acquisition policy, but like everyone else I've been influenced by my experiences.

As human beings, we learn well from the stories we hear or read as well as from the ones we live. I think I learned something from each of these experiences, and I hope that others may find something useful somewhere in them also.

This isn't a broken system that needs radical overhaul. It does need to be improved, and it can be. I believe, and the data support, that we have made significant improvements over the past several years, but there is more work to be done. We do have too much bureaucracy, and we do need to tailor and streamline our programs more. We can improve in almost every facet of acquisition, but that improvement is going to come from the hard work and professionalism of the people in the ring—industry and government—fighting every day to deliver high quality products to our warfighters. Those people deserve our respect and gratitude.

CONCLUSION

Adventures in Defense Acquisition

Reprinted from Defense AT&L: *January-February 2017*

For what is likely to be my last communication to the acquisition workforce as Under Secretary of Defense for Acquisition, Technology, and Logistics (USD[AT&L]), I thought I would share with you a few stories, all true, from my 45 or so years working in various aspects of defense acquisition, either in uniform, as a civil servant, in industry, or as an appointee. I've put them more or less in chronological order, starting with an experience I had while serving in Europe during the height of the Cold War. There has certainly been a lot of water under the bridge since then, and a lot has changed, but the things I've learned along the way are in many cases timeless.

During the 1970s, as an Army captain, I commanded a Hawk air defense battery in West Germany. We had a new battalion commander take over during that time. He immediately started a program he called "Victory Through Integrity" or VTI. This was the period of the readiness crisis and the "hollow force" following the end of the war in Vietnam.

Our new commander's ideas on logistics included that cross-leveling parts between units and cannibalizing down items of equipment, like our radars, was a violation of our integrity. We stopped doing these things and went nonoperational for several months while we stubbornly stuck to our "principles" about these maintenance policies. During that period, training as well as operational readiness suffered enormously. Eventually, the battalion commander was told to change his policies. He very reluctantly obeyed the order. I believe it is always important to act in a principled way, and in particular to act with integrity, but in this case I felt that my commander had confused integrity with reasonable choices in management policy. Leaders will always have initiatives and labels to describe them (e.g., Better Buying Power), but when they represent management choices they should be viewed as just that—choices that can be reversed or changed based on new information (data) about how well they are working, or not.

In 1980, while still an Army captain, I attended my first congressional hearing. I believe it was the House Armed Services Committee. I was there in support of my boss at the time, the Army major general who was the Army's Ballistic Missile Defense program manager. He was one in a series of program managers providing testimony that day. This was about 3 years before President Reagan announced the Strategic Defense Initiative (SDI) program.

One of my most vivid memories of that hearing was the lead professional staff member for the committee holding up a schedule and chastising a witness for the degree of concurrency in his program. What I can't remember is whether he was for or against concurrency—but, whichever it was, he was passionate about it. We've been for and against concurrency several times since that hearing. Like many other decisions, the degree of concurrency (overlap between development and production) in a program is a judgment call motivated by many factors, first among them being confidence in the stability of the design. Early in my tenure as USD(AT&L), I referred to the extraordinary amount of concurrency, and the specific decision to start production on the F-35 fighter jet before any flight test data had been accumulated, as "acquisition malpractice." The press loves pithy expressions like this, so the comment got a lot of exposure. Concurrency decisions, like many others in acquisition, require critical thinking, sound professional judgment and taking a lot of program specific factors into account.

Careers can take strange turns. One of mine may have hinged on a 2 a.m. flight from Andrews Air Force Base in Maryland to Nantucket Island in Massachusetts. I was the Assistant Deputy Director of Defense Research and Engineering for Strategic Defense programs. My boss' boss' boss, the Under Secretary for Acquisition, was on vacation in Nantucket and was tasked on short notice to come back to Washington for a hearing on the SDI. I volunteered to fly to Nantucket on the MILAIR flight that would bring him back to DC and to prep him during the flight for the hearing, which would be held the same day. We picked him up at about 5 a.m. Nobody had told him I would be on the airplane, so he was a little surprised to see me. He was also pretty impressed that I had gone the extra mile to stay up all night so I could brief him. I accompanied him to the hearing, which went very well, in part because I had a chance to prep him thoroughly. Just after that, I applied to be the acting Director of Tactical Warfare Programs when the incumbent left government. This job, overseeing all of the Department of Defense (DoD) conventional weapons system programs and reporting directly to the Under Secretary, was my dream job at the time. I got the job.

While I was still the acting Director for Tactical Warfare Program, a period of 2.5 years when I didn't know if a political appointee would replace me, there were four changes in the officeholder of Under Secretary of Defense for Acquisition. One of these was a former executive from Ford who was totally new to Washington and DoD and who had just come onboard. At the time, we were struggling to get the Advanced Medium-Range Air-to-Air Missile program (AMRAAM) through testing and into production. Late on a Friday afternoon, I received a preliminary report from the Air Force that we had experienced a flight test failure. There was very little information on what had happened, so I decided to wait until I knew more before informing the Under Secretary. On Monday morning, I was at Patuxent River Naval Air Station in Maryland, getting a medical so I could do an F-18 flight out to a carrier. A perk of my position was that there were often good reasons for me to experience firsthand the performance of our conventional weapons programs.

Just as the flight physician was about to take my blood pressure, I received a call from the Under Secretary. The press had heard about the flight test failure and had asked the Secretary of Defense about it. He was clueless so he asked the Under Secretary, who was also clueless because I hadn't informed him yet. When asked, the Air Force was understandably quick to point out that I had been informed right after the failure. The Under Secretary proceeded to rip me a new one, as they say. As soon as I got off the phone, the flight physician took my blood pressure. Eventually I did get to experience the F-18 flight, and eventually the "acting" status was removed from my title, but it took some time to recover from that initial impression. Nobody likes surprises, and the more senior one is the less one likes them. Bad news does not improve with age.

In addition to having problems completing flight test, the AMRAAM struggled for at least a year to demonstrate that it could meet one specific reliability requirement, the average number of hours it could be carried on an aircraft before a failure occurred. The requirement had been set arbitrarily at 450 hours. This was a totally unrealistic number that later analysis showed had no operational value or cost effectiveness. The requirement could have been dropped to 250 with minimal cost or operational impact. So why did we spend more than a year making holes in the sky to prove we could achieve 450 hours? Because we had failed operational testing and it had politically become a high-interest item. The program had a bad reputation and was at real risk of cancellation. The Services concluded that it was better to keep flying to try to achieve the requirement than to take the political risk associated with reducing it; so we kept flying. In those days, requirements were often set by relatively junior people with a high degree of arbitrariness. The missile AMRAAM was replacing had a mean time between failures of 200 flight hours. So what was a good number for the replacement? How about 450 hours? Seemed reasonable. Acquisition and operational people have to work in close cooperation. If you don't, this is the sort of thing that happens.

One of my programs in DoD was a special access Navy program to develop the A-12 stealthy fighter bomber. It had already started Engineering and Manufacturing Development when it fell under my portfolio. It was also touted as a new model for how to do acquisition effectively at the time—

little oversight, firm fixed-price development, an acquisition approach that in the development phase teamed two competitors who would later compete for production, and a very aggressive schedule tied to fixed-price production options. It was a disaster waiting to happen. The A-12 is taught as a classic case study in how not to do acquisition, and for good reasons.

We have a lot of programs that struggle to get through development and into production, but most of them do get there. Programs like the A-12, where we spend billions of dollars and get nothing, are travesties. I won't try to tell this whole story here; it is available elsewhere in great detail. At that time, the Secretary of Defense was Dick Cheney, and we were doing something called "The Major Aircraft Review." In one of my briefings to Secretary Cheney, I had told him that based on earned value data (but not what the contractor or military Service were saying) the program was in big trouble, and would overrun by at least a year and $1 billion. I found that out from the DoD Earned Value Management guru at the time, Gary Christle.

After the A-12 blew up, figuratively speaking, and was canceled (properly so, as the Supreme Court finally concluded about 20 years later) there was an investigation, led by a general officer, into who knew what when. It turned out that John had briefed a member of my staff several weeks earlier, but no one had informed me. The data provided compelling evidence of where the program was headed. That member of my staff who had been briefed was a very capable Navy officer. However, instead of informing me of the data, he had immediately called the Navy staff to warn them about this threat to the Navy's program in the Office of the Secretary of Defense. I was rather upset when I found out he hadn't seen any reason to inform me, the person he was supposed to be working for. During the investigation, I brought this up, and in the report that followed I was criticized for not having adequately trained this officer in the fact that he had a duty to inform me, his supervisor, of any relevant information about the program he was overseeing for me. I'm not making this up. Service loyalties run deep.

The A-12 cancellation came about in part because the Secretary of Defense had testified that the program was progressing more or less on track. I don't know for a fact, but my guess is that he simply forgot about the concerns I had expressed to him during the major aircraft review. He had no reason to dissemble, and he was put on the spot by a question he had not anticipated. A few months later, the contractors requested a bailout, embarrassing the Secretary, who subsequently ordered the program canceled. Two people on the Secretary's staff argued against cancellation—me and the Director of Acquisition Policy, Eleanor Spector. Our new boss, who replaced the previous Under Secretary for Acquisition at about that time, listened to us but kept his cards close. The decision meeting with Secretary Cheney took

Conclusion

place early one morning, and neither Eleanor nor I attended. A few hours later, another member of the acquisition staff, who had been in the Secretary's briefing room for a subsequent meeting, dropped off a hard copy of a set of briefing charts he had found at the podium. They were the charts my boss, the new Under Secretary for Acquisition, had used to brief the Secretary. The final chart read: Recommendation—Termination. I don't know to this day if that was the right decision or not. Most of the time, as Eleanor and I maintained, one is better off working through problems to get the needed capability. This isn't always the case, however. I do know that 25 years later the Navy still doesn't have a stealthy tactical aircraft operating from a carrier, but we are getting close.

The Advanced Self-Protection Jammer or ASPJ is another program that didn't make it through the transition from development to production and fielding. ASPJ was another product of the fad of fixed-price development that was tried in the late 1980s. A good deal of my time in the early 1990s was spent cleaning up the many messes that this policy created. I have good experience-based reasons for wanting to avoid fixed-price development. ASPJ had another problem, however, and it had to do with algebra.

ASPJ was a jamming system for tactical aircraft. Its job was in part to jam enemy air defenses so that tactical aircraft wouldn't be shot down. In order to get through the Operational Testing phase to transition to full-rate production, ASPJ had to demonstrate that it could adequately perform this function. The metric for success was expressed as an algebraic equation that had to be statistically tested. The equation was built in part around the success of the jammer at defeating a threat after an air defense missile was launched against the aircraft with ASPJ on board. We made the mistake of not including the cases in which ASPJ was effective at preventing the launch, so these successes didn't count as part of the test. Again, we found ourselves in a situation where changing the rules would have been viewed with suspicion in the political environment around struggling acquisition programs. In this case, we did make the needed changes, but for other reasons the program was canceled in the defense drawdown that followed the Cold War. It was later resurrected with a different name and ultimately fielded.

A few years later, I had taken a position at Raytheon as Corporate Vice President of Engineering. We were in a tight competition with our most ferocious competitor, Hughes Aircraft, to build the next generation short-range air-to-air missile, the AIM-9X. We thought we had a much better design than our competitor and were sure we could offer the customer much better operational performance. We had a problem, however. From what we could tell from the draft request for proposals we had seen and from discussions with the Air Force, there was no way our higher performance could be considered in the source selection. We also anticipated a price disadvantage because our missile design, though innovative, was more complex—and we believed more costly as a result.

I spent a lot of time in the Pentagon trying to get the program management, the operational community, or the Under Secretary for Acquisition to provide some way for our better operational performance (a bigger engagement envelope and higher probability of kill) to be considered in source selection. I failed. In this case, we lost—but this occurred just as Raytheon was buying Hughes. Hughes had bid very low; we speculated that this was done so Hughes could book the business to enhance its attractiveness as an acquisition. In some respects, this was a lowest price technically acceptable source selection, something many in industry complain about today and something I have tried to limit to cases where it is really appropriate. Most of the time we do want higher performance, if it is at a price we would consider reasonable. For the last few years, I have been encouraging or directing the military Services to provide bidders with a monetized adjustment in source selection as a means of encouraging innovation and obtaining best-value solutions. After several examples, it is clear that this approach is working. I wish it had been used in the 1990s when we were bidding on AIM-9X.

While I was in industry, I served for some time on the Army Science Advisory Board. One study we were involved in was a review of a weapon system that had featured prominently in the First Gulf War. It happened to be a weapon system that my company produced. I don't recall the reason, but as part of the study we needed some technical data on the system's performance. For reasons we didn't understand, we just couldn't get the program office to give us the data, despite several requests. Finally, one of the study group's members, retired Gen. Jack Vessey, the former Vice Chief of Staff of the Army, called the Chief of Staff to ask for some help. We got the data. I, however, got a call through my corporate headquarters to go to Washington to meet with a brigadier general on the Army staff responsible for the program to explain my reasoning, as I was associated with the request. The program office, fearing it might look bad somehow, had been slow-rolling us in providing the data and I was being called to task for having gone over everyone's head to the Chief of Staff through Gen. Vessey. My management wasn't pleased. Corporations know where their money comes from, and sometimes the people who control those funds have narrow ideas of what is right and what is wrong.

Another incident from my time in industry involved what I can only describe as abuse of power by a government acquisition official. At the time, my firm had two matters, totally unrelated and involving two programs, that we wanted resolved by the Service in question. One was a protest of a bid we had lost. It was not at all common for my firm to protest. We felt that it would upset our customers and that it was unlikely to succeed. In this case, we had lost a bid on something we considered a core business—a share of the market and a product that we had controlled for a very long time. We felt we had a legitimate reason to protest the source selection and it was important business—so we protested.

The other matter was a request we made of the same Service on another program that was coming up for source selection. We wanted some changes to the request-for-proposal language, changes we felt were fair and that just happened to be to our advantage. With these two matters on the table, we were visited by a senior flag officer from the Service involved. He asked us which of the two matters was most important to us and told us that the Service's decisions on them were "linked." I was shocked. In my view, then and now, the government should be resolving disputes or issues with industry on a case-by-case basis on the merits. I never found out if this conduct was illegal, but I'm certain that it was unethical. The government should not cut backroom deals in which it coerces a contractor to give up a legal right to a decision on the merits in return for a competitive advantage. The government has immense power over contractors, and has an obligation to not abuse that power. When it does abuse its power, trust is destroyed. By the way, my colleagues from industry and I did exactly the right thing: We ignored the question.

While I was in industry, I spent several years as an independent consultant. One of the projects I participated in was the Army's Future Combat Systems program or FCS. Like A-12, this program wasted billions of dollars and delivered basically nothing to the Army. It was hugely ambitious, driven by a "vision" that was divorced from reality and hobbled by totally unrealistic direction on schedule, imposed from the top of the Army.

The acquisition community within the Army took huge risks trying to execute the unrealistic 4.5-year schedule from start of development to a production decision—for the largest and most complex program in the history of the DoD. The acquisition strategy risks, including the contracting approach, a Lead System Integration, the immaturity of the requirements and the early loss of competitive incentives doomed the program before it started. The sanity check that the Under Secretary for Acquisition is supposed to provide failed under Service pressure to proceed. As soon as the responsible leadership departed the Army, the schedule was slipped 4 more years—but the damage had already been done. This is the most extreme example of something I have seen too many times; operational and Service leadership is always in a hurry and usually has no real understanding of what it takes to design, prototype, test or produce a specific product. This mistake cost the Army more than $10 billion of precious research and development funds and several years of modernization that can never be recovered.

The Services do have distinct cultures, and that includes how they relate to outside stakeholders and authorities. The classic allusion to "the dumb, the devious, and the defiant" isn't wholly accurate, but there are times when it seems apt. A better characterization might be that the Army knows how to salute to a fault, the Air Force likes to cite Office of the Secretary of Defense (OSD) direction as to why it is acting in a certain way, and the Navy would strongly prefer that there be no OSD direction. That is certainly an over-simplification, but it is a rough approximation of reality.

I could tell stories all day from my current tenure as USD(AT&L) about the Services, but here is one from my tenure as Principle Deputy Under Secretary: For some reason, we were having a meeting in my office with a brigadier general from the Army's acquisition community. We got into a discussion of several options for how to proceed on a specific program. It wasn't a decision meeting, and staff members were just tossing out ideas for discussion. We did this for about 20 minutes and the meeting broke up. About an hour later, I received a note from the Army Acquisition Executive complaining about all the direction the brigadier had been given. He walked out the room convinced that he had just been directed to do every one of the things that had been discussed, when in fact he had been directed to do none of them. Apparently, he went back to his office with his hair on fire and started ranting about all the crazy guidance he was getting from every member of the DoD acquisition staff. I'm guessing that the Air Force would have picked any guidance they liked and implemented it but made clear it was at the direction of the OSD. The Navy would probably have regarded it as an amusing conversation and largely ignored it. Try as I might, I don't know that I ever convinced the Services, at least at the program manager level, to not take direction from random staff members with no directive authority over them. My policy was that the staff was there to advise me as the Defense Acquisition Executive, not to provide direction to the Services—but implementing that policy isn't as easy as it should be. A program manager trying to get his program approved just wants it approved, and is likely to err on the side of accepting direction if he or she thinks it will help achieve the goal. I finally directed my staff to identify all comments on Service plans as "Defense Acquisition Board Issue," discretionary, or administrative. This meant that I would have visibility into anything the staff thought was important to change. I think this has helped, but there is still room for progress.

Conclusion

We spend a lot of time trying to devise acquisition strategies that will effectively incentivize industry to deliver more of whatever the government wants. Industry has two priorities. In order of importance, they are to (1) win contracts, and (2) make money on them. The first is a prerequisite to the second. Government people should never lose sight of the fact that these imperatives always motivate industry. We can use them to get better results, but we need to be careful about unintended consequences.

A case in point was the Joint Advanced Guided Missile or JAGM, an Army-led joint program. The Army was conducting a competition and had asked industry to build competing prototypes as risk reduction efforts in support of the competition. The prototypes were to be flight tested as part of the source selection. I had challenged the Army's intention to use a fixed-price incentive contract for the next phase of work—Engineering and Manufacturing Development. My concern was the degree of risk for the upcoming phase. I asked the Army to bring in the engineers for the program to walk me through both competitors' designs, the one they would use in the early prototype testing as part of the source-selection process and the production prototypes they were proposing to actually build in the next phase. What I discovered was that there was no traceability between the risk reduction prototypes and the production prototypes. Every subsystem of the missiles would have to be redesigned. The competitors were building "proof of principle" prototypes for the source selection. They were not reducing the risk in the designs they intended to build for production.

As a result of this, I directed the Army to change the contract type to one more suited for the remaining risk. Probably more importantly, the light bulb went on about what the competitors were trying to do. They were not motivated to reduce risk. That would have entailed taking some risk, and that was the opposite of what they were motivated to do. They were motivated to win, which meant that they wanted a low-risk and successful flight test so that they could win the contract. The government had asked for the things our policy supports and the Congress expects: competitive prototypes and flight tests. The government failed to insist on prototypes with designs traceable to the designs being bid for production and to the reduction of the specific risks associated with those designs. We can't blame industry for responding to the business incentives we provide. The government acquisition team must have the expertise it needs to understand what is required, and the professionalism to ensure that industry provides it. Industry will always act to maximize its return, and the government will get what it accepts.

It has been a great honor to have led the terrific men and women in the DoD's acquisition workforce. You are unsung heroes who, with equally dedicated and patriotic people in industry, provide our men and women in uniform with the products and services they need to defend our freedom. I hope that some of these anecdotes will prove useful as you continue your efforts to improve even more on the great work you do every day. Thank you. It has been wonderful to have been part of this team.

Made in the USA
Middletown, DE
08 June 2023

32294141R00126